PENGUIN MODERN CLASSICS
A Life in Words

Ismat Chughtai (1911–91) was Urdu's most courageous and controversial woman writer in the twentieth century. She carved a niche for herself among her contemporaries of Urdu fiction writers—Rajinder Singh Bedi, Saadat Hasan Manto and Krishan Chander—by introducing areas of experience not explored before. Her work not only transformed the complexion of Urdu fiction but also brought about an attitudinal change in the assessment of literary works. Although a spirited member of the Progressive Writers' Movement in India, she spoke vehemently against its orthodoxy and inflexibility. Often perceived as a feminist writer, Chughtai explored female sexuality while also exploring other dimensions of social and existential reality.

M. Asaduddin is an author, critic and translator. His work has been recognized with the Sahitya Akademi Prize, and the Katha and A.K. Ramanujan awards for translation. Among the books he has published are *The Penguin Book of Classic Urdu Stories*, *Lifting the Veil: Selected Writings of Ismat Chughtai*, *For Freedom's Sake: Manto*, *Joseph Conrad: Between Culture and Colonialism*, and (with Mushirul Hasan) *Image and Representation: Stories of Muslim Lives in India*. He is currently Professor, Department of English, Jamia Millia Islamia.

PRAISE FOR THE BOOK

'Translator M. Asaduddin has . . . done a remarkable job, catching all the nuances of Chughtai's luscious prose and extraordinary wit. This is a book for all to read and enjoy'—*Hindustan Times*

'Ismat Chughtai's candid words continue to be contemporary and cutting edge'—*The Hindu*

'Asaduddin's work is top-of-the-shelf stuff . . . it transports you to the world of the original . . . If you have not read Chughtai before, this will whet your appetite'—*Outlook*

'A youthful Ismat Chughtai jumps exuberantly from every page, outrageously outspoken, courageous, honest and very, very funny . . . there is never a dull moment'—*Indian Express*

'These essays showcase the best of Chughtai's range and mastery as a writer—they are erudite, self-aware and always probing . . . [Asaduddin's] work is nimble and nuanced'—*Time Out*

'Ismat Chughtai's memoir is a reader-friendly, breezy, almost racy read'—*Mail Today*

'The first complete translation of celebrated Urdu writer Ismat Chughtai's *Kaghazi Hai Pairahan* is a delightful and authentic account of several years of her life'—*Sunday Standard*

'Ismat's vivid descriptive style, her rich imagery, her wry humour and a rare ability to look critically at herself, all come together to etch an interesting canvas of an era gone by . . . a must-read for every modern, thinking, liberal Indian woman . . . This book is a compulsive page-turner'—*Business Line*

'Breezy and engaging'—*Business Standard*

'The book . . . has several gems in the sketches and descriptions . . . And it owes as much to Asaduddin as Chughtai that this is so'—*Financial Express*

'The first thing one notices on starting the short story writer, feminist, educationalist and iconoclast Ismat Chughtai's remarkable memoirs, *A Life in Words: Memoirs*, with due credit to M. Asaduddin's elegant translation, is how utterly unselfconscious, unaffected and natural the writing seems'—*Mint*

'This is a fantastic work, so detailed, so sincere, so intensely human'—*Free Press Journal*

'A must-read for anyone interested in literature, or for that matter, life'—*Reading Room*

'An honest and brilliant description of Ismat Chughtai's life and times'—*New Woman*

'[Chughtai's] memoirs are just as radical as her fiction'—*DNA*

'Eminently readable . . . superbly translated'—*Reading Hour*

ISMAT CHUGHTAI

A Life in Words

MEMOIRS

Translated from the original Urdu *Kaghazi Hai Pairahan*
by M. Asaduddin

PENGUIN BOOKS

An imprint of Penguin Random House

PENGUIN BOOKS

USA | Canada | UK | Ireland | Australia
New Zealand | India | South Africa | China | Singapore

Penguin Books is part of the Penguin Random House group of companies
whose addresses can be found at global.penguinrandomhouse.com

Published by Penguin Random House India Pvt. Ltd
4th Floor, Capital Tower 1, MG Road,
Gurugram 122 002, Haryana, India

First published in Viking by Penguin Books India 2012
Published in Penguin Books 2013

Copyright © Ashish Sawhny 2012
Translation and introduction copyright © M. Asaduddin 2012

10 9 8 7 6 5 4 3 2

ISBN 9780143420316

Typeset in Goudy by R. Ajith Kumar, New Delhi

Printed at Manipal Technologies Limited, India

www.penguin.co.in

MIX
Paper | Supporting
responsible forestry
FSC® C043100

This is a legitimate digitally printed version of the book and therefore might not
have certain extra finishing on the cover.

For
Shamim Hanfi
my Urdu mentor

CONTENTS

INTRODUCTION

Ismat Chughtai (1911–91)[1] has remained Urdu literature's most courageous and controversial writer and its most resolute iconoclast. Appearing on the scene during the heyday of the Progressive Writers' Movement, which changed the complexion of Urdu literature in significant ways, Ismat remained a progressive in the true sense of the term throughout her life, even though the movement dissipated shortly after Independence in 1947. Among her fellow fiction writers—Rajinder Singh Bedi, Krishan Chander, Saadat Hasan Manto—she was distinguished both by the themes she dealt with and the style she developed to treat them. As the subcontinent's foremost feminist writer she was instinctively aware of the gendered double standard in the largely feudal and patriarchal structure of the society she lived in and did everything to expose and subvert it. She

---

[1] Scholarship on Ismat Chughtai, both in English and other Indian languages, has remained marred by inaccuracies of dates; the author herself was delightfully sportive about this, and helped little to remove this confusion. Even the basic fact of her birth has been recorded erroneously in many books and articles as 1915, instead of 1911. The first book in English that discusses Ismat Chughtai in a theoretically informed way, i.e. *Literary Radicalism in India: Gender, Nation and the Transition to Independence* (London and New York: Routledge, 2005) by Priyamvada Gopal also demonstrates this confusion. While the chapter on Ismat Chughtai gives her year of birth as 1915 (p. 68), the appendix records it as 1911 (p. 164). In all fairness, I must admit that I had committed the same mistake initially, but after the current researches on her life and works, particularly after the publication of *Ismat: Her Life and Times* (New Delhi: Katha, 2000), there is no reason why this error should persist.

lobbied relentlessly—and successfully—to get an education, struggled fiercely to find her own voice and wrote with passion and panache to depict the visible and subtle tyrannies of contemporary society and her conflicts with the values that made them possible.

Kaghazi Hai Pairahan (henceforth, *KHP*), generally known to be Ismat Chughtai's autobiography, is a curious piece of work. It is certainly written by Ismat Chughtai, and it is about her life, her family and her growth and development as a writer. But it is not a straightforward autobiography inasmuch as it does not record the author's life story—from her birth to the point of writing the book—in a chronological order. It is fragmented, jagged, written in fits and starts when spurts of memory propelled her to record her reminiscences, without consideration for chronology, repetition or narrative coherence. Perhaps it is not realistic to expect a traditional autobiography from such an individualistic, temperamental and radical writer like Ismat Chughtai, who never moved on a straight or predictable path, much like the heroine, Shaman, of her autobiographical novel, *Terhi Lakeer* (Crooked Line).

The fourteen chapters of *KHP*, written for the Urdu journal *Aaj Kal*, were published from March 1979 to May 1980. The general tenor of the chapters and the manner in which they were written is illustrated by the following note from the author to the editor of *Aaj Kal* when she sent in the second instalment:

> I'm sending the second chapter. I am trying to record from my memory the events that affected me and what I had heard from conversations in the family, the tensions inherent in every class, new questions and their resolution—all this is so complicated. I will send you whatever gets written at any point of time. Let them be published under different titles. The sequence might be worked out while editing them [for the volume].

The writer did not have the opportunity to take a second look, much less edit what she had written because of other preoccupations and her failing health. It was at the initiative of the editor of *Aaj Kal*[2] that the instalments were put together as they appeared in the journal, where they were published as volumes in Urdu in 1994,[3] three years after her death. The editor, at his own initiative, also added the opening chapter, 'Ghubaar-e-Kaarwaan', written much earlier in the same journal in a series that went by the same name, in which many Urdu writers reminisced about their writerly lives. This underlines the fragmentary nature of this autobiography and raises significant questions about the motivation and intention of the author and about the notions of authorship, representation, selfhood and subjectivity, the answers to which will help us 'understand the peculiar tension between public and private realities that underwrites women's writing'.[4]

~

The span of the volume is limited to the years between when Ismat Chughtai entered high school to the time of writing her controversial story, 'Lihaaf'. In other words, the autobiography records the events of only a couple of years of her life. Even with the addition of the opening chapter there are silences and gaps that cry out to be verbalized and filled up. However, within this limited timeframe, we find encapsulated vignettes that point to the multiple and richly tapestried cultural matrix that went into developing Ismat Chughtai's artistic sensibility.

The real absence in *KHP* is any vignette from her married life, even though her husband, Shahid Lateef, figures in many places. One gets just a fleeting glimpse in the chapter, 'In the Name of Those Married Women . . .' It is a matter of speculation as to why a brutally honest

---

[2] Monthly Urdu magazine, published by the Publications Division, Government of India, Delhi.

[3] Ismat Chughtai, *Kaghazi Hai Pairahan* (New Delhi: Publications Division, 1994).

[4] Susie Tharu and K. Lalita, *Women Writing in India, Vol. II: The Twentieth Century* (Delhi: Oxford University Press, 1995), p. xvii.

and outspoken author like Ismat Chughtai shied away from talking about her married life. Was this reluctance to talk an admission of the failure of her married life? Or did she set herself a limit on how much she would reveal, since some facts are too personal to be chronicled even in an autobiography? Was she exercising her individual freedom to be selective, much as the iconic black feminist writer and folklorist Zora Neale Hurston had done in her autobiography, *Dust Tracks on the Road*?[5] These questions will tantalize readers as they go through the pages of this volume.

∼

The 'condition-of-women novel' began to be written in Urdu, albeit in a reformist mode, as early as the 1870s, much before its emergence in other Indian languages, with the fictional works of deputy Nazir Ahmad[6] (1830–1912), and continued through the works of Ahmad's

---

[5] Zora Neale Hurston, *Dust Tracks on the Road* (Urbana and Chicago: University of Illinois Press, 1984; originally published in 1942). This was written by the writer, rather reluctantly, at the instance of the publisher. Its reliability and authenticity has often been called into question. Hurston omitted a good part of her life from the text—she did not elaborate on the struggles she faced in her literary career and did not mention her second marriage. And though she chronicled her life from the moment of her birth she does not give a date. According to her biographer and editor of the 1984 edition of her autobiography, Robert E. Hemenway, all this was part of 'her general reluctance to locate personal experience in the common chronological record' which then contributes to a far more complex and complicit historical and political evasiveness (p. x).

[6] Nazir Ahmad's best-known novels are *Mirat ul-Uroos* (The Bride's Mirror, 1869), *Banat un-Naash* (Daughters of the Bier, 1870), and *Taubat un-Nasooh* (The Repentance of Nasooh, 1874). Two of these novels have been translated into English: *The Bride's Mirror*, translated by G.E. Ward (London: Frowde, 1903; rpt. Delhi: Permanent Black, 2001), and *The Repentance of Nasooh*, translated by M. Kempson (London: W.H. Allen, 1884; rpt. Delhi: Permanent Black, 2004).

nephew, Rashidul Khairi (1868–1936). But it would be many years before full-fledged biographical or autobiographical accounts by women in Urdu were written. Meanwhile there was a spate of women's journals; the big three were *Tahzib un Niswan* (1898), *Khatoon* (1904) and *Ismat* (1908), and the debates conducted in the pages of those journals animated the Urdu public sphere of the time.[7] These debates and the writings by women, most of whom observed purdah, seriously question the post-enlightenment assumptions of visibility and voice in the public realm as the only definitive markers of subjecthood. As Pathak and Sunder Rajan point out, 'It is not always the case that "to speak is to become a subject".'[8] The subaltern can express her agency and wield her influence in myriad forms. Accounts of Muslim women's resistance from behind the purdah have not been fully recognized, and their contribution to education and social reform has not been accounted for. A too easy analytical conflation of subjecthood and

---

[7] Ismat Chughtai's essays and reminiscences are replete with references to these journals. Aijaz Ahmad points out the extraordinary reach of these journals in his article, 'Jameson's Rhetoric of Otherness' in his *In Theory: Classes, Nations, Literatures* (London: Verso, 1994). His extended comment is relevant for our purpose here as it brings to the fore an essential facet of Urdu public sphere having its bearing on women, and the temporal and spatial contexts that Ismat Chughtai came to inhabit: '. . . Rashid-ul Khairi, for example, established a very successful publishing house, the Asmat Book Depot, which published hundreds of books for women and children, as well as four of the five journals that came into my family for two generations: *Asmat, Khatoon-e-Mashriq, Jauhar-e-Niswan, Banaat* and *Nau-Nehaal* . . . That these journals came regularly into my family for roughly forty years is itself significant, for mine was not, in metropolitan terms, an educated family. We lived in a small village, far from the big urban centres, and I was the first member of this family to finish high school or drive a car. The fact that two generations of women and children in such a family would be part of the regular readership of such journals shows the social reach of this kind of publishing' (p. 117).

[8] Zakia Pathak and Rajeswari Sunder Rajan, 'Shahbano', *Signs* 14, no. 3 (Spring 1989), pp. 570–71.

voice runs the danger of erasing or muting other narratives of agency and resistance to patriarchal structures from behind the veil or less visible spheres. The contribution of the begums of Bhopal in the social and educational sphere is living testimony to this. They were deeply religious, purdah-observing in some cases, and yet their vision was bold, independent and forward-looking for their times.[9] Segregation certainly acted against women's empowerment, as Ismat Chughtai makes clear at places in *KHP*, but to overemphasize purdah would run the risk of ignoring and erasing the work of women of remarkable grit and fortitude who were engaged in cultural and political resistance and reform. This fact needs to be stressed. In the normative nationalistic narratives of feminism in India, the Muslim woman is either erased or contained within the paradigms of veils or backwardness, a victim of her own community; in fact, she is the 'other', against which the emancipation and modernity of more visible upper-caste Hindu women is inscribed. The easy conflation between Indian and Hindu remains entirely assumed and unacknowledged in the work of many scholars in the field.[10]

~

[9] Shaharyar M. Khan, *The Begums of Bhopal: A Dynasty of Women Rulers in Raj India* (London & New York: I.B. Tauris, 2000); Siobham Lambert-Hurley, *Muslim Women, Reform and Princely Patronage: Nawab Sultan Jahan Begam of Bhopal* (London: Routledge, 2006).

[10] Geraldine Forbe's magisterial study, *Women in Modern India: The New Cambridge History of Modern India, Vol. IV* (Cambridge: Cambridge University Press, 1996), fails to chronicle the history of Muslim women and their struggle for subjectivity. Mahua Sarkar in her book, *Visible Histories, Disappearing Women: Producing Muslim Womanhood in Late Colonial Bengal* (Durham and London: Duke University Press, 2008), has dealt with this issue in the context of Muslim women from Bengal (India) and Bangladesh. She shows convincingly how Muslim women in colonial and postcolonial Bengal came to be marginalized in comparison with their Hindu counterparts. For meaningful insights on the contributions of colonial Muslim women from their seclusion, see Gail Minault, *Secluded*

There are two kinds of fiction writers. For the first kind, a biography may not be of great importance to their readers for uncovering the meaning of their works. Their works might make sense even without this frame of reference. For the other kind, a biography might contain vital information and clues for a comprehensive understanding of their works.

Whatever one might say about impersonality and self-effacement in literature, and even if one does not pitch for biographical criticism, knowledge about the biographical and social contexts of the writer might throw a specific light on them, and help readers gauge the impulse behind particular pieces of work. Among women fiction writers in Urdu, Qurratulain Hyder may be taken as illustrative of the first kind, while Ismat Chughtai is certainly representative of the second kind. Ismat preferred to characterize her writing as photography rather than painting; some of her plots are taken directly from real life with minimal changes, and biographical and historical contexts are extremely important for uncovering the significance of her works. A few examples: controversy around 'Lihaaf' has become part of Urdu literature lore and KHP gives the background of that story, the furore it caused and how the trial was carried out. Also, Ismat Chughtai's description of her journey with Manto (who was being tried for 'Bu') from Bombay to Lahore to attend the trial and her hilarious account of the actual court scene makes the readers realize how laughable the charges of obscenity against her and Manto were. 'Dozakhi' (Hell-bound), the pen-sketch of her elder brother, Azim Beg Chughtai,

---

Scholars: *Women's Education and Muslim Social Reform in Colonial India* (Delhi: Oxford University Press, 1988). For contemporary insights on Muslim women in India, see Zoya Hasan and Ritu Menon, *Unequal Citizens: A Study of Muslim Women in India* (Delhi: Oxford University Press, 2004) and Zoya Hasan and Ritu Menon (eds), *In A Minority: Essays on Muslim Women in India* (Oxford University Press, 2005). Of course, the most comprehensive source book to date on South Asian Muslim women remains Tahera Aftab's *Inscribing South Asian Muslim Women: An Annotated Bibliography* (Leiden: Brill Academic Publishers, 2007).

has acquired a lasting place in Urdu literature, but the sketch draws a rather effete and morbid image of Azim Beg; reading KHP gives us a fuller understanding of the man who was remarkable in many ways. Similarly, the protagonist of 'Bachchu Phupi', Ismat Chughtai's father's sister in real life, and an immortal character in Urdu fiction, comes across as rather quaint, eccentric and somewhat uncouth. The author's description of her in KHP adds important dimensions to her character, winning the reader's empathy. If the short story graphically describes who she was, the memoir uncovers the reason why she was so. The short story 'Bachpan' makes a deeper impact when the reader is aware of the larger context provided by KHP. Then, Terhi Lakeer, arguably the author's masterpiece, makes far greater sense if read in conjunction with KHP rather than without it, just as many of her short stories and novellas exist in an inter-textual relationship with Terhi Lakeer. 'Chauthi ka Joda' which deals with the plight of unmarried girls and their parents in middle-class Muslim families seem lifted directly from the life of Ismat's own cousin Hashmat Khanam, as one finds in the chapters 'Conflict' and 'An Incomplete Woman'. The desperate search for a husband for Hashmat Khanam drove her mother to the brink of madness. Even though she was married much below her social level, her husband turned out to be such a dissolute lout that she was compelled to live the life of a widow. Thus, all of Chughtai's works are mutually illuminating and a contrapuntal (Edward Said's term) reading of them will be immensely rewarding for the reader.

KHP thus demonstrates that as far as Ismat Chughtai was concerned, there was close correspondence between her life and her art. Any reader reading her stories, novels and plays closely will definitely arrive at her own assessment of the pieces, but familiarity with her autobiography would open them to other resonances and inter-textualities. It is in this sense that the memoir re-situates Ismat in her work.

Further, though Ismat Chughtai hardly mentions dates and years, thus undermining KHP's value as a historical document, as biographies and autobiographies often tend to, KHP often encapsulates glimpses of history and illuminates historical epochs through what looks like simple, even cursory, brushstrokes. For instance, one gets to know how Farsi lost its prominence in British India as the privileged language of administration, and an entire generation of scholars and aficionados who were making their living through this language suddenly found themselves treated as the dregs of history, through a character who finds himself anachronistic in the new cultural and linguistic configurations. There are also interesting insights into the uneasy coexistence of British India and princely India in the early decades of the twentieth century, and accounts of how the colonial masters never failed to stir trouble and wield clout even in the princely states.

Similarly, *KHP*'s value as a literary document of the time is considerable. It chronicles the stunning impact of the volume *Angarey*[11] on the Urdu scene, stirring debates that have become an important part of Urdu's literary history. Echoes of those debates, concerning the relationship between the individual and society, literature's role in holding a mirror up to society and exposing its decadent morality and hypocrisy, the question of obscenity, etc., reverberated on the precincts of Urdu literature for a long time. These debates had great salience for Ismat Chughtai and Saadat Hasan Manto, both of whom were charged with obscenity at about the same time. As noted earlier, *KHP* has a delightful account of how they both travelled together from Bombay to Lahore (along with Shahid Ahmad Dehalvi, their publisher) to attend their obscenity trials. From this account one can conceive the nature of the Urdu reading public and the Urdu public sphere of the time. The debates that were carried out in the pages of periodicals like *Adab-e-Lateef*

---

[11] *Angarey* (Embers, 1932), a collection of eight stories, radicalized the Urdu literary scene, creating an uproar of unprecedented heat. The group of writers who wrote these unconventional stories—Sajjad Zaheer, Ahmed Ali, Dr Rasheed Jahan and Mahmuduzzafar—has since been known as the 'Angarey Group'. For a detailed view of the contribution of the group, see Carlo Coppola, 'The Angare Group: The *Enfants Terribles* of Urdu Literature', *Annual of Urdu Studies*, Chicago, no. 1 (1981).

and *Saaqi* about the way the obscenity trial was conducted in Lahore were particularly salutary. Further, *KHP* draws vivid portraits of two of her literary mentors, her elder brother Azim Beg Chughtai,[12] whom she addresses as Azim Bhai in *KHP* and Rasheed Jahan, whom she calls Rasheed Apa 'Angareywali'. If Azim Beg nursed her literary talents from an early age, Rasheed Jahan divested her of all romantic and fanciful notions about man–woman relationships and brought her in touch with the reality of everyday life in which women occupied a secondary position. Ismat Chughtai acknowledges:

> The handsome heroes and pretty heroines of my stories, the candle-like fingers, the lime blossoms and crimson outfits all vanished into thin air. The earthly Rasheed Jahan simply shattered all my ivory idols to pieces . . . Life, stark naked, stood before me.[13]

Then there is the humorous portrait of Hijab Imtiaz Ali, a romantic, quaint and exotic woman writer of the earlier generation, who offered a sharp contrast to whatever Ismat Chughtai stood for.[14]

Perhaps the most important insight *KHP* contains is about the position of women, particularly Muslim women, in the society of the time. Ismat Chughtai was *writing silences*, recording the suppressed voice of women from different strata of society. The traditional

---

[12] Ismat Chughtai's immortal pen portrait of her brother, 'Dozakhi', known for its stark vividness and unsentimental detachment, has remained an unparalleled specimen of the genre in Urdu literature. It is available in English translation in M. Asaduddin (ed.), *Lifting the Veil: Selected Writings of Ismat Chughtai* (New Delhi: Penguin Modern Classics, 2009).

[13] *Women Writing in India, Vol. II: The Twentieth Century*, p. 118.

[14] Ismat Chughtai's essay/short story 'Bachpan' begins with a parody of Hijab Imtiaz Ali (neé Miss Hijab Ismail), contrasting the romantic portrayal of childhood drawn by Hijab Imtiaz Ali with her own. The story is available in English translation in *Lifting the Veil: Selected Writings of Ismat Chughtai*.

patriarchal society into which she was born contained women, muted their voices and screened out their agency. Her literary oeuvre, among other things, is a chronicle of restoring this agency if we look at it necessarily as a negotiation with structures, often subterranean and subversive, rather than visible and frontal. Her own fierce struggle to get an education against heavy odds is indicative of the challenges and the devious routes one had to take to circumvent those challenges. The virulence with which women's education was resisted is seen in the case of her elder sisters who were sent to a boarding school by their father. The entire family stood together against him for sending his daughters to a boarding school and threatened to ostracize him. He was warned that his daughters would never be married, and that he should be ready to keep them in his own house all their lives and maintain them. The spectre of spinsterhood and the associated social stigma must have loomed large in the mind of her mother, who was against the education of her daughters. The comment made by ostensibly sensible people in her extended family that 'educating girls was worse than prostituting them' only indicated the lengths to which people were ready to go in their opposition to women's education. The purdah was not merely physical segregation; women themselves internalized the mores of the patriarchal society to such an extent that they evinced symptoms of what may be termed as 'purdah of the mind'. That is why when Azim Beg Chughtai, himself a writer of considerable merit, tried to bring his wife out of purdah she herself resisted it. In another episode Azim Beg had to recant his support of the banned book *Ummat ki Maaein*,[15] make a public apology at the mosque after the Friday prayer and witness the burning of copies of the book he had wanted to promote. The episode indicates the social opprobrium any radical step evoked and the self-censoring that often resulted from it.

---

[15] *Ummat ki Maaein* (Mothers of the Muslim Community) (Delhi: Kohinoor Press, n.d.) by Rashidul Khairi was written mainly for female readers and recounted the lives of the Prophet's wives, each story containing a lesson to be learnt and emulated.

If this was the plight of Muslim middle-class women, the plight of Hindu women chronicled in the memoir was even worse. *KHP* describes the condition of child widows in Rajasthan. Society denied any dignity to these widows. Deprived of the right to marry again and of economic empowerment of any kind, they were compelled to look for a provider and find one in the maharaja of Jodhpur's family. Children would be born, sent to the palace and inducted into the maharaja's army or maharani's entourage. Deprived of any agency, they lived lives that were fashioned for them by those who dictated the patriarchal structure. It also gives the context of how an oppressive and brutal custom like sati evolved as a resolution of the women's question. Ismat's description of the royal crematorium in Sambhar, Rajasthan, where the walls were smeared with handprints of child wives who were burnt at the pyre, is disturbing, and brings out in lurid light the brutal injustice of the system.

Against this background, the contribution made by Shaikh Abdullah, the founder of the Aligarh Girls' School, and his wife, Ala Bi,[16] aka Alia Apa, appears nothing less than heroic. The school was a beacon of light in the dark firmament of women's education. The challenges these pioneers of women's education among Muslims faced were truly enormous. The generation of Muslim girls educated here constituted what Gail Minault so aptly characterized as 'daughters of reform'; many of these girls would contribute to the radicalization of the Muslim woman's consciousness. Rasheed Jahan, Shaikh Abdullah's daughter and Ismat Chughtai's mentor, was the only woman member of the 'Angarey' group who set the tone of reform in Muslim society, and Ismat Chughtai herself continued and reinforced this stream of thinking. In mounting a blistering critique of orthodoxies—Hindu, Muslim, Christian—*KHP* presents Ismat Chughtai in her true spirit as a champion of secular modernity.

∼

---

[16] Begum Waheed Jahan, popularly known as 'Ala Bi', was Shaikh Abdullah's zestful partner in pioneering women's education.

Ismat Chughtai is intimately related to the tradition of women writing in India that represents female subjectivity and feminine sensibility. The 'conjunctural terrain' that she occupied allowed her to make significant interventions in the way the women's question was sought to be articulated and the female body configured in the context of the existing power structures in society.

However, she was not a feminist in a narrow or reductive sense, her concerns being much wider and more inclusive than merely the world of women. Her works cannot be reduced to mere allegories of gender oppression. Anita Desai stresses this polyphony and plenitude in Ismat's works when she says:

> One could read her work as an exposure of Indian traditions, of religious bigotry, of the male hegemony and female illiteracy and dependence—but that would be a limited interpretation for—beside her obvious and instinctive iconoclasm—there was also her intimate involvement with that world, her delight in it—the unruly household with too many children, the squabbles and rivalries amongst the women, the displays of affection and indulgence, and the rich and colorful language, spiced with salty proverbs and aphorisms. Instead of contradicting each other, these elements came together to form such an indivisible—and infinitely rich—whole that one can only exclaim, on reading her work, 'Oh, human nature! Ah, the human race!'[17]

∼

Ismat Chughtai should also be seen in the context of the history of Muslim women's self-awareness. Her family took pride in its Mughal[18]

---

[17] Ismat Chughtai, *The Quilt and Other Stories*, translated by Tahira Naqvi and Syeda S. Hameed (New York: Sheep Meadow Press, 1994), p. viii.

[18] Her delectable story 'Mughal Bachcha' (The Mughal Brat), based on the life-story of her maternal uncle Shaikh Shamsuddin, brings out in vivid and witty detail the popular perception of the attributes of a Mughal male. The adjective 'Mughal' is frequently used by Ismat Chughtai to draw attention to some assumed and ingrained attributes of her characters.

descent and its Arab–Persian heritage. Even though Ismat fiercely asserted her Indian identity, it was a composite one articulated through an idiom which derives its salience from multiple lineages— Indian, Muslim, Mughal. It would not be far-fetched to speculate that she was brought up in an environment where pan-Islamism had its resonances. In the early decades of the twentieth century, Urdu women's magazines carried spirited and informed articles on women's movements in Muslim countries, mainly in Turkey and Egypt.[19] Ismat Chughtai mentions Halide Adib (1884–1964), the Turkish writer, activist and champion of women's rights, who visited Isabella Thoburn College, Lucknow, when Ismat was a student there. Adib had close contact with the leaders of the Indian freedom movement, visited India several times and spoke on the urgency of Muslim women's empowerment. Among her intellectual successors in the Arab world are Nawal el-Sadawi (1931–), the Egyptian feminist writer, activist and physician, Assia Djebar (1936–), the Algerian writer, and Fatima Mernissi (1940–), the Moroccan feminist and sociologist, all of whom, though younger than Ismat Chughtai, wrote and worked in more or less the same conditions and struggled with the same forces as Ismat did. These remarkable women, through their discursive strategies, sought to intervene significantly in reversing the male gaze that has traditionally characterized the construction and depiction of women and refiguration of the female body as a site to create multiple spaces of agency and social and political empowerment. The point here is that it would help if we try to locate Chughtai's radicalism and modernity in the larger context of women's liberation across the subcontinent and the world, rather than see her only within the paradigm of the Progressive Writers' Movement, and her allegiance to or discontent with it, as has been done so far both in Urdu and English. Her membership certainly lies with a greater community of

---

[19] Gail Minault, 'Muslim Social History from Urdu Women's Magazines', in her book *Gender, Language and Learning: Essays in Indo-Muslim Cultural History* (Ranikhet Cantt: Permanent Black, 2009), p. 94.

thinkers, as evidenced by the way her formidable legacy still animates the intellectual and academic realms, when her works are being increasingly available in translation in various languages.

~

A few words about her language and style: economy, naturalness, spontaneity, raciness, repartee, freshness of idiom and imagery and a witty turn of phrase are the hallmarks of Chughtai's style. These features allowed her to bring alive what has come to be known as 'begumati zubaan'— a pert, racy, earthy, graphic and colourful tone, which Gail Menault characterized as the 'voice of a sub-culture', and whose study, according to her, 'tells us a great deal about the way Muslim women lived, thought and felt, and believed, in Delhi and elsewhere, not so long ago'.[20] Ismat Chughtai also used the rich phonetic resources of Urdu to good effect in her stories and novels.[21] Above all, there is this impression of speed that Krishan Chander pointed out in his introduction to her collection of stories, *Chotein*.[22] The same speed is evident in *KHP* as well. As in many of her writings, her thoughts, here too, seem to outstrip her words, leaving many gaps. Her thought hops and jumps from topic to topic, with scant respect for coherence, and the language cannot keep up with the thought

---

[20] Gail Minault, 'Begamati Zuban: Women's Language and Culture', in ibid., pp. 116–34.

[21] This particular aspect of the phonic and the sonic has been stressed by Saadat Hasan Manto in his literary sketch, 'Ismat Chughtai'. For an English translation, see, M. Asaduddin (ed.), *For Freedom's Sake: Selected Stories and Sketches* (Karachi: Oxford University Press, 2001).

[22] 'One aspect of her stories that strikes the reader is the overpowering speed of the narrative structure, that is its movement, pace and vibrations. The story seems to gallop. And phrases, allusions, feelings, sounds and emotions of the characters move ahead with the destructive speed of a storm. Sometimes the reader lags behind, trying to keep up with the swiftness of the narrative pace and ends up cursing the writer.' (Krishan Chander, 'Foreword to Chotein', in *Ismat: Her Life, Her Times*, p. 174)

process. There are too many loose ends, sentences are mangled and incomplete, ellipses abound. At many places in KHP, readers wonder what is going on. They have to pause, think about the context, and have to be familiar with the general details of her life and her writings to make sense of the passages. They have to be alert, filling up the gaps before they move on. This also points to the challenges faced in its translation into English.

The translation of KHP in English fulfils a need that was sorely felt by those readers of Ismat Chughtai who can access her only in English, and those interested in the women's question. Researchers on Ismat Chughtai had to depend on the Devanagri version by Iftikhar Anjum[23] that has problems of its own. Only some extracts were available in the English translation, which were marred by inaccuracies.

I have tried to retain the flavour and nuances of the original, which entails tweaking of the accepted English idiom at places. More challenging were the areas of silences and ellipses, of subtle allusions and cryptic nuances, and maintaining a continuity of the narrative without any sense of rupture and repetition. I have not tinkered with the original text, except for leaving out a couple of lines at two places to avoid repetitions or details that were too jarring. Even so, repetitions could not be entirely avoided. Readers will see that the Ali Asghar episode appears twice in the narrative. I have added a few footnotes to facilitate intelligibility and continuity of the narrative, and to provide a helpful context for the understanding of the narrative. But it has to be said again that as KHP is essentially fragmentary it may not give the reader a satisfying account of the author's entire life. For readers interested in a fuller account of the author's life I would suggest reading autobiographical essays, such as 'Taraqqipasand Adab aur Main' (Progressive Literature and I), 'Bombai se Bhopal Tak' (Bombay to Bhopal), and personal sketches such as 'Mera Dost

---

[23] Ismat Chughtai, *Kaghazi Hai Pairahan*, Devanagri transcription by Iftikhar Anjum (Delhi: Rajkamal Prakashan, 1998).

Mera Dushman' (My Friend, My Enemy), 'Dozakhi' (Hell-bound), and 'Bachchu Phupi'. But, despite the fragmentary nature of *KHP* and its gaps and inadequacies, one cannot deny the fact that the individual and the social, the personal and the political come together to make it a unique document in the annals of life-writings by women in Urdu literature.

M. ASADUDDIN

DUST OF THE CARAVAN

I was weeping inconsolably.

Someone was being beaten brutally. The perpetrator was a giant-like monster, while the one being beaten was a tiny, dark-skinned child. I do not remember clearly the people involved as I was very small at the time. But I remember that when the big cane struck it made a horrific, slithering sound. The sound is embedded in my memory, and I often still hear it.

It was probably then that I realized that the big beat the small, the strong batter the weak. That was when the strong man implanted himself in my subconscious, like a tall pillar, the weaklings strewn like garbage about his feet. I lowered my head in deference to the strong and began despising the weak.

But there was something that lay hidden in the deep recesses of my mind, something of which I was not aware. Whenever I saw a magnificent palace eaten away by moss sprouting on its walls and grass growing over it pitilessly, in the heart of my hearts I would smile secretly. The power within those insignificant grasses and weeds would overwhelm me.

We were so many siblings* that my mother felt nauseated by the very sight of us. One after another we had tumbled to the earth, pummelling and battering her womb. Suffering endlessly from vomiting and labour pains, she looked upon us as objects of her punishment. Her body had flattened at a young age and looked like a platform. She had become a grandmother at the age of thirty-five

---

* Ten siblings, to be exact—four sisters and six brothers.

1

and suffered continual punishment. We children had been left pretty much to the care of servants, and we became very close to them.

Servants have two faces—one they show to the master, while kissing his hand and feet, and the other revealed only behind his back, while calling him names and giving vent to their feelings. There isn't a class of people more unfortunate and helpless than domestic servants. This is particularly true of India where unemployment and poverty have forced a large number of people to act as slaves to the small class that rules over them.

There were some servants who had been with our family for generations. Their minds had become enslaved along with their bodies. They were incorrigibly lazy, stupid and sly. If they were turned out they would wander about aimlessly for a couple of days and then return to the peg to which they had been tied. Just like pet dogs. However, now that the country has progressed and unemployment reduced, it is difficult to come by servants with such a slave-like mentality.

As a child I have seen servants treated with such contempt that I developed an intense hatred for the system that allows some to be masters and others to be servants. Servants appear as characters in many of my stories. Weak and helpless servants, lying, cheating and cunning servants—my stories have plenty of them. In my limited world, class differences manifested themselves in the relationship between servants and their masters, and it left a deep impression on my mind. But as I came in contact with the wider world I realized that the distinctions between the high and the low and between castes are only a sham. The real distinction is between wealth and poverty. This is the way of the world. A rich person, however devout and patriotic, treats the poor like a servant.

No one had the time for love and pampering. Tricks learnt from servants proved useful; whenever I needed something I would snatch it from anyone who had what I wanted.

All of us, brother and sisters, were adept at full-throated yelling. Disquieted, Amma would promptly give in to our demands. We were absolutely sure of this power that we had over others. It is only by crying and howling that children can express their likes and dislikes.

One day, in a majlis, I realized for the first time the significance of marsiya and nauha. When the narrator began to describe how Ali Asghar's gullet was pierced by an arrow, I was overwhelmed by grief and began to howl. The women observing maatam suddenly became quiet and stared at me in amazement. They thought that the long wait for the tabarruk, the consecrated food, had become unbearable for me, or that I had been hurt, or bitten by an insect.

'Why shoot the arrow? And why in the throat?' I asked in my usual, obstreperous manner. No one cared to reply. They thought I was crazy and stubborn, and turned me out.

Returning home, my brothers complained about my making a racket in the majlis and embarrassing them. They reported that I was most shamefully kicked out.

'Why did he shoot the arrow? He could have shot him in the arm, why in the throat, poor baby?' I demanded persistently.

'Enough. Now shut up and go to sleep,' I was reprimanded.

But how could I sleep? The moment I closed my eyes, an image of an arrow stuck in the face of the baby swam before me and I started howling all over again.

'Go to hell, you ill-fated brat! Just go to sleep, you witch, or I will strangle you.' One by one, the elders threatened to snuff the life out of me, but my sobbing did not stop. Then, overcome by fear, I sneaked into Shekhani Bua's bed. I was afraid to sleep all by myself.

'Why did they shoot the arrow?' I sidled up to Shekhani Bua and asked between sobs.

'That Yezid was a bastard,' she explained.

'Then why did they take the baby to him?'

'The baby was thirsty.'

'They should have given him milk.'

'His mother's milk had dried up.'

'He could have been given water to drink.'

'There was no water, because his army was guarding the stream.'

'Why?'

'How do I know? There was some problem, I suppose.'

'Then?'

'They took the baby to the river so that he could drink water, when the arrow was shot.'

'In the throat.'

'Yes.'

And large, thorny balls seemed to get stuck in my throat.

'You and your arrow! She won't sleep herself and won't allow anyone else to sleep!' My mother, who was listening, slapped me so hard and then punched me so that it certainly seemed like my own Karbala.

For years afterwards, this incident became part of my family lore, and it would be recounted gleefully, to my utter humiliation, to guests. 'She howled in the majlis and was kicked out. Then Amma gave her a sound thrashing!' my brothers would report to my deep embarrassment. This was my life's first major upset and it had a long-lasting effect. After this, going to a majlis became terrifying for me; I knew that allusion would be made to the shooting of the arrow in the throat, and thorny lumps would get stuck in my throat, disturbing the sacred ambience of the majlis.

Several years ago I saw a film about Hitler's exploits. The sight of millions of decaying corpses revived the consciousness of the arrow stuck in Ali Asghar's throat. There has been an ongoing veritable bloodbath in Vietnam for the last twelve years. Where are the people who can stop it? How long will humanity remain a helpless witness to such spectacles? Human beings have ostensibly given up cannibalism, but the truth is that they continue to devour human flesh in some form or the other. I couldn't care less for such a world, and detest the principles of the system which allows this.

There was another incident from my childhood that left a deep impression on me. My father was an enlightened gentleman. He met many Hindu families socially, that is to say, Hindus and Muslims of a particular class embraced each other gracefully and were aware of each other's sensibilities. From a young age we were aware that there was some distinction between Hindus and Muslims. Outward profession of brotherhood went hand in hand with discreet caution. If a Hindu was visiting, meat wouldn't be mentioned, and even sitting at the same table one had to take care not to touch any of their belongings. Their food would be served by a different set of servants; it would be cooked by a maharaj, a Brahmin cook from the neighbourhood, from where utensils would also be borrowed. I felt suffocated by this hypocrisy. They talked about enlightenment and liberal ideas, professed deep love for each other, and recounted tales of great sacrifice for each other. The English were held to be the main culprits. All this would go on while the elders were secretly nervous about the children doing something that would defile the purity of religion!

'Are some Hindus coming?' we asked, seeing restrictions being imposed on us and feeling bored.

'Don't be cheeky! Chachaji and Chachiji are coming. Just remember, if you are impertinent you will be skinned alive.'

We could guess that it wasn't Chachaji and Chachiji who were coming. If they were, then seekh kebab and roast chicken would have been cooked; lauki raita and dahi bade would not have been prepared. The difference between 'cooked' and 'prepared' was interesting.

A businessman, Lalaji, lived in our neighbourhood. His daughter was my closest friend. Children were not subjected to the restrictions of caste up to a certain age. Sushi used to eat with us frequently— well, there was not much defilement in eating fruits and snacks. As we children knew that Sushi did not eat meat we took great delight in tricking her into eating it. She never came to know of it, but I do not know what instinct in us derived pleasure from this mischief. We would be in each other's houses through the day, but on Bakr-eid, Sushi would be locked up. Goats would be slaughtered behind screens in our backyard, and meat would be distributed for several days after that. During those days our relationship with Lalaji would stand ruptured. And when there was a festival in their house, we would be placed under guard.

One day, there was a fun-filled celebration at Lalaji's house. It was Janmashtami. Large pans were set up on one side and snacks of one kind or another were being fried in them. Standing around like beggars, we were gazing longingly at them, drawn irresistibly by the appetizing aroma of the goodies. On such occasions, Sushi would turn very devout, even though we had many times, away from watchful eyes, taken bites of the same guava.

'Be off!' we were pushed away by others, but the next moment we were back. Which child could resist the sight of the fat pooris being fried?

'What is inside?' I asked Sushi, pointing to the room in the front which had been decked up like a bride, with flowers and leaves. One could hear the sound of bells ringing inside. We were dying of curiosity. 'Who is in there?'

'Bhagwan is sitting there,' Sushi said, turning her head in pride.

'Bhagwan?' I was overwhelmed by a sense of inferiority. How easily their Bhagwan came and went. And there's our Allah Mian—no one knew where He remained hidden. Motivated by an unknown urge I left the line of beggars and climbed on the veranda. No one in Sushi's family noticed me; after all, my religion was not written on my face. A lady with a tray of aarti appeared and began to apply chandan–chawal to everyone's forehead. She applied it to mine too. I tried to wipe off the dot but my mischievous nature took over. We had been told that the spot where the dot is applied would be consigned to hell. Well, I had a surfeit of flesh; it would be no big deal if such a tiny spot ended up in hell! Brought up in the company of servants one could learn a lot of worldly tricks. The certificate painted on my head now, I entered the room where Bhagwan was seated in regal splendour.

What delightful fancies the eyes of childhood weave! The room was filled with the aroma of ghee and frankincense. A silver cradle hung in the middle of the room. Nestled on mattresses and between silken pillows, decked with gold and silver edgings, was a silver infant swaying in the cradle. It was a beautiful piece of artwork. Hair drawn beautifully, he had a necklace around his neck and a diadem of peacock feathers on his head.

What an innocent face he had! The eyes shone as though lit with lamps. Maternal love welled up in my heart. The child broke into a laugh and spread out his arms longingly. I touched the child's cheek softly. My entire being danced with joy. Unable to control the impulse I picked up the child and clasped him to my breast.

A virtual storm erupted, and the child jumped out of my lap with a scream and fell down. Sushi's grandmother's mouth was a gaping hole. She was hysterical, as though by kissing the silver infant I had pierced his throat with an arrow.

Chachiji grabbed my hand, dragged me to the door and then threw me out as though I were a dead lizard. A complaint was promptly lodged with my family that I had tried to steal the silver image of god. Amma first beat her own head and then gave me a thrashing. Thank God we had a good relationship with Lalaji; riots broke out those days on much flimsier grounds. I was taught that the worship of images was a sin. Mahmud Ghaznavi was an idol-breaker. I didn't understand; the idea of worship had not occurred to me. I was not performing any puja, just hugging a baby.

After this incident, members of my family began to give serious thought to my afterlife. My heart was filled with the notion of Islam's superiority, that it was the best and the greatest of all religions on the face of the earth. The slogan of brotherhood among all people had its own place, but the fact of the matter was that a Muslim was after all a Muslim, they said. I was also introduced to the First Arabic Reader, the *Baghdadi Qaeda*. Sleep would overwhelm me as I repeated the endless conjugations. The sound of the rhythmic alliterations had the impact of a lullaby, but when Mullaniji's whack fell on a back with a thudding sound, any trace of drowsiness vanished. Mullaniji had impaired vision, was deaf and extremely bad-tempered. It was said that her late husband would tie her to a charpai and rip her skin off with wet twine. She would slap me a few times for every word I uttered. She taught about twenty children and would hit, slap and whack each of them. With her dry, skinny fingers she would pinch the flesh on my fat thighs. We would read ayats to wish death on her. I have

never hated any human being as intensely as I did that old crone.
Moreover, whatever she taught me seemed like a curse from Allah.

I got past childhood somehow. I never understood why people
sing such paeans to childhood.* Childhood exemplifies restrictions
and deprivation. When one grows up one acquires positions from
which one can fight injustice. Having suffered the love and affection
of eight brothers and sisters, I was eager to come into adulthood.
When nephews and nieces were born, a new sense of seniority proved
immensely comforting. A lack of equality is found not only among
the rich and the poor; it exists in a more intense form in the power
relationship between men and women.

My father was a liberal. On principle, he safeguarded the rights
of girls more than those of boys, but in practice, girls and boys were
equal in the same way as Hindus and Muslims were brothers. It was
considered necessary to pay lip service to some platitudes.

I don't know whether it was my good or ill luck, but by the time I
began to understand things my three elder sisters were already married.
To be the only sister among several brothers is not a bad situation at
all. At the slightest hint of my rights being violated the case would
be taken to Abba's court.

My sisters were adept in the art of housekeeping. They were not
only proficient in Urdu, Farsi and the Quran, but also in sewing,
embroidery and cooking. I was clumsy in everything . . . All I was
interested in was climbing trees and riding a bicycle like my brothers.
I felt like a write-off; I stood nowhere in comparison with my brothers
either. And why should they have felt sorry for me? Encouraged by
Abba, I was bent on competing with them in everything. Everyone
would take a turn in riding the horse, but the moment my turn came
my brothers would begin grumbling. If I played gulli-danda with them
I was given a crushing defeat. If I insisted on playing football with
them, all the kicks would land on my forehead. My brothers found

---

* Ismat Chughtai's memorable story 'Bachpan' (Childhood) takes a wry,
unemotional look at childhood.

my stubbornness extremely annoying. Before they got married, my elder sisters ran the household. They were in charge of the keys to the store-room, they stitched all the clothes, and for that reason my brothers did not mind being ruled by them. As for me, I was a pain in the neck.

Azim Bhai was always sick. I could not keep up with my brothers as I was a girl and he could not keep up with them because of his illness. He felt sorry for me. He said to me, 'Boys are like bulls, why do you want to be a bull? Take them on in the sphere of learning; there you will beat them hands down.'

He began to teach me very resolutely and got me two double promotions. At this time, my elder brother failed his exam. He was a year and a half older but three classes ahead of me. Then one day we found ourselves in the same class and when I began to help him with his homework, I felt as though I was older. Spurred by Azim Bhai I read the Quran in translation and the traditions of the Prophet and Muslim history. And then I began to take part in the discussions among Abba's friends, showing off my new-found knowledge. My mother was horrified and went for her shoes, as was her habit. But Abba's encouragement egged me on and I learnt many things in the company of my father's elderly friends.

My mother did not like my activities at all. She was worried about my future—'These manly pursuits do not befit a woman,' she would say. She had little understanding of my pursuits, and could not explain things to me either. Later I found out why my mother was so anxious. This was a man's world, she said, made and distorted by man. A woman is a tiny part of this world and man has made her the object of his own love and hatred. Depending on his whims, he worships her or rejects her. To make a place for herself in the world a woman has to resort to feminine wiles. Patience, prudence, wisdom and social graces—these will make a man dependent on a woman. From the start, she'd say, make a boy so dependent on you that he feels embarrassed to sew his own button and would die of shame if he has to prepare his own meal. Do all the small chores that a servant can do, bear with his injustices with quiet self-abasement so he eventually feels remorseful and falls at your feet to ask for forgiveness!

But I had spent my life in the company of my brothers. I was greedy to be like them and even outdo them. I considered femininity a sham, and looked upon compromise as falsehood, patience as cowardice and gratitude as duplicity. I was not in the habit of beating about the bush. Even decking up, wearing gaudy clothes and applying make-up to hide one's blemishes seemed a kind of deception.

'No boy will ever fall for such a girl,' my clever friends warned me. Frightened, I would try to act on their warning, providing a field day for my brothers. There was no place for formality amongst us that would make them hesitate in telling the truth; if I was candid with them they were even more so with me. I became the butt of jokes. 'Ah, decking up to snare boys!' Could I dare wear any make-up after that?

Experience has taught me that a woman needs neither light nor heavy make-up. I never had any dearth of friends, and some of these friendships bordered on love. When I met girls in Russia who did not take any interest in cosmetics and wore simple, workman-like clothes, I asked them why they didn't dress themselves up.

'Never felt the need! Why, do I look ugly?' one of them threw back at me.

'Not really. But you will look even more beautiful [if you wear make-up].'

'I would like to offer goods that are genuine. My own complexion, lips and femininity are good enough,' she replied with confidence.

In Europe too, the younger generation is fed up of cosmetics. To maintain the eternal relationship between man and woman it is enough for a man to be a man and a woman to be a woman. The Russian girls made a deep impression on me. In my stories I have written a great deal about women's economic subjugation and helplessness. If a girl obeys the men in her family simply because she is economically dependent on them, then it is not obedience but deception. If a wife stays with her husband simply because he is her provider then she's as helpless as a prostitute. The children born of such a mother will only display helplessness and a slavish mentality. Such a people would always be dependent on the munificence of developed nations. As long as the women of our country continue to suffer oppression without resistance we will be weighed down by a sense of inferiority in political and economic spheres too.

Rasheed Jahan left a deep impact on me when I was quite young. I tried to learn candidness and self-respect from her.

As a child, I had another very close friend, Mangu, the daughter of our coachman. She was a little older than I was and would often throw her weight around on that account. She was married at the age of thirteen or fourteen after which she left for Lucknow. When she returned with her first daughter she looked quite subdued. Her playfulness had vanished; there was no smile on her face. Her mother-in-law, I learnt, would beat her frequently for the crime of having borne a girl child. She also incited her son to beat Mangu.

When Mangu came back with her third daughter, Abba had retired and we had moved to Agra. In the exceedingly restrictive environs of Agra I observed the utter helplessness of women. Nearly all the women of the neighbourhood looked consumptive and depressed, exploited by their husbands and other members of their husbands' families. They somehow maintained a precarious existence on the strength of amulets and charms and back-breaking hard work. I felt even more repelled by the fate of being a woman.

Mangu too had the look of a tuberculosis patient. Her mother-in-law was planning to get her son married a second time, in the hope that the second daughter-in-law would produce male progeny. Mangu's parents were mourning this development, trembling at the thought of taking on the burden of Mangu and her three daughters. Mangu's three daughters—crying and loitering about—were like a gaping advertisement of the insignificance of womankind. I felt angry with God for the injustice of making me a girl, and prayed longingly to Him to somehow turn me into a boy.

Abba, through the superintendent of police of Lucknow, exerted pressure on Mangu's husband to call her back, threatening him with arrest if he dared to marry a second time. When she returned after a year she was unrecognizable. She had not produced a son, yet she looked healthy and plump. It emerged that Mangu was possessed by spirits. These were very dangerous and vile spirits who, after entering Mangu's body, inflamed her to give her mother-in-law a thrashing. One day she also bit her husband's ankle. Everyone was terrified of her. When the exorcists were brought they said that her mother-in-law was a cursed woman and if Mangu stayed with her she would bear seven daughters and all the kith and kin would be ruined. The poor mother-in-law was in dire straits. Mangu's husband took her with him to Daliganj where he had a new job, looking after the horses of the sahibs. That was when I realized that though illiterate and uncultivated, Mangu was not stupid. She did what she needed to, demonstrating that a woman may be weak but does not have to be stupid. The sense of inferiority that plagued me all those years left me. It is not necessary to be a boy, what you need is the intelligence and ingenuity of a boy; armed with this knowledge, I shelved sewing and needlework and concentrated on getting myself an education.

Religion was never imposed on us as an instrument to enter paradise or avoid hell. Abba's friends came from different faiths and beliefs. After listening to their conversations many of my superstitions and fears were allayed. Every person will go to his own grave and answer to God for himself. I had no fear of the ways of the world and, in any case, the Mughals are known to be somewhat crazy. My family was also so large that it seemed an entire world in itself; every member was absorbed in his own life and was self-reliant.

It was considered appropriate only for boys to have such an attitude. All the women in our family—Amma, my maternal and paternal aunts, my uncles' wives—were appalled at my conduct. For a woman, it was not proper to have such a sharp tongue. How would she adjust herself to her in-laws? Society has accorded a place for women, and if a woman sets her foot outside its boundaries, her feet would be cut off. Too much education was dangerous. In our family there were no restrictions on speech and action; but this was valid only for men, and if I wanted to exercise the same freedom I was reprimanded.

I do not know what pleasure Azim Bhai got from urging me on. After returning from office in the evenings, he would engage me in conversation for an hour or so which, in fact, meant he incited me to rebellion. Abandoning writing essays in a serious vein, as was his wont, he had begun writing stories. These stories achieved what his serious essays failed to do. His heroines would be extremely interesting women, full of mischief. What I have learnt from him was that if you want to say something, wrap the message neatly in a story or a narrative and you will draw less flak. People will read your stories and be influenced by them. Before writing stories I had written several essays which got little attention. However, as soon as I wrote two or three stories they created quite a stir. Just as no one can slap you if you say something over the telephone, you can say whatever you want through your stories, and no hand can reach for your throat.

In the beginning I did not know how people reacted to my work. I wrote only for *Saaqi*, and the letters that came for me were thrown away by the editors of the journal. Unfortunately, 'Lihaaf' was the first story that was published immediately after my marriage, and thinking I would be responsible enough, Shahid Ahmad Sahib* handed over all the letters to me. The tone of these letters was so frightening that initially I broke out into a cold sweat. Thoroughly chastened, I reined in my pen, and as far as I know, I haven't slackened it afterwards. But I bore the curse of the environs in which I was brought up. I could not give up the habit of speaking my mind. And when people, annoyed by my forthrightness, stooped to name-calling, I did not take it as a personal affront. I was accustomed to squabbling and fighting bitterly, and then making up. I enjoy teasing people and if, in return, anyone hurls stones at me, I do not hold it against him.

Books have affected me more than anything else in my life. Every book I have read has given me something. I have looked for answers

---

* Editor of *Saaqi*

to most of my problems in books and found them. Books have proved to be my closest friends, providing me succour in moments of sorrow. I have coped with my hours of darkness and a thousand deprivations with the help of these friends.

I developed a close affinity with the authors of the books I read. How many names can I recount? I started with Hardy and the Brontë sisters and went on to Bernard Shaw. But the Russian writers influenced me the most. When my mind and intellect needed a guide, I encountered these authors and their books. Political philosophy appeared drab and Russian literature informed every corner of my mind. I still read Chekhov for good luck. When I can't come to grips with a story, can't make out where to begin and where to end, I read a couple of stories by Chekhov as an intellectual exercise. All at once my mind lights up and my pen begins to move.

After books is chatting. My family is extremely talkative, and when a few members gather we forget everything else. We talk as we walk, eat or drink. One may need to go for a bath in the midst of a conversation but no matter; we continue taking part in the discussion even as we bathe. Every other minute the bather will pop his head out of the window, and continue to add his bit to the discussion even while rubbing soap on his body. I enjoy talking to everyone— shopkeepers, grocers, taxi drivers, even beggars. Teasing old men and women and hearing them hurling curses and calling me names gives me a special kind of pleasure. It is not essential for your interlocutor to be educated, wise and erudite. Talking to simple, illiterate people often opens windows of the mind. To understand human beings it is necessary to talk to them. I have had such practice in talking to people that in five minutes I can extract from a person information about his whole life. You have to ask only a few simple questions which will lead to a very productive meeting.

Talking is an extremely interesting activity. I talked with Sufia Jan Nisar Akhtar so much more in her short life than I have done with others for years. Talking to Manto sharpened my sensibilities; six or seven hours would pass as though they were a couple of minutes.

His wife, Safiya, was also quite chatty. Sultana Jafri is also a great one to have chats with. I have great fun engaging Sardar Jafri* in provocative conversations and bandying words with him. Those who have the experience of talking with him know that he can be as incisive, caustic and bitter in his use of words as he can be soft and sweet; if he so desires, he can leave anyone charred by the fire of his words. There was a time when, in literary gatherings, if anyone incurred his displeasure Sardar would use the power of his jibes and stop taunting only after reducing that person to tears. Ever since he has fallen ill, literary assemblies have become somewhat insipid and a cautious atmosphere has set in. One could never talk enough with Qudsiya Zaidi, and now when I talk with her daughter Shama Zaidi,** her memory revives. Just a few words with Salma Siddiqui leave you in a good frame of mind. Ainee*** has also turned out to be quite chatty. She talks very fast, as though there is so much to say and time is running out.

However, it must be said that in matters of chatting and talking, no one can beat my maternal cousins, Akhtar and Jamila. In their presence other people seem dumb. After talking with them for several hours I feel as if the rust in my tongue has been scraped off. Sentences tumble off our tongues of their own accord. Broken, incomplete and fragmented sentences—but full of meaning. The maternal side of

---

* Ali Sardar Jafri (1913–2000), Urdu writer, poet, critic and film lyricist from India. One of the foremost leaders of the Progressive Writers' Movement, he was also the co-editor of *Naya Adab*, the movement's journal. He has more than a dozen collections of poems to his credit in addition to several anthologies that he edited. He was married to Sultana Jafri.

** Shama Zaidi (1938–) theatre person, screenwriter, costume designer and documentary filmmaker.

*** Qurratulain Hyder (1928–2007) was the most celebrated writer of Urdu fiction of the twentieth century. She is particularly known for her magnum opus, *Aag Ka Darya* (River of Fire), a novel that spans several centuries of Indian history, culture and civilization. She was known as Ainee or Ainee Apa among her friends and admirers.

their family traces its lineage from the begums of Delhi, a connection which lent a peculiar charm to their conversations. The dialogues in my stories are borrowed from the language they used.

After chatting and meaningless conversations, comes writing. Farsi was considered to be the mother tongue of our family. My father's older brother fought as a lone soldier in defence of Farsi. He did not allow his sons to receive an English education. They used to read, write and speak Farsi with great fluency but could not find jobs.

Taya Abba died a pauper. Still, he insisted that all his nephews also study Farsi. Abba, who abided by all the decisions of his elder brother, took exception to this and decided that his sons would not study Farsi. Of course, the daughters were a different matter. I am talking of a time when my three elder sisters had studied Farsi and were already married. So, the only person who could be used as a drawing board was this humble self. My brothers seized upon this decision as a proof of their superiority and, declaring me inferior, teased me to such an extent that I developed an intense aversion to Farsi. But Taya Abba had nothing to do except say his prayers and teach me Farsi. Thus, my brothers won and I lost.

'Study Farsi and sell oil,' my brothers would hurl the popular adage of the time at me, adding insult to my injury, and I would shed tears while cramming Farsi. The moment I could exercise my will I rebelled against Farsi. However, by that time Taya Abba had taught me so much that later, when I wanted a bird's-eye view of ancient and modern Farsi literature, I found the language familiar. Taya Abba had died by then and I couldn't thank him. Still, I would think twice before using Farsi in my speech. Another thing—the language spoken at home was so rich that while writing stories I did not need to pause to search for suitable words. Man can express every thought in his language of everyday speech. At that time my language was closer to Hindi, as Hindi had not yet become so turgid. It was quite fluent and sweet, a quality that has survived in the tongues of women from Delhi and Agra.

I feel the same kind of pleasure in writing as in reading. I have enjoyed my most fulfilling moments while writing, and my writings have helped me cope with my most difficult moments. I have unburdened myself of many woes in my writings, as I have taken upon myself many other burdens. The pen is my provider as well as my friend and confidant, a friend who keeps me company in my hours of loneliness. While it was with me I have never felt alone. I can send for any person, and at any moment, through this udankhatola, and when they arrive I can say anything I want to them—make them laugh, cry, burn them to cinders and, if I so desire, tear them to pieces. I can make them dance like puppets before me. In those moments I feel some of the power of the Creator.

It would be easy for me to say who hasn't influenced me. All the people I have come across in my life have left their imprint on my mind: after Azim Bhai, so many of my friends, teachers and even people I ran into while travelling. Dr Ashraf has solved so many questions for me. Dr Ram Vilas Sharma helped me gather my dispersed thoughts and give them coherence. In Krishan Chander's stories I came across strange and delicate idols.

Whenever I meet Fazlur Rahman, the pro-vice-chancellor of Aligarh Muslim University, I use him as a 'ready reckoner'. If you allude to any play or verse from a poem, he can launch into a recitation from memory. Without knowing it, he has taught me a great deal. Shahid Latif* was more than a husband. When he related to me as a friend our relationship acquired another dimension. Though marriage usually spells a death knell for friendships, ours remained stubbornly firm. Shahid would look through each of my stories and novels before they were sent for publication. Though I never told him, I attached great value to his opinion. If he ever caught me out, he would put on such airs!

The children's novel, *Teen Anarhi* (Three Novices), is based entirely on my three nephews. In fact, it would not be wrong to say that the novel is their biography.

---

* Ismat Chughtai's husband. She married him in 1942, against the wishes of the members of her family.

Nathuram, our family dhobi in Aligarh, has remained a close friend. Whenever I visit Aligarh he comes himself to collect the laundry and, sitting on his haunches, chats for hours. I have heard stories from him which cannot be found in books. He mostly sings kathas, in his aged, trembling voice. He taps a beat on the threshold with the finger adorned with a silver ring and provides musical accompaniment by rapping his amulet. His guru is a water carrier who is very wise. Nathuram intersperses his narrative with his guru's sayings. He recites *Aalha Udal** stories with great zest. He charges five rupees for the recitation, and one rupee for the rickshaw fare, for a session that spills over to four to five hours. If you seek clarification he will provide a commentary in chaste Braj bhasha. I have learned from him the speech pattern of his class.

In college I learnt a lot about other religions from Dr Tucker's lectures and under her guidance I read quite a lot. The cobwebs that had formed in my mind about religion were all dusted away. Buddhism had a great impact on me. Soon after doing my BA I had the occasion to go to Agra in connection with a property issue. On reaching there I got to know that Sushi, my childhood friend, was getting married the following day. The entire family was invited. I was surprised that a conservative and obscurantist Hindu like Lalaji had maintained a family relationship with my brother. As for me, having broken all bonds I had reached a point where humanity was my only god. How could I relate to Sushi? Sushi is compelled to lead a fraudulent existence; she considers the chap chosen by her parents her spiritual god. I still

---

* *Aalha Udal* is a popular ballad in the Bundelkhand region telling the tales of two warrior brothers, Aalha and Udal. Its singing style is very dynamic and full of lyricism. Aalha and Udal were two Rajput brothers, in the service of the last Mahoba ruler, Raja Piramal. Prithviraj Chauhan attacked Mahoba in 1182 and the brothers fought valiantly to protect their raja, dying in the process. The court poet Jagnik Rao wrote an epic comprising 20,000 verses dealing with their valour, known as *Veer Kavya*. The *Aalha Udal* is sung all over Uttar Pradesh by the Yadavs and kshatriyas and reflects more of a martial than musical essence.

remembered what had happened on that Janmashtami, though we had left Agra after that incident and moved to Aligarh.

When Lalaji came to know of my arrival, he sent Suresh, his younger son, to fetch me. I was not keen on going.

'I'll come in the evening,' I said.

'Didi requests you to come now because the rituals will start soon and she won't be able to talk to you then,' Suresh persisted.

I went over to find Sushi, covered in turmeric paste, sitting in the room where one day Bhagwan Krishna's cradle had been set up. I had a momentary impulse to step back when Sushi leapt from her place.

'How are you, dear Chunni?' she asked, using my pet name. I had left this name far behind, just like my childhood, and had the strange feeling that she was addressing someone else, not me. She drew me to her and locked the door.

Outside, her grandmother was muttering, 'It isn't good to allow all sorts of people to come at a time like this.'

For a long time Sushi gazed at me as her eyes brimmed over. She was not taken in by my smile which was affected. She gave me a mischievous look, as one would to make up with a child who was sulking.

'Hai Ram, how tall you have grown, like a palm tree!' Still not finding any crack in the wall, she opened the cupboard and took out a plate of sweets. I was going to pick a laddoo, with the intention of throwing it in the dustbin later. Why should I eat something handed by those who consider our touch a defilement?

'No, no. Open your mouth.'

Reluctantly, I took a bite from the laddoo in her hand. Sushi placed the rest of the laddoo in her mouth. So, she too had not forgotten!

The walls spread out their arms. We put our heads together and, laughing to our heart's content, recounted the pleasurable misadventures of childhood. As I was leaving, Sushi placed a tiny brass image of the crawling Krishna on my palm.

'Hey you witch, this is for you. Happy now?'

I am a Muslim. For a Muslim, idol worship is strictly forbidden.

But devmala, in Indian mythology, is a part of my country's heritage. It has absorbed the culture and philosophy of centuries. Faith is one thing, the culture of one's country is quite another. I have an equal share in it, in its earth, sunshine and water. If I splash myself with colour during Holi, or light up diyas during Diwali, will my faith suffer an erosion? Are my beliefs so brittle and judgements so shaky that they will fall to pieces?

I have travelled beyond all limits of worship.

Well, what more is there to write? If one's eyes are open and ears alert one can see and hear so many things. A dot is formed in the mind. Such dots are connected to form words, and words form chains of a narrative.

Sometimes it also happens that instead of a dot there is a wound. Wounds cannot be connected to form words and a narrative chain. A vacuum is formed in its place. When I get the news of Hindu–Muslim riots from any part of the country, my pen mocks me, and the laddoo placed in my mouth by Sushi becomes a poisonous, thorny ball stuck in my throat, threatening to explode. Then I take out the image of the infant Krishna from my cupboard and ask him: 'Are you really the dream of a romantic poet? Haven't you been born in my own land of birth? Aren't you more than a fancy, a longing? Are you the imaginary creation of a helpless woman shackled by so many restrictions, who, after creating you, swallowed life's poison with a smiling face?

Can't you take out the arrow stuck in this earth's throat?

But the brass Bhagwan cannot even laugh at my stupidity, as he is frozen in his metal shell. Politics, the most profitable profession in the world, is the god on this earth. The blood of the innocent is used to wash the black stains of defeat suffered in politics. Human beings are led to fight one another like dogs in order to prove the rival's incapability.

Will god break out of his brass shell one day?

IN THE NAME OF THOSE MARRIED WOMEN . . .

whose decked-up bodies
atrophied on loveless,
deceitful beds

—Faiz Ahmad Faiz

It was about four, or perhaps half past four in the afternoon, when the doorbell rang loudly. The servant opened the door, and then drew back in fear.

'Who's there?'

'Police!' Whenever a theft took place in the mohalla, all the servants were interrogated.

'Police?' Shahid got up, peeved.

'Yes, sir.' The servant was shaking with fear. 'I haven't done anything, Sahib. I swear by God.'

'What's the matter?' Shahid asked, going up to the door.

'Summons.'

'Summons? But . . . well, where is it?'

'Sorry. I can't give it to you.'

'Summons for what? For whom?'

'For Ismat Chughtai. Please call her.' The servant heaved a sigh of relief. 'But tell me this . . .'

'Please call her. The summons is from Lahore.'

I had boiled milk for my two-month-old daughter, Seema, and was waiting for it to cool. 'Summons from Lahore?' I asked as I held the feeding bottle in cold water.

21

'Yes, from Lahore.' Shahid had lost his cool by then. Holding the bottle in my hand, I came out barefoot.

'What is the summons about?'

'Read it out,' said the police inspector dourly.

As I read the heading—Ismat Chughtai vs The Crown—I broke into laughter. 'Good God, what complaint does the exalted king have against me to file the suit?'

'It's no joke,' the inspector said dourly. 'Read it first and sign it.'

I read through the summons but could barely make any sense of it. My story 'Lihaaf' had been accused of obscenity. The government had brought a suit against me, and I had to appear before the Lahore High Court in January. Otherwise the government would penalize me severely.

'Well, I won't take the summons.'

'You have to.'

'Why?' I began to argue as usual.

'What's up?' This was Mohsin Abdullah, sprinting up the stairs. He was returning from somewhere unknown, and his body was covered with dust.

'Just see, these people want to inflict this summons on me. Why should I take it?' Mohsin had passed his law exams with a first class.

'I see. Which story is this?' he asked after reading the summons.

'It's an ill-fated story that has become a source of torment for me.'

'You'll have to take the summons.'

'Why?'

'Don't be stubborn,' Shahid flared up.

'I won't take it.'

'If you don't, you'll be arrested,' Mohsin growled.

'Let them arrest me. I won't take the summons.'

'You'll be thrown into prison.'

'Prison? Good. I've a great desire to see a prison house. I've urged Yusuf umpteen times to take me to a prison, but he just smiles. Inspector Sahib, please take me to jail. Have you brought handcuffs?' I asked him endearingly.

The inspector was flustered. Barely restraining his anger he said, 'Don't joke. Just sign it.'

Shahid and Mohsin railed against me. I was chattering merrily.

'When my father was a judge in Sambhar, the court used to be held in the mardana, the part of the house meant for menfolk. Through the window we would see thieves and robbers being brought in handcuffs and chains. Once, a band of fearsome robbers was brought in. They had a beautiful woman among them. A stately figure in coat and breeches, she had the eyes of an eagle, her waist was supple as a leopard's and she had a luxuriant crop of long, black hair on her head. I was captivated by her . . .'

Shahid and Mohsin confused me thoroughly. I had wanted the inspector to hold the feeding bottle so that I could sign, but he retreated with shock as though I had held a gun at him. Mohsin quickly snatched away the bottle from me, and I signed.

'Come down to the police station to sign the surety document. The surety is five hundred rupees.'

'I don't have five hundred rupees with me now.'

'Not you. Someone else must stand surety for you.'

'I don't want to implicate anyone. If I don't present myself in court, the money will be lost.' I tried to show off my knowledge of the law. 'Please arrest me.'

The inspector didn't get angry this time. He smiled and looked at Shahid, who was sitting on the sofa holding his head in his hands. Then he said to me gently, 'Please come along. It'll take a couple of minutes.'

'But the surety?' I asked, pacified. I was ashamed of my stupid behaviour.

'I'll stand surety for you,' said Mohsin.

'But my child is hungry. Her ayah is young and inexperienced.'

'Feed the child,' said the inspector.

'Then please come in,' Mohsin invited the policeman.

The inspector turned out to be one of Shahid's fans and flattered him so much that he forgot his irritation and began to talk pleasantly.

Mohsin, Shahid and I went to the Mahim police station.

Having completed the formalities, I asked, 'Where are the prisoners?'

'Want to see them?'

'Of course.'

There were ten or twelve men lying huddled behind the railings.

'These are the accused, not prisoners,' said the inspector.

'What crime have they committed?'

'Getting into brawls and drunken fights, violence, pickpocketing . . .'

'What will be the punishment for them?'

'They'll be fined or imprisoned for a few days.' I felt sorry that I had got to see only petty thieves. A couple of murderers or highwaymen would have made the visit more exciting.

'Where would you have put me up?'

'We do not have arrangements to house women prisoners here. They are taken either to Grant Road or Matunga.'

After returning from the police station, Shahid and Mohsin chided me severely. In fact, Shahid fought with me the whole night, even threatened to divorce me. I silenced Mohsin by saying that if he made too much fuss I would disappear and he would lose his five hundred rupees. Shahid could not bear the disgrace and humiliation of a public suit. His parents and elder brother would be terribly upset if they heard of it.

When newspapers published the news, Shahid received a touching letter from my father-in-law, which ran thus: 'Try to reason with Dulhan. Tell her to chant the names of Allah and the Prophet. A lawsuit is bad enough. That too for obscenity. We are very worried. May God help you.'

Manto phoned us to say that a suit had been filed against him too. He had to appear in the same court on the same day. He and Safiya landed up at our place. Manto was looking very happy, as though he had been awarded the Victoria Cross. Though I put up a courageous front, I felt quite embarrassed . . . I was quite nervous, but Manto encouraged me so much that I forgot all my misgivings.

'Come on, it's the only great story you've written. Shahid, be a man and come to Lahore with us . . . The winter in Lahore is very severe. Aha! Fried fish with whisky . . . fire in the fireplace like the burning flame in a lover's heart . . . the blood-red maltas are like a lover's kiss.'

'Be quiet, Manto Sahib,' Safiya reprimanded him.

Then, filthy letters began to arrive. They were filled with such inventive and convoluted obscenities that had they been uttered before a corpse, it would have got up and run for cover. Not only me, but my whole family, including Shahid and my two-month-old child, were dragged through the muck . . .

I am scared of mud, muck and lizards. Many people pretend to be courageous, but they are scared of dead mice. I was scared of my mail as if the envelopes contained snakes, scorpions and dragons. I would read the first few words and then burn the letters. If they fell into Shahid's hands, he would repeat his threat of divorce.

Besides these letters, there were articles published in newspapers and debates in literary and cultural gatherings. Only a hard-hearted person like me could endure them. I never retaliated, nor did I refuse to admit my mistake. I was aware of my fault. Manto was the only person who would get furious at my cowardice. I was against my own self, and he supported me. None of mine or Shahid's friends attached much importance to it. I am not quite sure, but Abbas* probably had the English translation of 'Lihaaf' published somewhere. The Progressives** neither appreciated nor found fault with me. This suited me well.

I was staying with my brother when I wrote 'Lihaaf'. I had completed the story at night. In the morning I read it out to my sister-in-law. She didn't think it was vulgar, though she recognized the characters portrayed in it. Then I read it out to my aunt's daughter who was fourteen years old. She didn't understand what the story was about. I

---

* Khwaja Ahmad Abbas (1914–1987), the progressive writer and journalist, who wrote both in Urdu and English.
** Writers belonging to the Progressive Writers' Movement.

sent it to *Adab-e-Lateef* where it was published immediately. Shahid Ahmad Dehalvi was getting a collection of my short stories published and included it in the volume. The story was published in 1942 when Shahid and I were fast friends and were thinking of marriage. Shahid didn't like the story, and we had a fight. But the controversies surrounding 'Lihaaf' had not reached Bombay yet. From among journals, I subscribed only to *Saaqi* and *Adab-e-Lateef*. Shahid was not terribly angry, and we got married.

We received the summons in December 1944 to appear before the court in January. Everyone said that we would just be fined, not imprisoned. So we were quite excited and began to get warm clothes stitched for our stay in Lahore.

Seema* was a small baby. She was weak and would whimper. We took her to a child specialist who declared that she was in good health. Nevertheless, it was not wise to expose her to the severe cold in Lahore. So I left her with Sultana Jafri's mother at Aligarh and set out for Lahore. From Delhi, Shahid Ahmad Dehalvi and the calligrapher who 'copied' the manuscript joined me. The Crown had made the calligrapher one of the accused as well. The suit was brought not against *Adab-e-Lateef* but against the book published by Shahid Ahmad Dehalvi.

Sultana had come to the station to pick us up. She worked in the Lahore radio station and was staying at Luqman Sahib's place, a gorgeous mansion. Luqman Sahib's wife had gone along with her children to visit her parents. Thus the place was at our disposal.

Manto had also reached Lahore, and soon we were flooded with invitations. Most of them were from Manto's friends, but many also wanted to have a look at a strange creature like me. We appeared before the court one day. The judge only asked my name and wanted to know if I had written the story. I admitted to the crime. That was all!

We were greatly disappointed. Our lawyer talked all the time. We couldn't make much of it as we were whispering among ourselves.

---

* Ismat Chughtai's daughter.

Then the date for the next hearing was announced, and we were free to do whatever we wanted. Manto, Shahid and I roamed around in a tonga, shopping. We bought Kashimiri shawls and shoes. When we were buying shoes, the sight of Manto's delicate feet filled me with envy. I almost broke into tears looking at my rough and graceless feet.

'I hate my feet,' said Manto.

'Why? They're so graceful.'

'They are completely womanly.'

'So? I thought you have an abiding interest in women.'

'You always argue from the wrong angle. I love women as a man does. This does not mean that I want to be a woman myself.'

'Come on, forget this man–woman argument. Let's talk about human beings. But do you know that people with delicate feet are very sensitive and intelligent. My brother Azim Beg Chughtai too had very delicate feet. But . . .'

And I was reminded of how his feet had swelled up before he died and become a detestable sight. And Lahore, decked like a newly wedded bride, with apples and flowers, was transformed into the sandy graveyard in Jodhpur where my brother was sleeping in his grave under tons of earth. Thorny bushes were planted on his grave so that hyenas would not dig out the corpse. Those thorns began to stab me, and I left the fine pashmina shawl on the counter.

Lahore was beautiful, lush and lively. It greeted everyone with open arms. It was a city of people who were amiable and loved life. It was the heart of Punjab.

We wandered about the streets of Lahore, our pockets stuffed with pistachios. We popped them into our mouths one after another as we walked along, deep in conversation. Standing in a lane we gorged on fried fish. My appetite was wonderful. In the salubrious climate of Lahore, anything one ate was digested easily. We entered a hotel. My mouth began to water at the sight of hot dogs and hamburgers.

'Hamburgers contain ham, that is, pig's meat. We can have hot dog,' Shahid said, and we, like good Muslims, stuck to the religious prohibition and abstained from eating hamburgers. We stuffed ourselves with hot dogs, washing them down with the juice of Kandhari pomegranate.

However, we soon realized how crafty the white race is. If hamburgers contain pork, hot dogs contain pork sausages. When he heard this, Shahid felt like vomiting though it had been two days since we had eaten the hot dog. It was only when a Maulvi Sahib expressed the view that if one ate pork unwittingly one may be forgiven that Shahid felt somewhat relieved of his emetic urges.

In the evening when Shahid and Manto got themselves drunk, the hamburger–hot dog debate was revived and raged on for some time. Eventually, it was decided that one should abstain from both because it was impossible to prove conclusively which was halal and which haram. Under the circumstances, they settled for chicken tikka.

We made the rounds of Anarkali and Shalimar, and saw Noor Jahan's mausoleum. Then followed endless rounds of invitations, mushairas and gossip.

And suddenly, my heart sent up a thanksgiving prayer to the Crown of England for providing us with this unique opportunity for enjoying ourselves in Lahore. I began to look forward eagerly to the second hearing. I did not even care if the verdict was that I be hanged. If it occurred in Lahore, I would certainly achieve the status of a martyr. The people of Lahore would give me a befitting funeral.

∽

The second hearing was scheduled for November 1946. The weather was very pleasant. Shahid was preoccupied with his film. Seema was now a healthy child, and her ayah was quite competent, so I left her in Bombay and flew to Delhi. Shahid Ahmad Dehalvi and the calligrapher joined me from there, and we went to Lahore by train. I felt sorry for the calligrapher. He had been dragged into this situation for no fault of his. He was a harmless and quiet sort of fellow, with a permanent grimace on his face. I felt guilty at the very sight of him.

Copying the manuscript of my book had brought all this trouble on him. I asked him, 'What do you think? Shall we win the case?'

'I can't say anything. I haven't read the story.'

'But . . . you've copied it.'

'I see each word separately and do not think about its meaning.'

'Strange! And don't you read the words after they are printed?'

'I do, to see if there are mistakes.'

'Each word separately?'

'Yes.' He looked down in embarrassment. A few moments later he said, 'I hope you don't mind if I say something?'

'Not at all.'

'Your writing contains many orthographic mistakes.'

'I know. I always confuse siin, swaad and thé, zwai, zwaad, zey and zaal. The same happens with the aspirates.'

'Didn't you practise spelling on the slate?'

'I did, and always got punished for these mistakes.'

'The fact is that just as I concentrate on the words but not on their meaning, you get so impatient to put across your point of view that you don't pay attention to the letters.'

I prayed for the long life and prosperity of calligraphers. They would rectify my mistakes, and I'd be spared embarrassment.

I went, along with Shahid Sahib, to stay at Mr Aslam's house. We had barely exchanged greetings when he began to rant about the alleged obscenity in my writings. I was also like a woman possessed. Shahid Sahib tried to restrain me, but in vain.

'And you've used such vulgar words in your Gunah ki Ratein! You've even described the details of the sex act merely for the sake of titillation,' I said.

'My case is different. I'm a man.'

'Am I to blame for that?'

'What do you mean?' His face was flushed with anger.

'What I mean is that God made you a man, and I had no hand in it. He made me a woman, and you had no hand in it. You have the freedom to write whatever you want, you don't need my permission.

Similarly, I don't feel any need to seek your permission to write the way I want to.'

'You're an educated girl from a decent Muslim family.'

'You're also educated. And from a decent Muslim family.'

'Do you want to compete with men?'

'Certainly not. I always endeavoured to get higher marks than the boys in my class, and often succeeded.'

I knew that I was being pig-headed as usual. Aslam Sahib's face was red-hot with anger. I was afraid that he would hit me or that his jugular vein would burst. Shahid Sahib was aghast, almost in tears. I assumed a softer tone and said humbly, 'Aslam Sahib, no one has actually told me that it was a sin to write on the subject with which "Lihaaf" is concerned. Nor had I read in any book that such a disease ... such aberrations should not be written about. Perhaps my mind is not an artist's brush like Abdur Rahman Chughtai's but an ordinary camera that records reality as it is. The pen becomes helpless in my hand because my mind overwhelms it. Nothing can interfere with this traffic between the mind and the pen.'

'Wasn't any religious education imparted to you?'

'Aslam Sahib, I've read *Behishti Zevar*.* Such revealing things are written there . . .' I said innocently. Aslam Sahib looked upset. I continued, 'When I read it in my childhood, I was shocked. Those things seemed vulgar to me. But when I read it again after my BA I

---

* *Behishti Zevar* (Heavenly Ornaments) is a volume of Islamic belief written by Maulana Ashraf Ali Thanvi (1863–1943), the famed Indian Islamic Sunni Hanafi scholar of the Deobandi school. It is a comprehensive handbook of jurisprudence, especially for the edification of girls and women. The volume discusses all aspects of life, including the sexual. This conduct book has remained a favourite with the people of South Asia for years, and is an essential gift, given along with other articles of dowry, to girls in marriage. For a commentary on the book and its partial translation in English, see Barbara Daly Metcalf, *Perfecting Women: Maulana Ashraf Ali Thanawi's Bihishti Zewar* (Berkeley: University of California Press, 1990).

realized that they were not vulgar but important facts of life of which every sensible person should be aware. Well, people can brand the books prescribed in the courses of psychology and medicine vulgar if they like.'

The storm subsided, and we began to talk in normal tones. Aslam Sahib had cooled down quite a bit. Meanwhile, breakfast was served. We were four, but the elaborate arrangement would have been enough for fifteen people. There were three or four kinds of eggs—omelettes, fried, scrambled, boiled—shami kebab, keema, parantha, poori, toast and white and yellow butter, yoghurt, milk, honey, dry fruits, egg halwa, carrot halwa and sohan halwa.

'By God, do you want to kill us?'

I had teased him enough. To make up for it I now began to praise his writings. I had read his *Nargis* and *Gunah ki Ratein* and began to praise them in superlative terms. Eventually he came round to the view that a deliberately stark style of narration made for both clarity and instruction. Then he began to enumerate the merits of all the books that he had written. Now he was in a genial mood.

'Tender an apology to the judge,' Aslam Sahib advised gently.

'Why? Our lawyer says that we'll win the case.'

'Nonsense! If you and Manto tender your apologies, the case can be wound up in five minutes.'

'Many respectable people here have pressurized the government to bring the suit against us.'

'Rubbish!' Aslam Sahib said, but could not look me in the eye.

'Do you mean the King of England or the people in the government have actually read the story and decided to file this suit?'

'Aslam Sahib, some writers, critics and people in high position have drawn the attention of the government to these books as detrimental to morality and urged that they be banned,' said Shahid Sahib in a subdued tone.

'If morally detrimental writings are not to be banned, should we offer homage to them?' Aslam Sahib growled and Shahid Sahib cowered in embarrassment.

'Then we deserve punishment,' I said.

'You're being pig-headed again!'

'No, Aslam Sahib, I mean it. If I've committed a crime and innocent people have been led astray, why should I escape punishment merely by tendering an apology? If I've committed the crime and if it is proved, punishment can bring peace to my conscience,' I said sincerely, without any trace of irony.

'Don't be obstinate. Tender the apology.'

'What will the punishment be after all? I'll be fined?'

'It'll bring you disgrace.'

'Arrey, I've suffered enough disgrace. It can't be worse. This lawsuit is nothing compared to that.' Then I asked, 'How much will they fine me?'

'Two or three hundred, I suppose,' said Shahid Sahib.

'That's all?'

'Maybe five hundred,' threatened Aslam Sahib.

'That's *all*?'

'Have you come into piles of money?' Aslam Sahib was incensed.

'With your blessings. Even if I don't have money, won't you pay up five hundred rupees to save me from going to jail? You are counted among the aristocrats of Lahore.'

'You have a glib tongue.'

'My mother had the same complaint. She used to say, "A glib tongue invites misfortune."'

Everyone laughed, and the tension in the atmosphere dissolved. However, a few moments later he began to repeat his plea for an apology. I felt like smashing his head and mine as well.

Then he changed the topic all of a sudden and asked me, 'Why did you write "Dozakhi"?'

There was an explosion in my head.

'What kind of a sister are you to characterize your own brother as being hell-bound?'

'He might be hell-bound or heaven-bound, what's it to you?'

'He was my friend.'

'He was my brother!'

'A curse on a sister like you!'

I haven't told anyone till today what anguish I went through while writing 'Dozakhi', what fires of hell I traversed and how much of me was burnt in that fire. It was late at night. The clock had struck two when I finished writing the sketch. What a terrible night it was! The sea had risen up to the steps of our house. The boundary wall had still not been erected. A storm was raging in my breast. Whatever I had written seemed to roll around me like a cinema reel. As I put out the lamp I felt suffocated. Afraid, I lit the lamp again. I was afraid of the dark. I was reminded vividly of the grave in which the body of my brother was lowered by the pall-bearers. After seeing his grave I could not sleep alone in my room for months. My aunt's daughter, much younger than I, would sleep beside me to keep me company. I felt suffocated in Jodhpur and ran away to Bombay. Of the ten pillars, one had caved in. Who could have fathomed the gulf it had created?

Without replying to Aslam Sahib, I quietly went to my room and began packing my suitcase. I phoned Sultana and asked her to come immediately and take me away. 'If Aslam Sahib tries to stop me, just blow him up,' I told her.

'What's wrong? . . . I'll be there as soon as the office shuts at 5 p.m.'

'Oh no! By then there will have been a murder or two. Come right away.'

Sultana arrived in a few minutes. Aslam Sahib refused to let me go, but Sultana, as instructed, would not give in. As the tug of war between them ensued, I split my sides with laughter. Eventually, I left with Sultana.

We appeared before the court on the day of the hearing. The witnesses who had to prove that Manto's story 'Bu'* and my story 'Lihaaf' were obscene, were all present. My lawyer instructed me not

---

* The short story 'Bu' (Odour) by Manto created fierce controversy in Urdu reading circles for its alleged obscenity.

to open my mouth till the interrogation began. He would answer the queries as he deemed fit.

'Bu' was taken up first.

'Is this story obscene?' Manto's lawyer asked.

'Yes,' answered the witness.

'Can you put your finger on a word which is obscene?'

Witness: 'The word "chest".'

Lawyer: 'My Lord, the word chest is not obscene.'

Witness: 'No. But here the writer means a woman's breasts.'

Manto was on his feet instantly and blurted out: 'A woman's chest must be called breasts and not peanuts.'

The court reverberated with loud guffaws. Manto also began to laugh.

'If the accused shows his frivolity a second time, he will be turned out or severely punished for contempt of court.'

Manto's lawyers whispered into his ear, and he understood the situation. The debate went on. The witness could find no other words except 'chest', and it could not be proved obscene.

'If the word "chest" is obscene, why not "knee" or "elbow"?' I asked Manto.

'Nonsense!' Manto growled.

The arguments continued. We went out and sat on the benches. Ahmad Nadeem Qasmi* had brought a basketful of maltas. He also taught us a fine way of savouring them. 'Squeeze the malta to make it soft, like one does a mango. Then pierce a hole in it and suck the juice.' Sitting there, we sucked up the whole basket.

The maltas only whetted our appetite, and we stormed into a hotel during the lunch break. Because I had been very sick when Seema was born and lost a lot of weight, I was not allowed any fatty food. However,

---

* Ahmad Nadeem Qasmi (1916–2006) was a pioneering Pakistani poet, dramatist, literary critic, journalist and short-story writer. Having written some fifty books in different genres, Qasmi was a major figure in contemporary Urdu literature.

the chicken served to us was as tough as an eagle. We garnished it with large black peppers and ate it with kulchas. And in place of water, there was Qandhari pomegranate juice. Involuntarily, a prayer came out from my heart for the people who had filed the lawsuit.

In the evening, Luqman invited a few writers and poets. There, for the first time, I met Hijab Imtiaz Ali. She was heavily made up, a thick lining of kajal in her eyes. She looked somewhat angry, somewhat melancholic. Whenever anyone asked her a question, she would gaze into space.

'A fraud,' Manto whispered into my ears, dilating his large eyes.

'No, she is lost in the world of dreams created by her pen and prefers to stay in that multi-coloured shell.'

Hijab Imtiaz Ali continued to look into space while I hunted out Imtiaz Ali and began talking to him. What a world of difference there was in the temperaments of the husband and the wife. Imtiaz Sahib was garrulous, open-hearted and full of laughter. The assembly was at its glorious best. It seemed to me that I had known him for years. His conversation was even more lively than his writings. Recently, when I went to Pakistan, I met Hijab Imtiaz Ali again. She wore light make-up and looked younger and lively. She was absolutely informal and friendly. It was as though she had been born again!

I had a great desire to see an *arghanoon*, allusions to which were too frequent in Hijab's stories. When I went to her house I asked her, 'Do you really have an "arghanoon"?'

'Yes. Do you want to have a look at it?'

'Of course. This word in your stories had an intoxicating effect on me.' I also told her that at one time I had written some prose verse in imitation of hers, which I had burnt later.

At the sight of the *arghanoon*, all my zest and anticipation of romance fizzled out. The instrument was the sort of baby piano that de Melo played in film songs! It was used as background music to produce tunes to suggest the heroine's mental state when she was angry! The word 'organ' is so dull; the addition of the Urdu letter 'ghain' (to make it *arghanoon*) made it sound like a lilting tune of Asavari.

The court was crowded the next day. Several persons had advised us to tender an apology. They were ready to pay the fine on our behalf. The excitement surrounding the lawsuits was waning. The witnesses who had turned up to prove 'Lihaaf' obscene were thrown into confusion by my lawyer. They were not able to put their finger on any word in the story that would prove their point. After a good deal of reflection, one of them said: 'This phrase ". . . collecting lovers" is obscene.'

'Which word is obscene—"collect" or "lover"?' the lawyer asked.

'Lover,' replied the witness a little hesitantly.

'My Lord, the word "lover" has been used by great poets most liberally. It is also used in naats, poems written in praise of the Prophet. God-fearing people have accorded it a very high status.'

'But it is objectionable for girls to collect lovers,' said the witness.

'Why?'

'Because . . . because it is objectionable for good girls to do so.'

'And if the girls are not good, then it is not objectionable?'

'Mmm . . . no.'

'My client must have referred to the girls who were not good. Yes, madam, do you mean here that bad girls collect lovers?'

'Yes.'

'Well, this may not be obscene. But it is reprehensible for an educated lady from a decent family to write about it,' the witness thundered.

'Censure it as much as you want. But it does not come within the purview of law.'

The issue lost much of its steam.

'If you agree to apologize, we'll pay up the entire expense incurred by you . . .' someone I didn't know whispered into my ear.

'Should we apologize, Manto Sahib? We can buy a lot of goodies with the money we'll get,' I suggested to Manto.

'Nonsense!' growled Manto, as his peacock eyes bulged out.

'I'm sorry. This madcap Manto doesn't agree.'

'But you . . . why don't you . . .?'

'No. You don't know what a quarrelsome fellow he is! He'll make my life miserable in Bombay. I'd rather undergo the punishment than risk his wrath.' The gentleman was disappointed that we were not penalized.

The judge called me into the anteroom attached to the court and said quite informally, 'I've read most of your stories. They aren't obscene. Neither is "Lihaaf". But Manto's writings are often littered with filth.'

'The world is also littered with filth,' I said in a feeble voice.

'Is it necessary to rake it up, then?'

'If it is raked up it becomes visible, and people feel the need to clean it up.'

The judge laughed.

I had not been terribly worried when the suit was filed. And now that I had won it I did not feel particularly elated. Rather, I felt sad at the thought that it might be a long while before I would get a chance to visit Lahore again.

Lahore! How beautiful the word sounds! Lahori salt crystals are like gems—white and pink. I felt like getting them chiselled and fixed in my chandan haar and then draping the garland around the swan-like neck of some fair tribal woman.

'Nammi nammi tariyan di lau'—Surinder Kaur's lilting voice was enchanting. The accompanying voice of Sodhi, her husband, was like the rustle of fine silk. The city of Lahore was reminiscent of the music of Surinder and Sodhi. You felt a tumult in your heart, and a great sense of contentment. The memory of the unknown, ethereal lover invaded one's being with the force of an anguished ache.

The air of Lahore is shot through with a special light. The bells tinkle in silence and one almost feels the fragrant ambience created by the writings of Hijab Imtiaz Ali. And one is transported back to that phase of life when one would get so lost in the twilight world of her stories. Then it all changed.

I read Charles Dickens' *David Copperfield* and *Oliver Twist, Tono-Bungay*, and Gorky's *Mother*, all of which brought me back from the

world of romance to the world of reality. I also read Chekhov, Émile
Zola, Gogol, Tolstoy, Dostoevsky, Maupassant . . .

All the castles of my dreams came crashing down! And it was as
if I was thrown back into the thatched bungalow near Lal Diggi in
Aligarh where we lived. This bungalow was made of raw bricks, and
if you hit a nail in the wall, the clay came down in a deluge of sand.
The floor was littered with the droppings of pigeons that made their
nests in the house. Bats hung from the beams. The bungalow had
an earthen floor, and whenever there was a dust storm, a whirlwind
would rage inside the house. There was neither electricity nor tap
water. The bhishti would carry water to the house in his camel-skin
bag. There were string cots on which durries and dirty khaddar sheets
were spread out. The pillows were sticky with oil. Amma had given
up wearing her baggy Farshi pyjamas that required twelve yards of
cloth and had taken to wearing a dhoti.

There was a time when we had a horde of servants in the house.
Amma would provide shelter to the needy who came begging for
alms. After Abba Mian retired, she had to exercise economy. Only Ali
Bakhsh, and his wife Shekhani Bua, who did the cooking, remained. In
addition to them we had to retain the kochwan and his wife because
we still owned two horses and a buffalo.

I was probably jealous of the poetic aura that Imtiaz Ali had.
Our family atmosphere was not at all conductive to romance. I had
written my first story, 'Bachpan', after a good deal of reflection. The
only journal our family subscribed to was *Tahzeeb-i-Niswan*, to which
I sent this story. It came back along with a letter of reprimand from
the editor, Mumtaz Ali Sahib, the father of Imtiaz Ali Taj. In the story
I had compared my childhood with that of Hijab Imtiaz Ali. The
point of his objection was that I had described in the story how I was
beaten by the Maulvi Sahib for my inability to recite verses from the
Quran correctly. I could never produce the sound of 'ain'; if I tried
hard, it would be 'qaaf'. He wrote that by making fun of the Quran I
had been irreverent and blasphemous.

Later, when my writings began to appear in journals, this story was published in *Saaqi*, and people liked it a lot. I also got fed up with Azim Bhai's stories and their stilted romantic ambience. They were false, and didn't contain any trace of the anguish of his own life. He wrote about the mischief and antics of his brothers as though they were his own.

I was a spoilt brat and would get thrashed often for telling the truth. But when the disputes were taken to Abba Mian, he would decide in my favour. My elder sister, who had become a widow at nineteen, was extremely bitter about life. She was greatly impressed with the high society of Aligarh, particularly the Khwaja family. I couldn't get along with the begums of that family even for a moment. I was a madcap, outspoken and ill-mannered. Purdah had already been imposed on me, but my tongue was an unsheathed sword. No one could restrain it.

The world around me seemed like a delusion. The apparently shy and respectable girls of these families allowed themselves to be grabbed and kissed in bathrooms and in dark corners by their young male relatives. Such girls were considered modest. Which boy would have taken interest in a plain Jane like me? I had studied so much that whenever there was a debate, I would beat to a pulp all the young men who were scared of the sight of books. They considered themselves superior to women merely because they were men!

Then I read *Angarey* on the sly. Rasheed Apa was the only person who instilled a sense of confidence in me. I accepted her as my mentor. In the hypocritical, vicious atmosphere of Aligarh, she was a much-maligned lady. She appreciated my outspokenness, and I quickly read all the books she recommended.

Then I began to write. My play 'Fasaadi' was published in *Saaqi*. After that I wrote several stories. None of them was ever rejected. Suddenly some people began to object to them, but the demand from journals kept increasing. I didn't care much for the objections.

But when I wrote 'Lihaaf', there was a veritable explosion. I was torn to shreds in the literary arena. But some people also wielded their pens in my support.

Since then I have been branded an obscene writer. No one bothered about what I had written before or after 'Lihaaf'. I was put down as a purveyor of sex. It is only in the last couple of years that the younger generation has recognized that I am a realist and not an obscene writer.

I am fortunate that I have been appreciated in my lifetime. Manto was driven mad to the extent that he became a wreck. The Progressives did not come to his rescue. In my case, they didn't write me off, nor did they offer me great accolades. Manto became a pauper in Pakistan. My circumstances were quite comfortable—the income from my career in films was substantial, and I didn't care much for a literary death or life. I continued to remain a follower of the Progressives and endeavoured to bring about a revolution!

I am still labelled as the writer of 'Lihaaf'. The story brought me so much notoriety that I got sick of life. It became the proverbial stick to beat me with and whatever I wrote afterwards got crushed under its weight.

When I wrote *Terhi Lakeer* and sent it to Shahid Ahmad Dehalvi, he gave it to Muhammad Hasan Askari for his opinion. After reading it, Askari advised me to make my heroine a lesbian like the protagonist in 'Lihaaf'. I was furious. I got the novel back even though the calligrapher had started working on it, and handed it over to Nazir Ahmad in Lahore. Lahore was then a part of India.

'Lihaaf' had made my life miserable. Shahid and I had so many fights over the story that life became a battlefield.

I went to Aligarh after many years. The thought of the begum who was the subject of my story made my hair stand on end. She had already been told that 'Lihaaf' was based on her life.

We stood face to face during a dinner. I felt the ground under my feet receding. She looked at me with her big eyes that conveyed excitement and joy. Then she cruised through the crowd, leapt at me and took me in her arms. Drawing me to one side she said, 'Do you know, I divorced the nawab and married a second time? I have a pearl of a son, by God's grace.'

I felt like throwing myself into someone's arms and crying my heart out. I couldn't restrain my tears though; and I was laughing loudly. She invited me to a dinner, which was fabulous. I felt fully rewarded when I saw her flower-like boy. I felt as if he was mine as well—a part of my mind, a living product of my brain, an offspring of my pen.

And I realized at that moment that flowers can be made to bloom among rocks. The only condition is that one has to water the plant with one's heart's blood.

Just one thing more.

I had asked a gentleman, 'Do you think "Lihaaf" is morally subversive?'

'Undoubtedly.'

'Why do you think so?'

'When one reads the story, one feels sexually aroused.'

'I see. And you want to snuggle into a lihaaf?'

'Oh no. Actually, Begum Jaan is very sexy. She's ravishingly beautiful, endowed with sap and sweetness, a well-proportioned body, warm lips, intoxicating eyes. She's a burning flame, a cup overflowing with wine.'

'So?'

'The devil tempts one.'

'What does he say?'

'To — her.'

'The devil is wise. My objective was just that. How I wanted that some brave fellow release her from Rabbu's* clutches, encircle her within his strong arms and slake her life's thirst. It is a virtuous act to provide water to a thirsty creature.'

'Could I have her address?'

'You've been born rather late in the day. By God's grace, she's now a grandmother. Many years ago a prince released her from the magic castle of the black giant and transported her to the spring garden of life.'

From a nearby apartment, the voice of Naiyera Noor** came wafting across. She was singing Faiz's verse:

---

* The young maid in the story 'Lihaaf'.
** A famous singer from Pakistan, known for her melodious rendering of Faiz Ahmad Faiz's Urdu poems.

In the name of those married women
whose decked-up bodies
atrophied on loveless,
deceitful beds . . .

And I wondered: where is the ideal Indian woman?

Sita, the embodiment of purity, whose lotus-like feet cooled the flames on which she had to walk.

Mira Bai, who put her arms around God himself.

Savitri, who snatched away her husband's life from the Angel of Death.

And Razia Sultana, who spurned great emperors and joined her destiny with that of a Moorish slave.

Is she getting suffocated today under the lihaaf? Or is she playing Holi with her own blood in Faras Road?*

---

* Prostitute quarters in Mumbai.

NANHE AND MUNNE

As soon as Nanhe Bhai agreed to the marriage, Amma abandoned the idea of committing suicide and sat up. Nanhe Bhai had agreed to marry on one condition: that there would be no extravagance during the marriage. Nanhe Bhai would go with Amma and bring the bride home—there would be no dowry, no gifts or offerings. The nikah would be held and that would be about it. Abba went along with this plan of Nanhe Bhai. After Abba's retirement, Amma had spent so extravagantly during Munne Bhai's marriage that it had left Abba strapped for cash. Amma acquiesced promptly, as she was apt to make false promises. If Abba showed the slightest reluctance to give money she would go ahead and take a loan, then spend the money as she liked. If Abba made any fuss when he learnt of this, she would sulk, even resorting to hunger strike. Checkmated in this way, Abba would accept defeat. He knew that it would be futile to impose restrictions on Amma's spending, because she would do whatever she liked. But this time Nanhe Bhai was with him, so Abba thought that Amma would not be able to do as she liked.

Amma, who just a while ago had feigned to no longer have any interest in this world, issued the command that the proposal be sent right away. Abba sent for his writing box and began to compose the text for the proposal. Bade Abba was promptly sent for so that this auspicious act could be brought into fruition by him. The text began to be composed.

'The proposal must be written in Farsi,' Bade Abba pronounced, as Persian was the mother tongue of the Chughtais. But Amma flared up.

'Ai, to hell with this cursed Farsi! To whom will Zafar Husain run to have the proposal deciphered? Just write a good proposal.' After much debate it was decided that the proposal would be written in Urdu.

Amma was greatly disheartened when she could not find the roseate paper to write the proposal on. She did not have the patience to wait till she had it. The proposal was written anyway and it was decided that it should be smeared with turmeric for auspiciousness.

Shekhani Bua ground some turmeric with alacrity, and all the children turned up to smear the envelope with turmeric. Several envelopes were spoilt. Eventually, Amma took charge of the situation, the envelope was sealed and the proposal sent.

Amma also called the draper and the goldsmith, though Abba did not get wind of this. The suits were ordered and the tailors got busy stitching them. We were sad that we would not be allowed to go with the wedding party, but Amma said, 'Just keep quiet. Each one of you will go.'

Away from the eyes of Abba and Nanhe Bhai, dress suits were being made for everyone, along with other elaborate preparations. Forgetting her promise about not inviting anyone, Amma sent out invitations to all the relatives and members of the extended family. When Mamu's reply to the proposal came, the date for the marriage was fixed. Apa came from Delhi and Baaji descended from Rampur.

Nanhe Bhai was furious that Amma had broken her promise. Her face innocent, Amma said, 'If they all want to attend the marriage at their own expense who are you to prevent them?' No one had an answer to that. However, Abba knew that eventually he would have to bear everyone's expenses. He also knew Amma very well, and how futile it would be to try to prevent her from extending invitations. He could not have his way. Amma would do whatever she had decided to do.

Munne Bhai tried to incite the groom, 'I know that everyone in the family has been invited to join the marriage party. They will join at Agra and then proceed to Jodhpur.'

'I will not marry, then,' Nanhe Bhai threatened.

'You have to. The proposal has been accepted. Amma will kill everyone. We cannot humiliate our own Mamu in this way.'

'But our family is so large! It will be so expensive. I do not earn even a penny. Abba is on a pension. He has to bear the burden of a large family. I do not want to burden him further. I will disappear from the scene.'

When Abba heard this he said, 'The proposal has already been accepted. Zafar Husain has already got the invitation cards printed. Nothing can be done now.'

'I won't marry. I am going to Nepal with Nawab Faiz on a hunting expedition.'

'Then I will have you thrown in jail.'

'How?'

'By slapping a charge of theft on you.'

'Will you tell lies?'

'Not me. Your mother will bring the charge. I will have her complaint sent to the police. I can't refuse her anything.'

'Even knowing that Amma is lying?'

'She will face the consequences of lying.'

'What charge will you slap on me?'

'Stealing jewellery and then running away.'

'Sir, this is so unfair!' Nanhe Bhai broke into a smile.

'I too have daughters. I cannot humiliate Zafar.'

'But is it wise to take everyone in our large family to the bride's house?'

'What large family?' Abba was taken by surprise.

'You don't know that Amma has invited everyone in Agra to go with the baraat.'

'Then she is being unfair.'

'Shall we cancel the invitations then?'

'No, we can't do this to people after inviting them. They will be annoyed.'

'Sir, this is sheer injustice.'

'I've got used to bearing with the injustices done to me by your mother.' Abba said, smiling. 'I have never made her unhappy if I can help it.' Amma's irresponsible acts were a source of both delight and misery for him. But his love for her always triumphed over his anger.

Both my brothers also began to smile. Amma was adorable. People duped her easily. She was most careless in matters of money, and she would not hold anything against people who may have cheated her. Everyone would remember this endearing trait in her character and forget about what seemed like trifles.

A heavy trousseau was made for the bride, and the amount of jewellery that had been made for Azim Bhai's bride was made for her as well, but in utmost secrecy. Amma took a loan from her 'moonhbola' chachaji, Girija Dayal, and had new dresses made for everyone. Abba had no idea!

Eventually, he began to ask Amma to have an ordinary trousseau and some jewellery made. Amma would tell him, 'Zafar will take care of that. I will take some gifts from him. After all, he is Nanhe's maternal uncle. Mattru [Farhat Husain Usmani, our younger maternal uncle] would also give bhaath. He will give me bangles weighing at least ten or twelve tolas. The same bangles I could give as offerings.'

Amma told all these lies with such an innocent face that Abba was taken in. He felt sorry and forced some money on her for her to do whatever she wanted with.

None of us knew about the loan she had taken from Chachaji. We did not breathe a word about our dresses to Abba. Amma had warned us that if Abba got to know about the dresses she would throw them into the fire and wouldn't take any of us to the marriage either.

Nanhe Bhai and Munne Bhai were secretly plotting to undercut Amma's plans. They asked for the guest list on the pretext that they would have the guests' tickets booked and an entire rail coach reserved for them, which would be economical. Amma was pleased to oblige them, but the duo sent postcards to all the guests informing that the bridegroom was down with typhoid and the marriage was postponed, and that they would be informed about the new dates.

Shamim and Chunnu, my brothers, and Jasim, who was my cousin and the bride's own brother, were not allowed to join the marriage party because their exams were close at hand. Abba did not go either because an adult was needed in the house to look after the children. The rest of us proceeded towards the rail station. Whenever our family travelled, two third-class coaches would be reserved in which we were stuffed along with bushels of grains. Abba would be in the first-class coach. Amma wanted two coaches to be reserved right from Aligarh so the guests would face no inconvenience. The organizers—Nanhe and Munne—had taken money from Amma but had only one coach reserved. The women had to travel in the same coach as the men, but we somehow managed.

When the train reached Agra station, Amma was really disturbed to see no guests. My two brothers made several rounds of the platform and informed her that there was no one to be seen.

'But why? They responded to the invitation and promised to join us,' Amma said. At that moment, Munne Bhai whispered something into Nanhe Bhai's ears and both of them ran into another coach.

Bade Abba had been standing on the other side of the platform and was taking note of what was going on. He had no luggage with him. He had not been too sure about the postcard informing him about the postponement of the marriage, and felt that someone might have played a trick on him. Seeing the marriage party, he stepped back and returned home. Amma had not seen him. She continued cursing the despicable people of her family who had betrayed her for fear of expenses!

'Maybe they are sick,' Munne Bhai said innocently, trying to console Amma.

'Ai hai, you mean the entire family has been stricken by the plague!' Amma broke into tears. 'How much I have done for them! And today my own people betray me. I never expected such callousness from my very own people. By God, I am not going to have anything to do with them for the rest of my life!'

We were not worried at all. The guests who had been invited were all elderly and would have found fault with whatever we said and did, exhorting us to behave properly, or cover our heads with dupattas. 'Ai, good girls do not sit with the stance of men!' they would have yelled every other moment. I could not stand them for a minute. My sisters would ignore their cutting remarks, though they would mutter curses under their breath. But I had a sharp tongue and I would talk back. Amma would threaten to thrash me, and would often throw shoes at me. But I always sat at some distance from her and she would miss her target—the shoe would hit the forehead of some unsuspecting individual. Amma's aim was not good at all.

Amma had great regard for these old men and women and she would be terribly embarrassed by our behaviour. She would complain about us to Abba who would reprimand us in his usual tongue-in-cheek manner, making it quite clear to Amma that he was indulging us.

'I fully understand what you mean. It is because of your indulgence that they have become so brazen!' Amma would say, venting her anger on Abba.

'Shall I give them a lashing?' Abba would say, seemingly menacingly, and Amma would recoil and begin to defend us. She knew that Abba had practised wrestling in his younger days, and just his touch could crush someone. When he got really furious and actually beat someone, he would be ruthless and turn into a brute. He never raised his hand against his daughters, except once when he had beaten me with a cane. But after the first lash of the cane, Munne Bhai came running and shielded me with his body. His body was burning with a fever, and after two or three lashes he lost consciousness. I ran from the scene and seeing Munne Bhai's condition, Abba got worried and forgot about me. It is because of Abba's violent temper which showed but rarely that whenever any of us committed a nasty act Amma would hide it from Abba, and if Abba was there, she would start beating us herself to pre-empt Abba from getting angry. Her beating seemed like a shower of flowers in comparison with what Abba would have served us with.

I had to undergo the worst travails during this journey. I had to wear a burqa for the first time, and I cannot put in words the sense of humiliation I had to suffer. So intense was this feeling of debasement that several times I thought of jumping off the train and committing suicide. In those days Azim Bhai had created quite a stir by writing such articles as 'The Quran and Purdah' and 'Hadith and Purdah'. There were fierce debates both in favour of and against purdah. In Bombay, Begum Atia Faizi, Zohra Faizi, Begum Humayun Mirza and some other gutsy women had gatecrashed a conference which was strictly out of bounds for women. This had created a commotion. Though all of them were wearing burqa, the Muslim community felt deeply humiliated by their action. If these women did not come from highly influential, educated and aristocratic families, they would have been severely dealt with. No one knew how many young minds these women had inflamed by their action, by removing the idea of purdah from their minds. Azim Bhai was against purdah. He forbade his wife to observe purdah but the family stood behind his wife and he was outstripped.

One day Azim Bhai brought to his room his friend Khwaja Muhammad Ishaq who stood face to face with his wife. 'Bhabi Jaan, adaab!' Ishaq Bhai said demurely, lowering his glance. Dulhan Bhabi let out a scream and ran away. She threw herself into Amma's arms and began to cry volubly. Everyone was astir. Azim Bhai was summoned before Abba and Amma gave the ultimatum that if the dissolute, wayward fellow (Azim Bhai) was not severely punished she would go on a hunger strike.

'What is it, dear fellow?' Abba asked Azim Bhai without looking at him.

'Nothing at all, sir,' said Azim Bhai, coughing. He had had a bout of asthma the night before.

'Stupid boy, why didn't you wear a sweater?'

'Sir, I was wearing one. I've just taken it off as it got dirty.'

'Just see, he is indulging him once again!' This was Amma. Abba continued to read the newspaper.

'To hell with this newspaper!' Amma slapped the newspaper down.

'All right, tell me why you are doing all this?'

'I have done nothing, sir.'

'You, the son of nothing!' Amma was furious.

'Amma, I am not the son of "nothing". You two have given birth to me . . .'

'Just see!' Amma was in tears. 'Ask him why he forced Dulhan to come before Ishaq?'

'Amma, you too come before Ishaq, don't you?'

'Just listen to him. He is like my son, a baby born the other day. But Dulhan . . .'

'Ishaq is like my brother. He is devar to your Dulhan.'

'Just shut up. I say, why don't you tell him off?' Amma had a go at Abba once again.

'Oh yes, tell me why you forced her to break purdah?'

'Whose purdah?'

'Dulhan's.'

'Dulhan is my wife, and I have the right to instruct her to maintain purdah or break it.'

'This will not be allowed in my house!' Amma held in the rein and descended on the arena, finally. Abba heaved a sigh of relief.

'Then I will shift to a friend's house tomorrow itself. He has a room vacant. All of us—my wife, the two children and I.'

'Nuzhat will not go.' Amma had brought up Nuzhat, her granddaughter, from when she was a tiny baby. And she would sleep beside her grandma. She had never been close to her parents. She called her grandma 'Amma', and her mother 'Dulhan', in imitation of her grandma, and called her father, 'Bhai Sahib'. She did not even know that she was Dulhan's daughter, not her grandma's. She was a sickly, wretched girl, always clinging to her grandparents.

'If I leave, my children will go with me.'

'To hell with you. Don't try to show off your affection for the children. I brought them up and now you're claiming your rights over them! Everyone knows that Dulhan is too clumsy to manage her children.' Manjhli Baaji was planning to take Midhat, the younger daughter, with her. She would come to attend the marriage and then adopt her. Dulhan Bhabi was heavy with a baby in her womb. How could she bear with the stress of moving house in this condition and stay all by herself? Azim Bhai was completing his LLB. At night he worked as a clerk in a lock factory on a monthly salary of forty-five rupees. On top of it, he was always sick.

Amma began to cry and Abba became restless.

'No! Dulhan will not break purdah. I will ask her not to stay with you. She will be given a separate room.'

'If she does not abide by my orders, I will divorce her.'

'Are you insane?' Abba thundered.

'So, tomorrow I will move along with the children . . .'

'You can go wherever you want. Dulhan and the children will stay here,' Amma announced.

'No one will go. He has had a bout of asthma only yesterday, and today he is moving about in his shirt sleeves!' This was Abba.

Amma was furious at her defeat. She got up and strode away.

It was said that this news had reached Dulhan Bhabhi's family. Dulhan Bhabhi was the daughter of Baaji's jeth; in fact, it was Baaji who had been instrumental in bringing her to our family as my brother's wife. She tried to scotch the rumour by saying that it was only a rumour and that no one had tried to break purdah. This had become necessary because Dulhan Bhabhi's brothers had got wind of it and declared that if their sister was forced to break purdah and made to dance in the marketplace they would decapitate both their sister and her husband. Azim Bhai remained subdued after this.

Seeing me angry and helpless in the third-class coach, Azim Bhai realized that my gloom stemmed from the burqa. When I had worn burqa for the first time, my brothers teased me no end, laughing all the while to their heart's content, and as I lunged at them, Amma, instead of saying anything to my brothers, chose to give me a good drubbing. My mother was very free with her hands.

Azim Bhai came to the window where I was sitting and began to whisper into my ear the way to tackle the situation. When the train reached Jodhpur station the servants were called to fold the beddings. The beddings were gathered in giant heaps which were tied tightly in a network of ropes from all sides. This made for economy. Ten beds were tied in two bundles. Since it was winter, there were both quilts and mattresses. If all the beds were tied separately, the porters would have asked for much more money.

All the women began putting on their burqas before getting off the train. The cap of my burqa was not to be found, though like a very docile woman I was wearing the lower portion which now looked like a coat, and I was earnestly looking for the upper part. Others also participated in the search.

'It has probably got into the bundle of beds by mistake,' I said quietly.

'You nasty, ill-fated brat!' I was showered with blows from all sides. 'You've done this intentionally.'

I took those blows as though they were sweet laddoos. I knew there was no question of untying the network of ropes around the bundles that had taken half an hour to tie up to dig for the cap inside them. I was made to wear a shawl and I got on to the platform like a triumphant victor. When my eyes met Azim Bhai's, he laughed out so loudly that it set off a bout of coughing. I masked my laughter by pretending to cough. The shawl would slip off my shoulders frequently and I would be deluged with whacks.

Only the person who had tasted the excitement of victory can imagine the moment I lived on the platform that day. Soon people got to know that my rebelliousness was encouraged by Azim Bhai; rather, he had ignited it. This was because the message that was being communicated through our glances soon became evident to everybody.

Our maternal uncle was standing on the platform, along with his friends and relatives, to welcome us. Our taya, Ibrahim Beg Chughtai—oops, I've forgotten to add 'Mirza'—was there too. He had already lectured us several times over about the greatness of the terms 'Chughtai' and 'Mirza'. We should not forget, under any circumstances, that we were among the descendants of the great Changez Khan, and that Chughtai Khan was the son of Changez Khan. Then the term 'Mirza' had its own importance, but only 'Mirza' did not have the same kind of aura. This was the title that my forefathers had acquired after killing scores of people and shedding rivers of blood. One was not talking about cows and goats, but about mounds of human skulls and horse hooves that were dipped in human blood!

It must be the dull, thin blood inherited from my mother's side that, instead of flaring up in pride, brings tears to my eyes, brimming over like the saliva of a timid and nervous mouse.

I was in a fix. From my mother's side, my lineage went back to Uthman Ghani, the third caliph after the Prophet of Islam; and from my father's side, my lineage was traced back to human skulls and rivers of blood. What a mess was created by my father when he married among the Shaikhs! Well, Bade Abba and Zahoor Nana, who was Amma's maternal uncle, had already reached Jodhpur. They had gone there at the invitation of Mamu and thus were not trapped in the snare of postcards.

Their presence threw cold water on the exuberance of Azim Bhai and Nasim Bhai. These two venerable old men were held in great esteem by the family. Abba and Amma greatly respected them and were bent upon transferring this inheritance on us.

The illuminated faces and dresses of these two gentlemen indicated their imperial descent. With his snow-white robe and sacred white beard, Zahoor Nana looked like a saint or seer. I have never seen him in soiled or crushed clothes. He wore white Islamic pyjamas, above his ankles, white angarkha and a cap worn by hakims. From a distance he exuded the scent of camphor. Ill-fated that we were, his appearance reminded us of a graveyard, because that is the ultimate destination for everyone!

Bade Abba was often afflicted with some unknown ailment, which did not allow him to take a bath too often; he would bathe only once in a while. The day the barber came to give him a bath he would look quite worried. And no matter whether it was summer or winter, water was heated in big pots. He would repeatedly remind everybody, 'I have to take a bath today', as though he was going to a battlefront.

After a bath he looked so fair and handsome, just like an Englishman, that it left us spellbound. However, in a couple of weeks his complexion would look dull once again. His ideas about the Mughals were similar to what Hitler thought about the superiority of the German race. There were no people born on the face of the earth who were as valorous, just, wise, humble, generous and so on, as the Mughals. And Bade Abba was every inch a true-blue Mughal, because, like the emperor Taimur, he too was born lame.

The baree was supposed to go at four. Mamu had brought out thirty trays covered with gold-embroidered coverings from the royal warehouse, the toshakhana, and had them sent. Amma had arranged for five maunds of dry fruits and candy. She filled the trays with nuts, pistachios, raisins and copra. Then there was one trousseau for the baree and one for the suhaag. The jewellery was placed in Apa's custody by Amma.

The baree was sent with the accompaniment of music and song. We went along too. Amma was the bride's only real phupi; that is why both the Mamus gave bhaath to her. They gave dupattas to the sisters and turbans to their husbands, which the wives later tore off to make dupattas. They gave suits to Abba and, to Amma, suits and gold bangles. They gave suits to the maidservants too.

'I have a share in the baree as well,' Amma said. Mumani Jaan brought a tray that had ten or eleven nuts and dry dates, a coconut and a couple of pistachios and raisins.

'What on earth is this? I am the only phupi of the bride and you are giving me this meagre offering? I will take an entire tray.' Amma sounded really indignant.

Mumani Jaan was Mamu's second wife. His first wife, the bride's mother, had died when she was a tiny baby.

'Apa, everyone was given one or two pieces, for luck.'

'By God's grace, I have brought five maunds of baree. Why do you have to give away one or two pieces?'

'Five maunds?'

'Oh yes. Your own Majju Mian has brought it, and I have filled up twenty trays with my own hands. One maund of sugar, one maund of laddoo and three maunds of dry fruits. The trays were so heavy that the women were finding it difficult to carry them.'

'Apa, why don't you come to the other room and see the baree?'

When the covers were lifted from the trays, they saw ten to twelve coconuts sitting forlornly on the trays, two to four sers of dry fruits and twenty to twenty-five laddoos.

'Oh God, what a calamity! I brought full five maunds of baree, and . . .' There was squabbling. Amma guessed that Mumani Jaan had sent off all the baree to her parents' home in Gulab Sagar. Great bitterness ensued. Mumani Jaan strictly observed prayer and fasting. In the morning she would recite the Quran for a couple of hours and pray eight times through the day. She had a tall and delicate physique, and beautiful, long, black hair. She looked somewhat like Hazrat Maryam. She was sitting in a corner, shedding tears. Amma flew off her handle and gave the relatives on the bride's side a piece of her mind. Whenever my simple-minded mother found someone simpler than her, a particular vein of hers twitched and she became terrible to that woman. Mamu doted on her, and would give his life for her. When he got to know that his wife had sent off the baree to her parents he unsheathed his sword. As the guests left he turned to her. He blasted his wife and his in-laws. Her people had slunk away by that time.

Mumani Jaan remained silent through all this. She continued to read the Quran through the night in the light of the burning lantern. Mamu kept spewing venom and she swallowed it without demur. Mamu called her all kinds of names but she did not so much as say 'ah'.

'There's a limit to shamelessness! What's the use of trying to wash away your sins by reading the scripture and saying prayers? You have broken my sister's heart. I will never forgive you for this.' He went down and sat on the stairs holding his head between his hands.

The next day, the baraat got under way to reach the bride's house. Mamu had used his influence to procure the maharaja's special elephant and led horses. The Arab horses were all white, of the same height, and decorated with gold and silver jewellery. The elephant was wearing a jhumar of ten sers of gold, anklets weighing twenty sers, and clothes with zardozi work. Then there was the moving throne, i.e. there was a beautiful dancing apsara on a throne. The baraat would stop every few steps, the throne would be lowered and the dancer would give a demonstration of her art.

The horse that had the groom on it was of unparalleled beauty. It had two bearers holding peacock fans on either side and a parasol bearer at the back.

But the groom was kicking his heels. No kimkhwab achkan fitted him. Every time he wore one, puffed his chest and shrugged his shoulders, it gave way from the back with a 'phrr' sound. It was a matter of coincidence that Mamu had sent several achkans from the toshakhana. However, none fitted the groom. Eventually he wore the black achkan which was his university uniform. The Banarasi silk turban obdurately refused to be tied properly, slipping off his shoulders. Finally, it had to be replaced by a pink, cotton turban. The groom refused to wear the sehra and slipped it in like a garland around his neck.

Azim Bhai was in dire straits. If the achkans for the groom were tight, his was loose enough for two men to slip into. He wore two sweaters inside and draped the dazzling achkan over them, and with great effort wore the turban rejected by the groom by fixing it with pins. When he looked at himself in the mirror he realized why others were smiling. He smiled too.

The baraat had to make a round of the city and then reach the bride's house. Naseem Bhai was a trained horse rider. He had advanced a couple of steps only when the horse began to act up. The horse, who should have been accustomed to carrying grooms in wedding processions, went crazy and turned into a growling tiger. He would advance a little, then dig his heels in the ground and kick back. The procession was accompanied by seven kinds of bands. The bands were exhibiting their skills in turns, but the horse was spoiling the show. We also got the news of the horse turning wild, though we were seated in cars at the tail end of the procession.

'Nanhe is up to mischief,' Badi Apa was muttering.

'Oh no! I do not think so. Is he so crazy as to spoil his own baraat?' Amma asked.

'You know, Munne is at the root of all this. He must have advised him to do this. Look, everybody is upset, while Munne is coughing away.' What she meant was that whenever Munne wanted to laugh he started coughing.

And then the worst happened. The groom had all but slipped off but managed to hang on to his seat while the horse left the procession and galloped ahead. The fan-bearers were stunned and the parasol bearer looked dumbfounded.

Nevertheless, the baraat advanced at a snail's pace without the groom. From a distance, others could not make out that the groom was not there and that the peacock fan and the parasol were hanging in the space. On his part, Mamu was standing with garlands and flowers along with the aristocrats and smaller rajas before the glittering entrance gate when the horse carrying the harassed and tired groom reached the main door and stood still. The groom leapt down and, huffing and puffing, began to clamber up the stairs on his wobbly legs.

'Oh Mamu, it's only God who saved me. This devil of a horse was bent on tearing me to pieces. Don't ask what I had to go through on the way!'

'How about the baraat?' the people gathered to welcome him asked.

'Coming,' the groom said, taking the support of the stairs and wiping off invisible sweat.

Mamu was not a fool. He had witnessed Nanhe Bhai's horse-riding skill several times. Riding the horse at a normal pace, Nanhe Bhai would suddenly tug at the rein, causing the horse to leap and gallop dangerously. Seeing this from behind the bamboo curtain, the chik, Amma would begin to scream nervously.

'Hey Begum, Nanhe is manipulating the horse for a manoeuvre. He's riding the horse, the horse isn't riding him,' Abba would reassure her.

'For God's sake, stop him. My heart is coming to my mouth.'

'Five rupees,' Nanhe Bhai would demand for stopping the horse.

'You pig. I won't give you more than a rupee.'

The bargaining would go on. Sometimes Nanhe Bhai would settle for two, sometimes for three rupees. Once the deal was struck he would make a deft manoeuvre and come near Amma.

'Amma, the money.'

'Come down first.'

'Oh no. First give money or I'll take the horse inside.'

'Hey, naughty brat, loathsome pig,' Amma would call him this and other names, and throw out the money from behind the curtain. Nanhe Bhai would tug at the rein and bring the horse to the spot, then leap down in such a fashion as to make the onlookers feel that the horse had thrown him off its back. Amma would let out a scream while he would pick the money nonchalantly and run away from there.

At the time of the nikah, Bade Abba and Zahoor Nana moved close to the qazi. Nanhe Bhai looked at them endearingly from the corner of his eye.

'Why are you taking the trouble? It is written in the traditions of the Prophet that people sporting a beard cannot be a vakil or a witness in the nikah.' Both the elderly persons were stunned. Only a couple of minutes ago they were conducting an erudite discourse as to whether the salat performed by clean-shaven young Muslims of the day would be considered below par. They had concluded that it would be much inferior in status to that performed by bearded Muslims.

The groom declared that no person with a beard could become the witness, unless he . . . I cannot describe the scene that ensued. Well, the nikah had to be conducted. Eventually Chhote Mamu and Azim Bhai became the witness and the vakil respectively, and the nikah was done.

We returned to Aligarh with the bride. However, when we reached Aligarh, a bomb exploded. Nanhe Bhai and Azim Bhai brought some boxes before Abba.

'What's there in them? I don't want to see the dowry. It is a stupid custom. I have nothing to do with whatever the parents of the bride had given to their daughter and son-in-law.'

'This is not the dowry, sir.'

'What is it, then?'

'The booty!' saying which they opened the boxes which were stuffed with pistachios, nuts, candies and bags of sugar.

'These are the five maunds of baree that Amma had bought for offerings. We got to know of it when the women carrying the tray came down. We took back all of it except half a maund of dry fruits and candy mixed together.'

Amma was in the kitchen. She did not get to see the sparkle in Abba's eyes.

'If the begum gets wind of it, then?'

'We will hide it in the room behind yours and have the room padlocked. We will seal the boxes.'

'Good. The fruits and sugar will come handy during your walima.'

'But we must have some carrot halwa before that!'

Munne Bhai handed to Amma some of the stuff from the boxes, saying, 'Amma, my friend Fayyaz has sent these fruits and bags of sugar. He thinks that the best chef cannot make carrot halwa as you make it.'

The halwa was made. Some was sent to the Nawab Sahib. Friends partook of the rest. After many days when Amma got to know the truth she began to beat her forehead and howl.

'Oh my God! I levelled false charges against my brother's wife who is an angel. Please forgive me, God. What can I do now? I wish I had been barren and not given birth to such offspring . . .'

Seeking forgiveness, Nanhe Bhai joined his palms and placed his head in Amma's lap.

'Here you are, Amma. Give me a good thrashing.'

But Amma withdrew her feet and turned away her face angrily. Nanhe Bhai's face fell.

'Munne, Amma is really angry.' If Amma had thrashed them, they would have felt relieved. Munne also became worried.

Nanhe Bhai had agreed to marry on the condition that Abba would bear the expenses of his education till he completed his LLB and, apart from board and clothing, would give him and his wife thirty rupees a month.

'Nanhe, you will not have pocket money for six months,' Abba declared.

'Why?'

'As a punishment for this mischief.'

'Be reasonable. The boy is studying . . . On top it, he has to maintain the new bride. I can't allow this injustice as long as I am alive,' Amma declared.

And Abba began to wonder—mothers have so many shades to them. No one knew what to make of their love or hatred!

CONFLICT

It is more difficult getting out of a third-class rail coach than getting into it. The Agra station was teeming with people. On top of it there were vendors displaying wares of all kinds—dolls playing with cymbals, old men shaking on spring shoulders, papad, sesame laddoos, miniature Taj Mahals and other sundry things. Passengers who wanted to come out of the coach pushed from behind, and in the front there was a bundle of sugar cane. What do you call the creature who ties with a rope many crooked sheaves of sugar cane with leaves and then shoves it into the rail coach before the passengers can get in? Of course, you can't see the person. There are perfumed ladies, someone balancing earthen pitchers with one or two bamboo poles, turbaned men and children with runny noses. Oh God!

Then there was Shaukat Apa! She was going to her grandmother's at Agra with the intention of staying with her for the entire period of her pregnancy. I invited trouble upon myself by wishing to spend a couple of days at Agra after my exam. Shaukat Apa had put on her most loveable face and wanted to come along with me. Now I realized why she was so persistent. Naim, her two-and-a-half-year-old roly-poly son, had taken after his father's side as far as his physical features were concerned. To lift him on to your lap was akin to picking up a live, pulsating and kicking bomb. The only difference was that he would not burst but the one who had picked him up would certainly shatter in a sudden explosion. Oblivious of his own weight, this winsome personality had the hobby of dropping with a thud on people who were sleeping. He also liked punching and biting. However, he had to give up on me as I, after sustaining bruises on various parts of my

61

body, shoved a pinch of quinine powder in his mouth in self-defence. After that he never tried to bite me again.

Well, we managed to get off the train in one piece. I had just one suitcase but Shaukat Apa had several as she intended to spend a couple of months in Agra.

'Drop me off at Maithan,' she said when the tonga started off.

'Drop you off—what do you mean?' I asked.

'I mean what I said.'

'How about me?'

'How do I know?'

'Aren't you coming to Panja Shahi?'

'Come on; am I crazy to go there at this hour? The cleaning can be done in the morning. The rooms are in a mess, filled with scraps and tons of dust. I will go there after two–three days.'

'So, you think I should go to that house littered with scraps?'

'Suit yourself.'

'Or?'

'Or what?'

'Shaukat Apa, in that case, I will also go there tomorrow, or after two–three days.'

'Where will you stay tonight?'

'With you.'

'Are you insane?'

'Why?'

'I am going to Amma's.' She addressed her maternal grandmother as Amma who, unfortunately, was my one and only Badshahi Phupi Khanum aka Bachchu Phupi.* People around her preferred to pronounce her name with *zer*, rather than a *zabar*** (behind her back, of course). I had only seen her calling names loudly and cursing our entire family from Rahman Bhai's window that opened into

---

* Ismat Chughtai wrote a riveting story with the same title on her father's sister.

** With the addition of *zer*, 'bachchu' becomes 'bichchu', i.e. scorpion.

our courtyard. She had a running battle with my Abba that had been ongoing, in true Mughal style, since much before my birth.

She would sit in front of Rahman Bhai's window quite regularly and the fusillade would start. Amma, Abba and other adult members would immediately take cover in the trenches, i.e. behind the veranda. The children used to stand below the window and look up at her in amazement. She never came to our house, nor did we go to hers. But as a rule, on Eid and Bakr-eid Abba would go to Maithan to pay a visit to his sister, along with his young sons who went to Eid prayer with him.

It was a strange battle. As happens with warfare where there is an interruption during Christmas, in our family feud there would be a temporary respite on Eid. Phupi Amma would place herself behind the purdah while Abba sat in the courtyard, and an exchange of jibes and taunts would ensue. This would go on in full steam for fifteen to twenty minutes. Phupi Amma wept and cursed as Abba made witty repartees and guffawed.

One might wonder why Abba went to pay his visit at all. The explanation given in our childhood for this was convincing enough. Amma felt that Phupi Amma's curses and abuses proved auspicious for our family; in fact, it was because of her curses that our family was thriving. Not a single baby had died. On the other hand, of the thirteen or fourteen children born from Phupi Amma's womb, only Hashmat Khanam, whom everyone called Khanam Sahib, had survived. Phuphi Amma's elder daughter, Musarrat Khanam, who was married to our older maternal uncle, Zafar Husain, had died when Shaukat Apa, her daughter, was nearly two years old.

'That wretch Zafar Husain devoured my darling daughter,' Phupi Amma never forgot to repeat when she sat at Rahman Bhai's window.

'Why did Zafar Mamu devour Mumani?' I asked all the elderly members of the family by turns. But in our family, elderly people hardly responded to queries made by children.

'Shut up. Don't get on my nerves.' This was the answer I got, which would sometimes be accompanied by whacks. This was enough to frighten me into silence, particularly because from childhood I suffered from nightmares and would scream in them.

Bade Mamu [Zafar Husain] was stunningly handsome, with a fair complexion, broad face, thick and curly golden hair, big liquid eyes and evenly set pearl-like teeth. He doted on us, and would bring sweets and toys for us. He lived in Jodhpur with his older son, Mazhar Husain. Younger than Mazhar was Azhar Husain, who must have been older than Shaukat Apa by nearly two years. He lived with our family. Shaukat Apa too lived with us when she was small. Once or twice in a year Bade Mamu came for a visit to our family and it was an occasion for festivities in the house. Amma doted on him, much more than she doted on Chhote Mamu, Farhat Husain.

There must be some truth in people's pronouncement that I am somewhat crazy. When Mamu let out a guffaw exposing his white teeth my imagination would soar. My younger brother, Chunnu, felt the same. When we were alone together, we would comment on the sharpness of Mamu's teeth. How he must have devoured Mumani! First, he must have chewed the fingers, then put the bones on one side. Was there marrow in human bones? Chunnu was a real terror. He was still a tiny boy when he trapped birds with dalia ki phatki before twisting their necks. Of course, he would, in imitation of Abba, utter 'Allaho Akbar' while twisting the neck. One must say 'Allaho Akbar' before shooting prey. If one does so, even if the deer dies before the zabeeha—the halal slaughter—it would still be halal. Both the bullet and the knife that killed the prey became consecrated with the utterance of 'Allaho Akbar'. After killing a bird, Chunnu peeled it like an orange and devoured it raw. Being a girl I was squeamish and felt nauseated at the sight.

Chunnu would comment in great detail on the activities of Mamu's teeth and I could barely stop myself from throwing up. I do not remember when I learnt that Mumani had died of TB and was not devoured by Mamu. Phupi Amma was accustomed to using poetic metaphors.

Shaukat Apa and I continued to squabble. She kept saying that if

I stepped into Phupi Amma's house, it would be doomsday. I was of Mughal descent; who could frighten me with doomsday?

'And if she turns you out?'

'How would she turn me out—by pushing me? I am not a Shekhani like you, but a Mughal woman.'

'Will you raise your hand against Amma?' Shaukat Apa broke into tears. I felt sorry for her.

'Oh no! Don't be afraid. I have never seen Phupi Amma from up close, but from a distance she looked like Abba Mian. I haven't seen her in nearly fifteen years. I have just a blurred image of her in my mind. Even if she pushes me out, I will still be able to see her face. After that I will proceed straightaway to the station, and from there to Aligarh.'

'Suit yourself. I am terrified of Amma. She might get angry and turn us out.'

'Then you can also go back with me.'

There was some problem with Shaukat Apa's pregnancy. It was feared that she might have a miscarriage, which was why she had come to Amma. What would happen to her if Amma turned her out? I tried to tell her if that happened we could go to Hakimonwali Gali and stay with Musharraf Aunty or Rifaqat Aunty.

'Oh no!' Shaukat Apa exclaimed. 'If I do that, Amma will not look at me for the rest of her life.' Shaukat Apa had larger eyes than most people, which was why she was apt to shed tears too easily.

Eventually we reached Phupi Amma's house. Shaukat Apa implored me not to get down, but I got off the tonga and went inside the house.

Phupi Amma was standing right before me, feeding guava wedges to the parrot in the cage. Hearing the sound of footsteps behind her she turned around to look at me.

'Is it Shaukat? Have you arrived, darling?' she said absent-mindedly.

'Shaukat Apa is sitting in the tonga and crying. I . . . I . . .'

She looked at me up close. The piece of guava fell from her hand. The tiger and the goat were measuring up each other carefully. Who was the tiger and who was the goat? It was difficult to decide at that moment. A spark flashed in her big, heavy-lidded eyes. I looked her straight in the eye and advanced. Amma said that my eyes remained dry while I cried. When I was beaten in my childhood I would scream at the top of my voice but not a single teardrop would fall from my eyes. If you raise a ruckus then the attacker gets confused and the intensity of attack is lessened. If you begin to scream even before you are hit then the person beating you thinks that you have been beaten enough and lets you off, and you can pre-empt shedding tears. But at that moment my eyes misted over.

And when Shaukat Apa peeped out from the gate fearfully, she was in such state that the forecast of the doctor was all but going to be true—two silly women were clasping each other and weeping volubly.

Perplexed, Khanam Sahib stepped out of her room and, seeing me, stood still in her tracks. I wiped Phupi Amma's tears and saliva from my cheeks and greeted her.

'May you live long!' She opened her arms.

Shaukat Apa was standing sheepishly. Naim had started chasing chickens the moment he entered the compound.

'She has taken after her father. Thank God she hasn't taken after her mother's side which is corrupted with the dirt of big, black Bedouins.' She started making jibes.

'God forbid, Amma! You've started all over again,' Khanam Sahib said, sounding annoyed.

'Am I lying, then? If there's no Bedouin blood in them, how could they come to have such broad shoulders, flat noses and curly hair! My brother is a true-blue Mughal.'

'Oh yes, I have never thought about it,' I said. 'It's true. Someone on my mother's side must have married a Bedouin woman.'

Sparks began to fly from Phupi Amma's eyes. However, seeing me smiling, she said, 'But you have also inherited shamelessness from your mother's side.'

'God forbid, Phupi Amma. How can those descendants of Uthman who thrive on watery lentils compare with us, the Changezis? We have ruled this country for several hundred years. We have planted banners proclaiming our shamelessness in every corner of this country.'

'Of course, it is the job of no Shaikh Chilli to rule.' Phupi was accustomed to hurling her weapons so fast that the enemy did not get time to recoup. 'Let alone the caretaker of cemeteries . . .'

This needs a bit of explanation. I did not know how from our mother's side the lineage was traced back to Saleem Chishti.* There could have been some kind of link, or maybe Phupi Amma had invented it to taunt my mother. She used to assert that Hazrat Saleem Chishti, who shared some family lineage with our maternal grandmother, was a caretaker of cemeteries.

'He was a powerful caretaker, nevertheless. Emperor Akbar lowered his head at his feet for an heir.' That made Phupi Amma flare up.

'The python has been reduced to dust, leaving the offspring of snakes to sting me. Your mother has poisoned your mind against me. Hey Shaukat, get out this moment.'

'Why, Amma?' Shaukat Apa was close to tears.

'Why did you bring this wretch with you?'

'I tried my best to dissuade her from coming.'

'Oh yes, Phupu. She tried her best to stop me, but I was determined to come.'

'Why?' Phupi Amma growled.

'Amma!' Khanam Sahib tried to intervene.

'You shut up. All right, tell me why you have come?'

'To see you. I never had a clear idea of how you looked. Then, so many years have passed. I have never seen you up close.'

'So you have come to see me up close?'

'Yes,' I said in a feeble voice.

'Why? Have you found an oldie for me to marry?'

I was overtaken by a fit of laughter. Phupi Amma looked a bit flummoxed. Unable to control my laughter I threw myself on the nearby bed.

---

* Saleem Chishti was a famed Sufi mystic, revered by Emperor Akbar.

'Arrey, what do you think you're doing? This is Amma's bed. She doesn't allow even Naim to climb on it.'

I stood up instantly.

'Sit!' Phupi Amma said firmly. I promptly sat on the bed. She turned to Shaukat Apa and said,

'So, she won't sit on this bed? Is it your father's bed?'

'Amma, for God's sake!' Khanam Sahib interjected.

'You shut up, Hashmat Khanam. Yes, you tell me why she can't sit on this bed?'

'This is your bed. You do not allow anyone, including me, to sit on it.'

'Are you worthy of sitting on my bed?'

'Did I say I was?' Shaukat Apa began to sulk and threw herself on the settee.

Phupi Amma sat beside me, placed her hands on my shoulder and said, 'You thankless girl, a phupi and her niece come from the same stock, and a grandma is thrice removed. This is my brother's offspring, you see, and you?'

Shaukat Apa began to cry. Phupi Amma called Naim and took him in her lap. 'And this is my brother's grandson. My elder brother had the heart of a lion. Once someone beat up Chhotey, my younger brother [my father's younger brother, Nasim Beg Chughtai], who came to him crying and complaining. My elder brother gave him two mighty whacks. Do men cry? From that day the two brothers began to practise on the wrestling ground. For three full months they practised push-ups and other manoeuvres. They ate bowlfuls of ghee and butter. At the end of the fourth month both my brothers went out in the street and while going past Nadir Pahelwan, gave him a push. Nadir began to bluster, "Are you blind? Can't you walk straight?" My brothers, waiting for this, pounced on him and beat him to a pulp. Girl, we're Mughals. Don't forget that we have razed to the ground the high and mighty of the world.'

I concealed my laughter in a yawn. I felt like telling her—'How about the dirt of the Bedouins mixed in my blood, and what about your calumny that my mother had liaisons with coachmen and grass cutters and thus gave birth to dark offspring like us? Wasn't your lion-hearted brother impotent? I remember you sitting in front of Rahman Bhai's window and reeling out my entire family tree.'

But at that moment love welled up in my heart for Phupi Amma. She did not allow anyone, except Khanam Sahib, to touch her earthenware pitcher, her bowl, her plate, bed, bed sheet, quilt and pillow. And when Phupi forbade Shaukat Apa, she wouldn't touch any of these again.

I had seen Khanam Sahib for the first time in Dhankot School, which was the worst school in Agra. There, sitting on gunny sacks, I fought with filthy children through the day. We—nine or ten girls—would go to school in a big litter, the doli. The doli would be so crammed that it looked like an inflated balloon. We would manage to get a foothold and then hang by the bar above our heads. Three on one side, three on the other and three, sometimes four, in the middle. Those in the middle experienced death throes. Sometimes their earrings would be pulled and blood would begin to flow, and sometimes their nose rings would be pulled. I had already lost my earrings in the fights with my brothers and used splinters in place of earrings. And, I would tuck my pigtail inside my kurta. There was also the fear of being strangled by the dupatta; so I would take it off and stuff it in my bag.

I had no idea why Khanam Sahib had come there. I had never seen a more beautiful woman. She must have been twenty-four or twenty-five at the time. She was five feet six inches tall, had long hair, high ankles and a slender waist. She was wearing a blue, baggy silk *gharara*, a white long-sleeved kameez and a white dupatta of delicate texture. I kept staring at her. Wearing an outsized pyjama, with a cheap print, a dirty, striped kurta and a dirty, rough mull dupatta, I was sitting on gunny cloth and writing 'alif', 'bey', on my slate.

'So, this is our maternal cousin!' It was as though she looked down from the sky at the gutter. I wished I could turn myself into an ant and crawl under the gunny cloth. She left, and my tears and my runny nose combined to make a veritable map of Panja Shahi on my slate.

On top of it, the teacher had served me a mighty whack as a result of which my head hit the slate. Being cornered from all sides I had scratched my dearest friend, Bakku, who was teasing me.

After fourteen or fifteen years Khanam Sahib was still beautiful, though her body had filled out. Her face looked a bit swollen. Her ivory complexion looked somewhat faded and sagged. Still, she looked stunning, like a queen. Her smile was still enchanting.

The meal at night was laid on the takht. I do not remember what I ate. I was in a trance. Phupi Amma fed me with her own hands, from her own plate. She allowed me to drink water from her pot and later, she also drank from it without a wash. Amazed, Shaukat Apa kept staring at us and probably felt jealous of me. But Phupi Amma was a great politician. She knew how to make up after hurting someone. She gave Shaukat Apa a box filled with knick-knacks, talcum powder and soap cakes for Naim. Shaukat Apa looked contented. She went to her room to sleep with her son.

It was arranged that Phupi Amma, Khanam Sahib and I would sleep on the chauka inside. Four settees were placed alongside each other with mattresses and bed sheets on them. There were only two quilts—the one Phupi Amma used was quite big. She allowed me to share it. It was bitterly cold. Two braziers were lit.

'Phupi Amma, from childhood there have been many questions in my mind regarding the hostility between you and Abba. No one gave me any answer. They would simply say that you were full of vanity.'

'Why don't you say upfront that I'm pig-headed, that I'm a bitch. I do not like mincing words.'

'But Phupi Amma, think for a minute, why should I have such wrong notions about you?'

'It is because of the poison injected by your father and mother. Have you heard any good word about me and my daughter from members of your family?'

'No. But why is that?'

'Your mother keeps up only with people from her maternal side.'

'For my mother, maternal and paternal sides are one and the same.

She also looked after Bade Abba and his children. She brought up the three children of her nand. She also brought up children of people outside the family. How well she looks after the needs of Chacha Mian! The whole family appreciates her. I haven't heard anything against her from anyone except you. It is difficult to find another couple as loving to each other as Abba and Amma. My mother did such a lot even for her moonhboli behn; very few people in the world would have done that . . .'

'Of course, you will support your mother,' she flared up, and pulled away, taking the quilt with her.

'Phupi Amma, if I die of cold, then the funeral expenses will cost you more than your quilt.'

Phupi Amma threw back the quilt over me, turned on her side and lay down. I tried to place the quilt over her but she became livid. With great difficulty Khanam Sahib managed to pacify her and persuaded her to share the quilt with me.

'Are you asleep, Phupi Amma?'

'Your Phupi Amma is dead!'

'For God's sake, Phupi Amma. We were talking of something else but you digressed. Tell me, what was the issue between you and Abba?'

'It's a long story.'

'Tell me . . .'

'Shall I?' Khanam Sahib volunteered. 'She, the darling sister of three brothers, had a volatile temperament. When girls are doted on as much as boys, they do not prove to be good wives.'

'Why is that so, Apa?'

'How can I tell you?'

Hashmat Khanam was the first girl in our family who had passed middle school and was a teacher in Lucknow. I am talking of the time when my Badi Apa had already been married, but the second and third sisters were still small. Abba Mian had admitted both of them into Karamat Husain Boarding House. As I was attached to the second sister, I was allowed to go with them. I do not remember much of the place except that after Baaji left for school I would stay with the maid and cry a lot.

Then I do not know why I was called back. When I grew up I asked people but did not get a satisfactory answer. Sending us to boarding school had caused a great uproar. The entire family threatened to boycott us, saying that my father was making his daughters Christians, that it would be difficult to marry us off and that he would have to maintain us all our lives. Amma shed bitter tears. Abba finally gave in. His friends also advised him to withdraw my sisters from school as, according to them, to educate a girl was worse than prostituting her.

I was fortunate that I was born later and got the opportunity to educate myself. That, too, after facing many hurdles.

Well, to come back to the point, Hashmat Apa resumed: 'In fact, Amma was a bit educated too. That had made the situation worse.'

'Why don't you say clearly that you consider me responsible for everything?' Phupi Amma growled again, but Hashmat Apa did not pay her any heed.

'When Amma was quite young, her mother died. My maternal grandfather, your paternal grandfather, i.e. Karim Beg Chughtai, married my maternal grandmother after his first wife had died.'

'I know. The first wife had given birth to my taya, Naim Beg Chughtai, and phupi, Umrao Khanam. I have never seen but only heard about them,' I said.

'Yes, Taya was married to Umda Khanam, who was our relative.'

'His son, Mirza Waliullah Beg, aka Dillu Chacha, who was as tall as a bamboo pole—we do not know why we called him chacha though he was our cousin—took opium and was addicted to sweets. Nanhe Bhai teased him a lot.'

Dillu Chacha was not married. In fact, he was a good-for-nothing and spent his life as a hanger-on. He looked very dirty; even the servants teased him.'

'And do you know, his father was the governor of Gwalior.'

'I have heard that he stayed in our house. His wife lived in Agra, and the son was a hanger-on. The importance of Arabic or Farsi had dwindled; scholars in these languages could not eke out a living. People say that Dillu Chacha carried his collection of Farsi writings with him.'

'Yes, he was thought to be intelligent. However, after the father fell on bad times, he too fell on bad days. And do you know who did him in finally?'

'No.'

'Your grandfather!'

'You mean, his own father destroyed him?'

'Yes. He was a man given to sensual pleasures. Wine and women were his main weaknesses. One day, the mehfil was in full steam—the hall and the garden were lit up and the courtesans were dancing. Someone went and reported to Nanajaan, i.e. his father, who came thundering out, pulled him by his hair and gave him a thrashing with a shoe. People were so terrified of Nanajaan that a veritable stampede ensued. Nanajaan was an influential person. He got him suspended immediately from his job, saying that his son was a worthless degenerate, not worthy of his position.'

'Oh God, that's too much!'

'He had not acquired any property. He spent some years selling family jewellery and other wares. When he began to starve and came to depend on the charity of neighbours, some provisions were made for him.'

'But grandfather had left behind a lot of property, hadn't he?'

'But he had disinherited his son. He did not give him a penny. It was such a shame for him that he could not show his face to people.'

'Why didn't he look for another job, in some other princely state?'

'First, who would have given him a job after this infamy? Secondly, he had got even the first job because of his father's influence, but drinking and licentiousness destroyed him.'

'It must be said that Dadajaan was too harsh.'

'The people of that age were a bit like that. The Mughals have always been a bit crazy. Then the English had engendered a sense of inferiority in them. Somebody who did not know English was considered worthless, even though most of the work was still done in Farsi or Urdu. Oh yes, do you know that I have started studying Hindi too.'

'Hindi?' I was taken aback. No one talked much about Hindi. Whenever a 'katha' was held in any family, Panditji would come with his dog-eared, brown 'pustak' and recite from it. Chachi also recited from a Hindi pustak. But Chacha knew both high Urdu and Farsi.

'But when Amma got to know of it she was really angry.'

'Why?'

'I don't know. I told her that I wanted to read Hindu mythology and she became furious. She thought that I was going to be a Hindu.'

'Why?'

'For getting a divorce.' This was Phupi Amma, who was pretending to be asleep.

'Will she get a divorce if she becomes a Hindu?'*

'Or you can become a Christian and you get a divorce.'

'. . . Hashmat Jahan, if you cannot maintain your faith then what's the use . . .? You will be cursed and reprimanded.'

'But I'll get the divorce.'

'By murdering your religion?'

'How about my life that is being murdered? You can outwardly become a Hindu but remain a Muslim in your heart. What is in your heart is what really matters.'

'Don't talk like a mad woman. This is the same Bedouin blood that is speaking.'

---

* This statement has to be understood in the context of the Hanafi school of Islamic jurisprudence as practised by a majority of subcontinental Muslims. It stipulated that a Muslim marriage was automatically annulled if one of the spouses renounced Islam and embraced another religion. This school is also the strictest in matters of divorce and gave women almost no ground to initiate dissolution of marriage. Desperate women locked in cruel and abusive marriages took recourse to apostasy to get out of the stranglehold of a loveless union. As the number of such women increased, it alarmed the society and nudged community leaders and jurists to institute reforms in Muslim law, to arrest this trend. For a wider view on the issue, see Gail Minault, 'Women, Legal Reform and Muslim Identity', in her book, *Gender, Language and Learning: Essays in Indo-Muslim Cultural History* (Ranikhet Cantt: Permanent Black, 2009).

'Look Phupi Amma, do not badmouth the Bedouins. I have deep appreciation for black people. Did you ever hear Paul Robeson's "Old Man Rose"?'*

I had asked the question to Hashmat Apa, but Phupi Amma cut in, 'Who is this blasted fellow?'

'A great musician of America.'

'Is he a godly person?'

'Oh yes, very godly.'

'All right. Now, go to sleep.'

'No, I want to keep awake tonight. How did this great mishap take place? How was an angelic woman like Hashmat married to a baboon, Liaqat, an illiterate and ugly fellow who was a mere chaprassi? He was not rich either.'

'If he was a real chaprassi, that would have been something. I also have a job. What is high and low? It's only a difference of salary. At least, he should have been a man!'

'What happened to you all, then?'

'My hands were tied,' Phupi Amma groaned.

'Who tied your hands and why did you agree to this marriage?'

'I was not even sixteen at the time. I had just completed reading the Quran. I had learnt some Farsi, though I knew Urdu well,' Hashmat Apa said.

'Phupi Amma, tell me.'

'Look, if you harass me more, I will break my head against the wall,' Phupi Amma muttered. 'Darling, don't ask me, my heart will give way.' Phupi Amma began to sob.

'No, Ma. No.' Khanam Sahib began to pat her mother like a baby. I was lying in between. Khanam Sahib's hand went over me to touch her mother, while tears were streaming down Phupi Amma's eyes.

All of a sudden sleep overtook us. It was as though someone had thrown some medical spray on us to render us unconscious. The emotional turmoil had left all of us exhausted.

---

* This is probably a reference to the song, 'Ol' Man River/ Mighty Lak' a Rose'.

An Incomplete Woman

Wisps of carded cotton were entering my nostrils. Whirlwinds of mists were tumbling over. A stained figure wrapped in mist was grinding some white stuff on the sil, the stone slab. Someone was probably preparing rice for kheer. Somewhere in the distance the sound of women wailing was faintly heard. I was gasping. I had difficulty breathing in. I was dying.

Bad dreams have continued to chase me from my childhood, but I was determined to live. I had decided to pull in my breath to the lungs and stuck to it all along. The burden on my chest kept increasing. The wisps of cotton had entered my lungs and were swelling. I was wide awake now but yet to regain my breath. I am running—towards the distant horizon—to grab fresh air in my fists. I must get back my breath or I will die!

But I didn't die. I was released from the shackle of this nightmare. The air gripped my lungs. With a groan I flung away the quilt and stretched myself limp on my bed.

Where was I? Who brought me here? This was a strange room—I had not seen it ever.

'God's curse! Why are you kicking up all that dust?' thundered Badshahi Phupi.

I got it now—I was at Maithan, in my father's sister's house. The sweeper woman was gathering dry leaves shed by guava and berry trees with a broom made from bamboo sticks. My bitter and harsh aunt was growling. There was an innocent rhythm in the sweep of the broom. It was as though some ghilman was playing the strings of a santoor with his heavenly fingers.

When I think of this nightmare it seems as though I have returned from the dead. Who knows whether one can die for a few moments; however, after going through purgatory I find myself more alert and active. My mind begins to scale distant horizons. Life's magic elixir courses through every pore of my body. A few years of my lifespan have been drained, but I draw new strength from every storm. I begin to laugh without reason, my heart wells up in happiness. The gentle aroma of the newly wet earth fills my nostrils.

~

As I came out of the room I saw Phupi Amma going through the contents of a box that lay open before her. The sunshine had lit the courtyard. When I greeted her she stared at me like a stranger with her bloodshot eyes, as though to ask who the hell I was.

I was not in the least bothered by her bloodshot eyes. I had found out that she was a paper tiger. Despite her threatening exterior she was a tiny scorpion who was made to shed tears of blood all these years by my sadistic father.

'Live long . . .' she muttered. 'Shaukat . . . hey Shaukat.'

'Yes, Amma.'

'Enough! Pick up your things and get lost!'

'Amma!' Shaukat Apa looked tearful.

'Yes, Shaukat Apa. You go clean up the house. I'll come by evening tomorrow.'

'Are you crazy!' Shaukat Apa yelled.

'Yes, you go. Throw your knick-knacks into the garbage dump.'

If Phupi Amma's eyes had poison darts I would have turned into a blue corpse long ago. I have tackled great challenges simply through tenacity. I have fed big, poisonous snakes simply by ignoring their hisses. My growling, jabbering aunt looked like a doll to me. She did not know what weapon to use against me.

'You just get lost. I have no place in my house for the offspring of snakes.' She who had clutched me in her arms with much love at night had turned herself into a stinging scorpion. Nevertheless I felt a fountain of love welling in my heart for her.

'I'm not in your house; I am Hashmat Apa's guest.' I darted out towards the water tap where Khanam Sahib was squatting on the chabutara and brushing her teeth with charcoal. She gave me a piece of charcoal and I began to chew it.

'You use toothpaste, don't you, memsahib that you are!'

'Yes, but I also use this stuff occasionally. It whitens the teeth.' Abba Mian would often catch the children and examine their teeth as people examine a horse's teeth before buying it. If there was a slightly shaky tooth, he would pull it out right there. Sometimes he would hold the packet of toothpowder in his hand and start brushing the children's teeth in the house. Even my elder brothers were not spared. After brushing their teeth he would trace moustaches on their faces with his blackened finger. When he was thirty or thirty-two he had to get all his teeth pulled out in one day because of pyorrhoea. Amma too had pyorrhoea but she would chew paan constantly and would not agree to have her teeth interfered with.

'Do not take offence at Amma's words,' said Khanam Sahib.

'Take offence! You have no idea how hard-hearted a creature I am. I haven't had anybody chastise me in many years. When I go home on vacation Amma looks after me with such solicitude that it seems as though I am getting old. No one teases me any more. Even Apa has begun talking to me affectionately. This is what you get when you become an adult and get yourself an education. Everyone begins to treat you with esteem. It's been years since I've had a beating.'

'Does your back itch for it?'

'Quite often. You too had your share of beating?'

'God forbid! No one has ever touched me with even a garland of flowers, but . . .'

'But . . .?'

'What's the point in telling you?'

'Lamps are ignited from lamps . . .'

'There's neither any oil left in this lamp, nor any wick.'

'But the flame has reached me. You have crushed the stones that came your way, crossed jungles infested with snakes and scorpions. You have doused rivers of fire with your tears. This is the first time I'm seeing you. The glimpse that I had of you in my childhood is still etched in my mind. After coming of age I have not been able to come to Agra ever. To tell you the truth, in the hurry and bustle of my own life I had forgotten you. It was fated that we should meet, so we are meeting now.'

'How did *you* find the opportunity to get an education? After middle school when I underwent training and took up a job, the entire family stood up against me and made my life hell. They threatened to burn down our house. For years, Abba would spend most of his time outside the house. Sometimes he would be away from home even during nights. Only we know how we—mother and daughter—managed to get by in this desolate house. Moreover, I spent most of my time in Lucknow. No one knows what Amma had to go through.'

'But you have such a large family.'

'Family? Whose family? Your mother instigated everyone against us.'

'Come on. My harmless, innocent mother cannot even write her own name. She can read magazines, though.'

'You can't bear to hear the truth about your mother.'

'It's not that, by God. I rebelled against my mother. I could persuade Abba through my rational reasoning, but not Amma. She beat me right through my adolescence, up to the age of fourteen or fifteen. Do you think my parents have educated me out of their free will?'

'Shaukat says that you're foul-mouthed and obstinate.'

'She's right. If I ever get the chance I will tell you what battles I've had to fight. Today, when I've passed BA, people in my family cite me as an example to others, as though I've achieved something remarkable. My mother does not feel ashamed of me any more either. The only regret is that if Shamim, my elder brother, had passed BA rather than me, Mamu would have found him a lucrative job in Jodhpur. Having failed his matriculation exam four times in a row he got bored, dumped his books and became a clerk in the municipality.

I have no complaints against Amma; I was the victor. One does not feel angry with the vanquished; one feels pity. She tried to organize my life according to her own understanding and experience but I proved to be too stubborn for her. She who opposed me tooth and nail is now repentant. But it'd be an exaggeration to say that she instigated every member of the family to take her part.'

'I do not care even a bit if you feel bad,' Khanam Sahib said, wiping her face with a towel. 'Your mother may be an ignoramus, but she is not a fool. Call it intelligence or cunning or politics—she got the entire family to her side with the help of her wealth. For her, the two families—her own and that of the in-laws—were the same. Your maternal grandma, too, was a crafty woman. Your mother has always been generous—if someone liked the dress she was wearing she would take it off her body and give it to her. She ensured that each member of the family got a monthly stipend. Whenever she visited Agra she spent money with open hands. Most of the members of our family were poor and indigent. They got stuck to her like houseflies.'

'Phupi Amma could have weaned them away to her side.'

'Amma did not have the knack. She could not hold on to even her own husband. Bibi, you have no idea what an incomplete woman Amma is! Her mother died in her childhood. She was the only sister among four siblings—her three brothers doted on her. Their stepmother was scared of her. A daughter is taught manners and etiquette by her mother, and how to keep the husband under her thumb, how to pull down the in-laws cleverly, making it appear that it was they who were to blame, how to support one's brothers at every step. I have heard that if your Mamu ever came to your house empty-handed your mother would secretly send someone to bring sweets from the market and give it out that it was her brother who had brought them. She would buy gifts for her brother-in-law, suits for her sister. She would arrange all this herself and tell the world, "Look how generous my brother is!"' And I remembered whenever Mamu came to visit he would give away money to children but Amma would snatch the notes away from us.

'Wow! My Amma was such a great politician.' I felt proud.

'On top of it she has a sweet tongue. My mother, on the contrary, has a sting in her tongue. I am the only child she has, but she doesn't spare me. Sometimes when she gets after my life I feel like jumping into the Jamuna and making an end of it. I planned to jump from the tower of the Taj Mahal several times but could not muster the courage. The daughter of an incomplete woman is no less incomplete herself.'

'People say that you are vain.'

'Those who are cowardly and weak use vanity as a kind of shield. Amma used to lord over everyone in her family. She did the same in her in-laws' house. However, her husband turned out to be spineless.'

'Everyone is scared of her and she is proud of it.'

'No. She often cries, but so secretly that even I have never seen tears in her eyes. She conceals her hurt from everyone, letting out her frustration through her invectives.'

'We do not know whether she ever loved her husband.'

'People say that he was crazy about her for the first ten or twelve years after their marriage. During this time she gave birth to fourteen children—some of them were born premature. Only two of us—sisters—survived. This proved her undoing. Like other men, her husband too began to look for greener pastures. If Amma were an ordinary woman she would have cried and lamented, shed tears or sought help from her brothers. But she didn't do any of it—no one had taught her to equip herself with womanly wiles. True to her temperament she expressed her sorrow through her rage. When she got to know about his affair with the sweeper woman she crushed her bangles and started to wear a white dupatta from that day.'

'And from then on she'd refer to Phupa Miyan as "the dead one"? The poor fellow!'

'It seems you have not yet been reined in?'

'I believe in wriggling out of all reins.'

'Haven't you lost your heart to anyone yet?'

'Lots of them. But I moaned and cried and consoled my heart.'

'Don't get me wrong, but how did *you* remain incomplete? Your sisters have all turned out to be ideal women. But I am afraid it is not in you to become an ideal woman. God help the poor fellow who gets saddled with a woman who is like a speeding train running off its tracks!'

'I am a hard-hearted creature, you know. In Bahraich malaria had spread like an epidemic. Everyone in the family was down with fever and shivered badly, but not me. Probably the poison in my blood did short work of the mosquitoes who dared to bite me. When I was a child, I longed to fall ill. In those days romantic heroes of most stories were doctors. I prayed to God to bless me with some disease so that a doctor, filled with compassion, would come and fall in love with me. After that I could die with the simple hope that the doctor, grieving, would wander about in deserts and then one day fall on my grave and give up his life.'

'Enough. Stop your nonsense. Amma's turning on her side. At any moment the volcano might erupt and the lava will begin to spill out.'

I went over to Phupi Amma and said, 'I'm starving.'

'Then eat me.'

'I see! I had no idea I could eat you. Great!' I got closer and pecked at her cheeks. 'Mmmmm . . . delicious, like ice cream. You can also savour it,' I said, inviting Khanam Sahib.

'Arrey, your mother has devoured my entire family. Now only these bones are left. You can chew them over.' When Phupi Amma gets herself into a rage she begins to talk in a strange rhythm, her voice quivering, as people recite the *bayaan* in a majlis before the reading of a *nauha*. I mimicked her voice exactly and said: 'Arrey, Rahim Beg's only daughter, the only audacious sister of three hefty brothers and the solitary phupi of this innocent niece, if you are not going to offer me breakfast and tea, it does not matter much, as I need to be on a strict diet. But won't you give me some water, or is the river of Furrat*

---

* Euphrates. This is a reference to the battle of Karbala, between Husain ibn Ali and his followers, and Yezid and his army. Husain and his followers were prevented from accessing the water of the river Euphrates. The water blockade continued up to the end of the battle on Muharram (10 October 680 CE).

still being guarded by the army of Shimar?' I went over to the pitcher and poured some water in a glass from it.

'Don't you dare drink the water without first cleaning your mouth!' Phupi Amma growled and the glass almost slipped from my hand. Shaukat Apa had said that once when Phupa was carrying hot water to the bathroom in a jar Phupi Amma had let out such a scream that the poor fellow dropped the jar on her feet and burnt her ankle. She, however, says that the 'dead one' had thrown the jar on her feet on purpose! If I had dropped the glass on her in this chilly weather it would have been great fun to see how she reacted.

Phupi Amma sent for a sumptuous breakfast which was prepared earlier. 'Devour it and fill your belly. I give it to you lest Khanam Sahib pulls a long face and goes on a sulk.'

I began to eat.

'Don't you have any shame? You could have shown some takalluf, by feigning reluctance to eat!'

'Takalluf! If we Mughals were accustomed to observing takalluf, we would not have been able to conquer India and rule over it. Plunderers do not feign reluctance. Moreover, my lineage goes back to Saleem Chishti, the Sufi mystic. I am eating up the entire spread so that all your sins are washed away by the good act of feeding me.'

Phupi Amma stared at me, dumbfounded. Hashmat Apa broke into a guffaw.

'Your mother appears dumb like a wet cat. Where did you get this razor-sharp tongue?'

'Our kochwan was a talkative fellow!' This was an allusion to Phupi's accusation against my mother that she was a loose woman. 'My brother is impotent. These dark children are bred by the kochwan and the gardener,' she would say.

Phupi understood immediately, and said, 'Who knows who will come to grief [by marrying you]?

'I wish you had a son whom I could elope with.'

'Do you have any shame at all?'

'He who has shame loses the game!'

'God's curse on you!'

'It was as a result of your curse that a shameless creature like me was born in the womb of Nusrat Khanam. You invoked curses on my mother all the time. At least one of your curses has come true. And then the kochwan . . .'

'How dare you! I will crush you under my shoes. Nusrat Khanam may be my enemy. But she's the daughter of my cousin who had the strength of a tiger. Even the high and the mighty would cringe before him. You know, one day Fattu the wrestler bashed up Mustaqim in the marketplace in broad daylight. My daredevil of a brother saw it and . . .'

'Ma, you've told this story earlier,' Khanam Sahib butted in.

'You shut your trap. What kind of a Mughlani are you that you couldn't keep even that wimp of a husband?'

Khanam Sahib looked dashed. Her face first turned ashen, then blue. It was as though all the poison accumulated within her had come over her face.

I countered Phupi: 'Did you spare your young, handsome husband who earned a decent salary? You turned him from a man into a puppet. People say he was well known to the police for his activities.' I improvised further, 'You turned him into a wet rat. And now you're finding fault with Khanam Sahib!'

Whenever she had a fight with her husband, she would threaten him. 'Behave yourself,' she would say. 'I am not a hapless, miserable woman. I am the pupil of the eyes of three brothers. If they get to know of this you will be dead. The eldest [brother] has spiritual power. He mutters the name of God all the time. If he wants he can shake the heavens. He will simply ruin your fate. The younger one [i.e. my father] is a magistrate. He will throw you in jail and you'll be working the chakki your entire life. The third one is a criminal of the worst order. He has already committed three murders. He won't think for a second before pulling out your entrails and handing them to you!'

'What's its name?' Phupa said; he used the phrase as a mannerism. He was dead scared of Phupi Amma's tumultuous ways. He had not thought of this shrew of a woman even in his dreams. He was accustomed to seeing gentle, docile women all his life.

'What's its name . . . the woman in my house is insane,' he would tell people. He thought her to be really a mad woman and was scared of her. 'She lost so many children that it turned her brain upside down.'

'But she seems to be in her full senses,' people would argue.

'What's its name?' he would go on muttering under his breath. People were not very fond of him. No one loves a henpecked husband. He was a blot on the fair name of manliness. Bade Abba had fallen foul with him long ago. Bade Abba was a great admirer of Mustafa Kemal Pasha who had brought about a revolution in Turkey. He literally worshipped him and took his name with each breath, along with the name of God. He was narrating some wondrous tale about Turkey to Phupa Mian.

'What's its name, who is this Mustafa Kemal Pasha?'

'Don't you know Ataturk?' Bade Abba was flabbergasted.

'What's its name, no.'

'Then I don't know you.' Bade Abba simply got up, turned his back on him and never saw his face again. Phupa Mian was dumbfounded.

Phupi Amma's condition might have got worse because of the death of her children. Nevertheless, this streak of eccentricity was inherited by all the members of the family. Well, you could not expect a real Mughal to be one hundred per cent sane. Their brain is always a little off-centre.

'Phupi Amma, you avoided the issue last night. Now tell me why you married Khanam Sahib off to a peon when boys in decent families would have given anything to marry her.'

Phupi Amma took a deep breath. 'Why rake up old ashes?' she said. 'Blood will begin to be shed. You are aware that the marriage of Musarrat Jahan took place against my wish. I tried to dissuade her in all possible ways, but she had gone crazy about the fellow. She was barely sixteen. She was so beautiful that Khanam Sahib was not even a patch on her. When she was born I looked at her for hours and yet I would not have my fill. Allah had blessed me with a miracle. She grew in leaps and bounds like cucumbers. She was older than Hashmat by twelve or thirteen years. Three babies that were born in between did not survive. Imami Khanam, my aunt, was in her death throes. The entire family had gathered. Your Amma and Mamu had also come over. Then God knows what happened—one day the old woman got up from her bed and asked people to send for the qazi. Just think of it! Instead of thinking about her encounter with malk-ul-maut, the angel of death, the woman was calling for the qazi. It seemed that at night, when Musarrat Jahan was keeping vigil, Zafar Husain, let worms feed on him in his grave, had come there for a few moments. We were all sleeping at the time. The crone just refused to die.'

'Didn't she die twenty years after Mamu's marriage?'

'Yes, indeed. But she was engineering the whole thing. They cast the net to trap my child. She was married, just like that. I had cursed Musarrat Jahan at the time. Your mother felt triumphant and left with her brother and his wife. They arranged for the walima with great fanfare just to spite me. And here in my house there was mourning.'

I was thinking . . . what a loveable fellow Bade Mamu was! He doted on all of us. He mourned his wife for twelve years. She had taken to bed when her wound had turned gangrenous. The ordinary fever had turned into tuberculosis. She had withered like a wilted flower, leaving her three children behind.

'I was not even fifteen at the time,' said Khanam Sahib.

'Yes. But Zafar had evil in his mind.'

'Apa had probably begun to have suspicions, as Zafar Bhai would often tease me for fun. He was scared of her disease and would not sit beside her. Apa's blood would boil.'

'It is the blood of Hashmat Jahan's father which is speaking now. You had just spat out my milk as though it were poison. Zafar had an evil eye. There was evil in his mind. What do you know of it?'

Khanam Sahib kept quiet.

'The shroud of my daughter had not yet been soiled in her grave when Zafar asked for the hand of Hashmat Jahan. My dead daughter had extracted a promise from me that I would never agree to marry off Hashmat Jahan to Zafar Husain. I had placed my hand on her head and taken the oath that I would rather give poison to Hashmat Jahan than give her hand to Zafar Husain.'

'Did you—I mean—give her poison?' I egged her on.

'Yes. I crushed her under my feet—she who was a part of my being, the only hope of my life, the last ray of light in the dark night. I sent my flower-like daughter to the mouth of a python, burnt her to ashes, and then I kept burning myself in the flame all my life. It's a flame that has burnt in my mind and heart all these years. It's a poison that has spread to every pore in my body.' Phupi Amma said all this in a mournful voice and kept swinging her head back and forth as though she were reading a wazifa.

'Didn't you find anyone else [for her]?'

'Who would have agreed to an instant marriage? I had no one to turn to. My husband would return late at night and then leave home early in the morning. I begged and pleaded with him to find a way out but he only muttered "what's its name". You would know that Hashmat Jahan was engaged to Nanhe [Naseem Beg, my elder brother, who had married Shaukat] at the time of her birth. Before the episode involving Zafar and Musarrat took place my brother and his wife doted on me. The entire family stood together. What great fun all of us had! My mind yearns for those days as I remember them.'

'Did they break the engagement?'

'Hear me out. Zafar Husain had said—if ever Hashmat Jahan is married it has to be to me. Or I'll shoot the groom. People do get to know these things, you can't keep them a secret. Forgetting my shame, I wrote to my brother to make good his promise, to take away my daughter and lighten my burden. Everyone in Agra and in this Maithan mohalla had got to know of Zafar's threat, God's curse on him!'

'I could guess what Amma might have written back. She must have issued the royal command.'

'How could I—the mother of a luckless daughter—have written to him that the loafer who was itching to cut his teeth on my daughter was none other than his adorable brother-in-law. My brother wrote that the boy was still studying, that he was a wayward lad of seventeen or eighteen. It wouldn't be wise to get him married right then. I could marry my daughter to whoever I liked, he said. He wouldn't stand in the way. I asked him to have at least the nikah done. However, in the meantime Zafar got to know of this and wrote to his sister, "I know Naseem is my nephew, but I wouldn't think a second before shooting him and then committing suicide.'"

'Uff. Mamu was a real . . . oh God!' I swallowed the word that had come to my lips.

'I was at my wits' end. My baby—she must have been turning in her grave. I would pace up and down all night in those days. I and my daughter. Zafar Husain had threatened to have Hashmat Jahan kidnapped. Like a cat with a burnt paw I would roam around the house all night. My heart would beat uncontrollably at the slightest sound. I felt sleepy but would splash water on my face and keep the vigil. Ya Allah! How many miles would I have traversed during those nights! Sometimes sleep would invade me so completely that my eyes would close even when I was standing and I would fall asleep. Then, when I opened my eyes, I would crash down where I was. Sometimes I felt like throttling Hashmat Jahan and getting some moments of sleep, and then grieving for her I would not be able to sleep. Do not think that there was lack of effort on my part. When I got that rude reply from my brother I remained in a state of shock for a few days. After her husband's death your maternal grandma had started living with your mother. She had instilled in your mother great love for her brothers. For your mother, her two brothers were dearer to her than her own offspring. The younger brother of your mother, Farhat Husain, also lived with your mother from the time of her marriage. I had called Farhat once to come over. The way he looked at Hashmat gave me hope. I called him once again, and forgetting all shame asked him to marry Hashmat. He began to shake all over. Tears streamed down his face. When I asked him the reason he said that it was not his fate to marry a girl like Hashmat. "Bhai Sahib is a capricious fellow. He says he will shoot whoever dares to marry Hashmat and then climb the gallows. How can my mother survive the death of two of her sons? I have never done anything for my mother. I can't be the cause of her grief in her old age," he said. After some time your mother got Farhat married.'

'Oh God! The punisher of tyrants and oppressors! Why do you land human beings in such dire straits?'

'I made another effort in this direction and managed to call Ishaq Husain over. He had completed the seventh and eighth grade and was spending his time roaming around. In another instance of shameless overture, I asked him to marry my daughter. He was baffled by the proposal. He did not dare disobey my brother as he was one of his hangers-on. Besides, Zafar's threat must have been working on him. By that time I had gone half mad. I would shove Hashmat into the attic in terribly hot weather, put a big lock on the door, then drag my cot near the door and go to sleep. Hashmat spent the nights crying in that dark room infested with mosquitoes, boiling with heat and cursing Zafar Husain, "May Allah deal with Zafar Husain as he deserves! Let him die a dog's death!"'

At that moment I had only hatred in my mind for Zafar Husain who was Shaukat Apa's father and my older maternal uncle. He had mourned his wife's death for twelve years and then remarried. His new wife was an innocent-looking, religiously inclined woman who was busy reading the Quran and saying her prayers. Mamu doted on us, particularly me. This episode that had taken place long ago had become a family joke. I had no idea what Mamu had done before my birth.

'There was just one thing left for me. Liaqat, my husband's nephew, was employed as a peon in some office. However, this was just for appearance's sake. He was involved in many shady activities. People said he was working as a pimp in Gwalior. His father had died in his childhood, and his mother brought him up with great difficulty. He was from a good family, though. I did not see right or left but called him over and he and Hashmat were married.'

'And after one night . . .'

'I turned him out. He was a brute. My daughter was terrified of him. She was so desperate she was going to slash her wrists when I intervened. Now, you tell me, what was my fault in all this?'

For the first time in my life I realized how sorrowful a woman my aunt was. No one had taught her how to survive in life, how to use her womanly wiles.

My mother was a fully realized, complete woman.

And my aunt was an incomplete woman.

~

Throughout the night Khanam Sahib and I chatted.

'Why don't you get a divorce?'

'The Indian ulema have not included khula in Muslim law.'

'How's that?'

'After consolidating their position here, the English concentrated on framing civil laws. The wise men of our community did not mention khula, i.e. the right of a Muslim woman to divorce her husband, while framing these laws. Since then no one ever fought for this. The enlightened parents were in favour of drawing a different contract for khula at the time of marriage, but people generally did not look upon it with favour.'

My own brother Jaseem declared on the day of his marriage that he considered a woman's right to divorce a bad omen. The girl's parents were in dire straits and had to acquiesce to his tantrums. The members of Khwaja Abdul Majeed's family were an enlightened lot. They were often invited to conduct the marriage ceremony and they insisted on khula. If the groom refused to accept it they would refuse to conduct the ceremony. Their efforts had considerable impact on the Muslim society in Aligarh and many families had begun to insist on khula at the time of marriage.

~

I did not need to stay there for the second night. Nanhe Bhai came and took me to Panje Shahi. First of all, I tried to engage him with the issue as he was a lawyer. I asked him why he did not try to get Khanam Sahib a divorce.

'Forget it.' True to his nature he skirted the issue. I blabbered on as he kept smiling and swinging his knees nonchalantly. Helpless, I changed the topic.

'I want to sell that Ghoriwala Ghar, the house with the mare. The papers are with you,' I said.

'Yes, they are. But why do you want to sell it?'

'I want to go to England for the teachers' training course.'

'What will you get out of it?'

'I will work.'

'Why?'

'What do you mean "why"? Why do you work as a lawyer?'

'It's a mistake on my part.'

'I'll also commit the same mistake.'

'We won't allow you to do it. You are our dear sister.' He was an incorrigible tease. You couldn't get the better of him in any argument. Then he smiled and said: 'I've sold that house.'

'How? I didn't sign any papers.'

'I faked your signature.'

'This is plain betrayal.'

'Yes, it is.'

'Why did you do this?'

'Just like that.'

'There can be a legal suit against you.'

'No doubt about it. But I have spent all the money.'

'What did you spend the money on?'

'On sundry things. Some I gave to Shaukat as she is pregnant. I also had some gold bangles made for her. Shaukat, show her the bangles. You know, I instructed them to make them using eight tolas of gold.' He said all this with such undisguised simplicity that I could not be angry with him however much I tried.

'If you lose the suit in the court then . . .'

'Then what?'

'You will go to jail.'

'Of course.'

I did not know what to do. I was angry but felt an irresistible urge to laugh as well. Nanhe Bhai was throwing sweet glances at me and smiling. Finding me silent he said:

'You want to go to vilayat?'

'Yes.'

'Then go.'

'You have sold the house. How can I go now?'

'You know how to swim?'

'Not too well. I practised swimming for a couple of days in the swimming pool at Aligarh.'

'Why don't you come with me for a swim in the Jamuna every day? You will be an expert in a week.'

'Come on. What does swimming has to do with going to England?'

'Didn't you understand? You can swim your way to England.'

'And what about the luggage? The way you talk, Nanhe Mian!' Shaukat Apa chided him.

'What's the need for any luggage?'

'Come on. How can one manage without some stuff? You're talking nonsense.' Shaukat Apa was peeved. 'Won't she die of chill in winter? She needs sweaters, a warm coat, other clothes.'

'No problem at all. You can stuff all this in a gunny bag and tie it with a cord around your waist.'

'And the fish? The giant whales who can gobble up elephants. Come to your senses, Nanhe Mian.'

'In that case take a long bamboo pole to thrash about. The fish won't come near you.'

~

When I reached Jodhpur I wanted to kick up a row. One day I asked Bade Mamu upfront:

'Bade Mamu, I learnt that you wanted to marry Hashmat Apa?'
Bade Mamu stared at me as if I had grown horns in my head. Amma
was puzzled.

'He must have taken a fancy to her, just like that.' This was Shamim
butting in. Mamu pretended not to have heard my question at all. He
began to talk to Amma about the price of ghee that he was going to
send for from Sewaye Madhopur.

'Shall I give you the money?' Ammi asked.

'No, Apa, I'll take the money later.'

Just think of the situation. How would you feel when you have
prepared an elaborate speech and then you find your audience starts
playing kabaddi? I was disappointed but did not give up.

'Didn't I catch you out, Mamu? You fancied her?' Shamim wanted
to press the issue. He was bent on making a big joke out of it.

'The food they prepare in Maithan is always tasty. Don't you agree?'
Mamu asked me in his light-hearted manner.

'Yes, I do.'

'And you must have eaten gajar ka halwa at breakfast, no?'

'It was good. But I am more concerned with Khanam Sahib's life ...'

'This is not you but the gajar ka halwa speaking,' Mamu said in
the most heart-warming way, got up and walked towards the garden
to have a chat with Abba.

'What a way to talk to elders!' Amma muttered.

'What about Khanam Sahib's life?'

'Shut up. Don't blabber too much. And don't try to boss around
just because you have passed BA.'

'But I . . .'

'Hey Dulhan, the pan is burnt to ashes.' Amma changed tack.

'But you supported Bade Mamu,' I persisted.

'Yes, I did.'

'Why? When . . .'

'I did because I wanted to. Did I have to take your permission?
Begum, when you start earning and feeding us, then you can beat us
with your shoes.'

'That's not the issue.'

'Did you ever listen to me? You always did whatever you wanted to do.'

'I . . .?'

'Then why have you set up this inquisition? Keep to your senses. If you accost Zafar again with this it will not be good for you. Ai Dulhan, if the meat has softened, throw in the ghia now.'

'Curse on it. Every day they cook ghia!' Shamim was in tears.

I felt terribly depressed. How insensitive the world was! My heart went out to Khanam Sahib, but no one was ready to spare a thought for her.

I received a letter from Azim Bhai asking me to reach Jawrah. He had become the chief judge of the princely state of Jawrah and was inviting me with great fanfare. In any case, I spent most of my vacations with him.

I gathered my few things and reached Jawrah. I had sent him a wire. Everyone had turned up at the station—Dulhan Bhabi with her five children and our other relatives. They were upset to see me without a burqa. Sarfaraz Chacha turned his face away and left the spot.

Away from the family, Azim Bhai felt lonely. He prevailed upon Nanhe Bhai to come there and managed to get him the position of the revenue secretary. Nanhe Bhai would arrive there in a few days.

Munne Bhai was regaining his health. He would now cough only a couple of times at night. They had an extensive garden. Dulhan Bhabi was very happy. She looked after me well. The children would always cling to me.

My arrival at Jawrah created quite a stir. A woman who was a BA, and that too a Muslim woman! This was a miracle. There were only a few graduates in the whole state, and most of them were Hindus. Only the headmaster of the school was a BA and BT.

Nawab Sahib was very happy that I had arrived there and attempts were afoot to settle me down.

Leaving Aligarh Once Again

Nanhe Bhai always lived the life of a calf not reined in. He was incorrigibly wayward, stubborn and lazy. He liked to lord over and terrorize everybody except Munne Bhai. As Munne Bhai remained sick, he spared him, thinking him to be frail and helpless. In fact, he pitied him. Paradoxically, he also loved him very much. Munne Bhai envied him for his carefree ways, his good physique and his smartness. Munne Bhai did not have the physique to carry off any outfit whereas Nanhe Bhai looked quite fetching even in his vest and shorts. Munne Bhai felt embarrassed to bare his shrunken feet with protruding veins.

However, everyone knew that if one had a beautiful physique the other had an unusually sharp tongue. Whenever Munne Bhai saw his elder brother riding his horses and galloping over fences with ease his face would go pale and he would try every possible means to make him look ridiculous. Paradoxically, again, he loved him the most among all brothers and sisters. When he had bouts of coughing and writhed in pain he would call Nanhe Bhai for help rather than our parents.

Nanhe Bhai, too, did not mind . . . He would look at Munne Bhai in such a way that the latter would feel embarrassed, as though he was saying, 'You're an incomplete human being. You are an object of pity.' It was a strange love and hate game between the duo.

Nanhe Bhai was a hefty, cheerful fellow. He was both liked and feared. The two brothers, born of the same mother, had no similarities—neither in physical feature nor in nature. Munne Bhai felt bad that people took pity on him, showed special consideration for him but he was really impressed with Nanhe Bhai. Despite his sickness he passed his BA quite easily. Following his example Nanhe Bhai too first did his FA with a second division and then one day managed to do his BA. The funny thing is that no one had ever seen him studying. No one knew where he studied.

In my childhood, when I was asked who I would marry, I would promptly say Nanhe Bhai. And when Shaukat Apa at the age of nine or ten declared that she would marry Nanhe Bhai I had a fight with her and complained to Nanhe Bhai about her.

He tied her to our four-poster bed and said to her, 'Now tell me, are you still bent upon marrying me?' Shaukat Apa apologized immediately to secure her release. Everyone had forgotten about the incident, except her.

And one day she did win over the most handsome and smart-looking man of the family. Sometimes an uncertainty overcomes me: was Shaukat Apa really in love with the person of Nanhe Bhai or was she infatuated with his personality and his position in the family? She wanted to acquire a dominant position in the family by marrying the 'heir apparent'. She would dream many sweet dreams. One day she said, 'Nanhe Mian will go to London to study for his law degree and will be employed in a high position. The government will confer titles on him and I will be called Lady Naseem.' Everyone made her an object of joke for this and the poor girl burst into tears. Nanhe Bhai too teased her endlessly and when he called her Lady Naseem she would burst out crying.

Shaukat suffered much psychological travail. Her mother's death had shaken her to the core. What with Mamu's job at Jodhpur and what with his involvement in the affairs of his friends, he was not up to the task of bringing up two small children, i.e. Jugnu and Shaukat. So he left them with my mother. Amma, who did not have time for her own offspring, who felt nauseated by our sight, could not be expected to care a lot for them.

Jugnu was born with a strangely calm temperament. He was simple and serious from an early age. He was not one to get up to any mischief himself or complain about anyone. He was the only child in the family who was never beaten or chastized. He was robbed of his parents, one by death and the other by circumstance. Naughty as I was, I was often smacked and teased by my own brothers, but never by Jugnu. Everyone in the family loved him. The servants, who were unhappy with us for our mischief, were all fond of him. In intellectual pursuits and sports he was beyond his years. He would never do anything that could be called childish.

Shaukat Apa doted on Bachchu Phupi, our aunt and her maternal grandma, who was our family's enemy. Her visitations were considered a kind of betrayal in our family. Jugnu would not mention her ever. He would neither praise nor blame her, he just kept quiet. Shaukat Apa— only God knows what went through her child-mind—would insist on visiting her grandma. If she was in a good mood, Bachchu Phupi would show her affection. However, sometimes she would remember that Shaukat was the daughter of that wretched Zafar Husain who had inflicted untold pain on her daughter Musarrat Jahan and sent her to her death and she would fly off her handle and shoo her back to our home. Then everyone would tease and taunt her.

In what different ways human beings shed the blood of fellow human beings! And no one bothers about what happens to innocent children when they are caught in the crossfire of adults. Children who grow up amidst hatred bear its scars in unknown ways and the wounds bleed whenever they are prodded.

Shaukat Apa grew up with the storm of hatred raging around her. She also received protection (at least she thought she did) from a stout husband and began to consolidate her position. One only wishes that God had given her a bit of the poise, patience and wisdom that were so evident in her elder brother, Jugnu. When one grew up as a hanger-on of a relative, it was simply not possible to demand honour and love on terms of equality. Jugnu was a favourite even with the servants. He treated them with respect and did not order them around. The servants would do his errands of their own accord.

When all the children clamoured for money, Jugnu would be busy doing some work. Seeing Jugnu Bhai, Amma's heart would go out to him.

'Hey Jugnu, why didn't *you* ask for money?'

'I have some, Amma.' Jugnu addressed his aunt as Amma.

Amma would reprimand him and thrust some money into his palm. However much he liked some fruits or sweets he would never make a scramble for them. That is why Amma would first take out his portion, but would always forget about Shaukat Apa.

Shaukat Apa's ideal was Bachchu Phupi, whom I met much later in life. She would show affection to this orphan when she was in a good mood, but would shoo her away when old wounds surfaced.

Women have always been Nanhe Bhai's weakness. Then, Shaukat Apa was like a newly bloomed flower, all of sixteen or seventeen. He fell for her head over heels. In the mornings, he would have breakfast in his own room and then go to college. When he returned from college he would enter his room directly and lock the door again. They would have dinner brought to their room also. The door would be locked. The brother who spent most of his time with us was now a rare sight. Earlier, the moment he entered the house there was pandemonium—he would tease others, get on their nerves, swing children up in the air, tickle them, bandy with Abba about hunting and sidle up to Amma. However, after marriage he spent all his time with Shaukat Apa.

Everyone in the house began to recoil from Nanhe Bhai and Shaukat Apa, though no one said anything. As opposed to them, Munne Bhai and Dulhan Bhabi who were married some years ago would spend less time in the privacy of their room. They had three children by then. Seeing Nanhe Bhai occupied they began to spend more time with us. Munne Bhai would occasionally make suggestive comments about Nanhe Bhai's absence. Dulhan Bhabi also began to spend more time with Amma.

Earlier, the moment Nanhe Bhai entered the house we would surround him and raid his pockets. We would often come up with something or the other. If there had been a function at Agra College his pockets would be stuffed with toffees and dry fruits. We robbed him of everything that he happened to have with him. Now Shaukat Apa would hold the toffee wrap in her hand and say 'finished' to us.

Dulhan Bhabi, though a stranger, seemed closer to us. She would play cards and pachisi with us. Shaukat Apa had no interest in such games, so Nanhe Bhai also stopped playing. Today, I understand why mothers-in-law and nanads are jealous of daughters-in-law. Thank God, there was no dearth of brothers, sisters-in-law or nieces in our house. We pretended Nanhe Bhai and Shaukat Apa did not live in the house.

An event happened at this time that left a trail of bitterness. A letter had come for me which Nanhe Bhai opened and gave to Shaukat Apa. She called me for a scolding about chasing boys. My blood began to boil and I almost gave her a good thrashing.

Munne Bhai used to teach me every evening. Seeing me fuming he asked what the matter was and I told him.

'Who's the boy?' he asked.

'How do I know?'

'Well, it was not your fault. Why should you worry?'

One day we were sitting in the courtyard when Nanhe Bhai came out of his room. 'Hey, Wasim, Jasim, Shamim, Chunni, Channu, Habbu, Majju, Naiyer, listen to me carefully.' Shaukat Apa too came out. We were all ears.

'Look, from today you will not address Shaukat by her name but call her "Bhabi Jaan". Are you happy now, Shaukat?'

For a while we stared at each other's faces. Then all of a sudden the crowd began to oppose the move and voiced its protests. Abba Mian was sitting on the four-poster, leaning against the bolster and eating some fruits. In the evenings he only ate fresh and dry fruits. Amma had split an orange and was handing him bits of it. He looked upon this domestic drama as he smiled through his Kaiser-cut moustache. Hearing the commotion, Munne Bhai came on the scene too, holding a bowl of curry and a roti in his hand. Dulhan Bhabi followed him, holding Najju in her arms. Their servant followed them, carrying the food tray. It was as though hearing the clink of swords the fighters of a tribe were descending on the arena wearing their armours.

Hearing the details of the issue Munne Bhai said:

'If you are talking of etiquette then you and Shaukat too should address my wife as "Bhabi Jaan".'

'By no means,' the crowd chorused in one voice.

'You shouldn't say that.'

'What can you do to us?'

'Now, tell me, Shaukat, how to deal with these brats? They do not agree,' Nanhe Bhai said in his classic style.

'How can I say?' Shaukat Apa was not in her element. She was pregnant and left the scene to throw up.

'The way she gives herself airs, the ghoul!' Shamim muttered.

'However, if you look at it from the point of view of family lineage, the claims made by Nanhe Bhai and Madame Shaukat are quite valid. What do you say, my Lord?' This was Munne Bhai flinging the question to Abba.

'Let the arguments be presented,' Abba said in the voice of a true-blue magistrate.

'My Lord, Madame Shaukat is the wife of the heir apparent. She is the future queen. She has absolute right to demand full respect.' Then he said to us, 'All of you call my wife "Dulhan Bhabi". Then why is this injustice with poor Shaukat, err . . . Bhabi Jaan?' Munne Bhai was always ready to add fuel to the fire. When there was an issue for debate he would coin such strange phrases and give such a convoluted picture of the situation that everyone would be stunned. Phrases would fly thick and fast; there would be fireworks of words. They would provide children a chance to sharpen their verbal skills. We children would have our blood coursing through our veins.

'Nanhe Bhai, what will you do now?'

'Well, let Shaukat return after throwing up. She'll decide what is to be done.'

'Indeed! You are such a slave to your wife that you dance to her tune.'

'Undoubtedly. I am certainly an obedient slave to my wife. My Lord, you too are one.'

'Hey, come to your senses!. . .'

'If you do not agree, ask Bachchu Phupi!'

'Every peace-loving person is a slave to his wife,' Munne Bhai asserted.

'Ai hai, what a slave to his wife, who pours the bowl of curry down the drain [if he doesn't like it]!' said Dulhan Bhabi.

'The wretched husbands can only dump the bowls, not their wives.'

'Hey Shaukat, come along now. How long will you keep throwing up?'

'Well, why does Nanhe call his wife by name?'

'How should I call her?' Nanhe Bhai was taken aback.

'Like Abba and Munne Bhai you can call her "biwi" or "begum",' the crowd opined.

'I also call my wife "khanam" occasionally,' Munne Bhai added.

'This is weird. What if I call Shaukat "biwi" or "begum" and then Amma or your wife appears on the scene? It will be such a shame.'

'It's a mess! The demand made by Madame Shaukat aka Bhabi Jaan is valid and the public should accede to it.'

'Let her go to hell! We are not going to call that vamp Bhabi Jaan,' Shamim fumed. He had given Shaukat Apa quite a few drubbings when they were children.

'We can call her what she wants but . . .' Chunnu had an idea.

'But . . .?'

'Give us some money.'

'Money?'

'At least two rupees per month.'

'Are you crazy? I'll give you a shoe beating in place of money.' Shaukat Apa was furious.

'Per person.' Chunnu was adamant.

Shaukat Apa was incensed. The two had got thirty rupees as pocket money only the day before . . . Uff! It made one dizzy doing the accounts. 'Forget it. I am not going to give you a penny! All you good-for-nothings want two rupees each! What an evil world!'

'Well, if you are ready to shell out two rupees per month I am ready to call you Bhabi Jaan,' Nanhe Bhai said with mock bashfulness. 'You always keep such a grip on your purse strings.'

'My Lord, what is your verdict on this?' Munne Bhai asked Abba.

'I do not want to interfere in this matter.'

'But it is sheer bad manners for small children to address Shaukat by her name. Nanhe Bhai will be justified in thrashing them.' Munne Bhai was always ready to spice up any issue.

'I am always ready for this job. I can give them a thrashing now.' Nanhe Bhai began rolling up his sleeves. The public swallowed the insult without demur.

'My Lord, would you like to say something?' Munne Bhai asked in a hushed tone.

'No. I am not one to interfere in the affairs of my children, provided the reason for thrashing is valid.'

Now we were in trouble. Nanhe Bhai was a sturdy fellow. He could bash us on any pretext. With so many mischievous children around he didn't have to even look for a pretext. There would always be a valid reason for him to hand out a flogging. Promptly a secret meeting was called in which Jugnu, who was Shaukat's own brother, was also present. He didn't side with his sister, and after great deliberation came out with the strategy to boycott Shaukat altogether. We decided not to have anything to do with her under any circumstances.

Jugnu was a believer in Gandhian principles and everyone abided by his suggestions. He used to help Chunnu, Shamim and Mujeeb with their homework, and taught me geography. He was Jaseem Bhai's buddy. If he had supported Shaukat Apa, whom he loved dearly, we would have been in real trouble.

The satyagrah began in earnest. We were all on one side, she was on the other. After Nanhe Bhai went to college she was alone. She wanted to open a separate front by drawing Dulhan Bhabi to her side, but it didn't work. Dulhan Bhabi was fond of playing cards and pachisi but Shaukat Apa hated all games.

Shaukat Apa began to feel suffocated. We had stopped talking to her altogether. If she said something we pretended that we hadn't heard her.

We whispered among ourselves and broke into guffaws. Nanhe Bhai did not seem to notice. Next, we boycotted him as well. If we saw him coming we quickly dispersed in different directions as though we had important work to do, and then rolls of laughter would reverberate from those directions. Munne Bhai would gladly join our gang and we would begin playing cards in different groups. Nanhe Bhai had no interest in cards. Jugnu was always wrapped up in his books. If Shaukat Apa called him he would go over to her, but Shaukat had nothing to say except complaining about us. He would listen to her with attention and then get busy with his studies. To save himself from the battle raging at home he would go to his friend's house to study.

If anyone had the right to be called Amma's son it was Jugnu. Aunt and nephew shared many traits. His relations with his maternal grandma, i.e. our Bachchu Phupi, were quite formal. On both the Eids he would visit her along with Abba Mian and my brothers.

Badshahi Phupi would greet him with harsh words. She taunted him, saying that he lived on the leavings of his aunt [my mother]. Instead of being hurt, Jugnu would smile sweetly which made Phupi's blood boil. In the same way, Amma would smile when Phupi abused her right and left. When people asked her if she did not feel bad about being unjustly accused, she would say innocently, 'Why should I feel bad? She is older than I am. She can say whatever she likes.'

Our two Mamus held Abba Mian in high reverence. They loved him more than they loved their sister. Abba did not hold it against them that they were responsible for the sad death of his niece who was the daughter of his only sister whom he loved dearly. He did not meddle in the affairs of others. Of course, Phupi held the view that he was slave to his wife, as he had been fed the flesh of an owl.

All of us loved Jugnu. But when word got around regarding our probable marriage and Shaukat Apa conveyed the news to me, I lost all control.

'Do you know, they are planning to marry you to Jugnu. But I wouldn't let it happen. I do not want Jugnu's future ruined by his marrying a stubborn and foul-mouthed girl like you.'

'Hunh! Who wants to marry an ass like him? Curse on him! I hate the wretched fellow.' In my eagerness to dismiss the suggestion I blurted out what I did not feel about Jugnu at all. I liked Jugnu a lot, though I had never thought in terms of marrying him. Jugnu was the only person in the family with whom I did not bandy words or behave nastily. I was quite impressed with him. Though he was only a few years older than I was he used to teach me quite well. At that point I did not even know that he was not my real brother; I regarded all boys around as my brothers. I did not yet think of any other relationship. However, it was as though a wall stood between us from that day.

Jugnu would tell interesting stories of ghosts and fairies in an arresting way. He never teased me, nor did he tear my doll. He was the first person to give me information about Allah. He had read the entire holy Quran. Waseem Bhai teased him endlessly, even thrashed him, but he never complained about him. He would laugh it off. They would jostle against each other all the time while walking.

I have always been fond of Jugnu. If we had got married then I would have ended up being a devoted wife. I like tall men, and he was the tallest in the family. Today, when I look back at the protagonists of my stories, they all look like Jugnu. I cannot say for sure what he felt about me. But he has always been my soulmate. Uff! How would Jugnu react if he stumbles upon these words?

For both Jugnu and me this reaction does not matter any more. He is now a very successful physician, a good husband, a good father, and, by the grace of God, a grandfather too. If he had married me he would have turned me into a mound of earth, robbing me of my mercurial elements. All the windows of thought would have closed.

~

Shaukat Apa gave birth to a boy, adorable and healthy. But we did not show the same kind of enthusiasm as we had done when Munne Bhai's son, Zaim, aka Najju, was born. Abba was also very happy at the birth of a grandson after the birth of two granddaughters. Naim was not the first. We tried to shower our affection on him but Shaukat Apa placed too many restrictions. 'He's sleeping now and will bring the house down if he is woken up,' she would say. We treated Munne Bhai's children as dolls. The moment we returned from school we would take them up in our arms, never mind whether they were awake or asleep. Dulhan Bhabi wouldn't say anything. If the baby decided to be fussy and started crying we would dump him on his mother and look for other distractions. If Dulhan Bhabi was peeved she would rather smack the baby than reprimand us.

The situation was this: to tease Naim we would dote on Zaim, play with him, tease him, make him cry. He was accustomed to it. If Naim appeared on the scene we would ignore him. How nasty these devars and nanads could be! We were indeed nasty.

Nanhe Bhai loved all the children. Munne Bhai's children would keep away from their sick father and would cling to him. He would throw them up in the air, would make them stand on his palm. Zaim was shrunken like his father. He was lightweight but very sharp and agile. Naim was fat and spoke with a stutter. We dealt with him harshly just to tease Shaukat Apa.

On her request which she made to us in words dripping with affection, Naiyer and I began to call her 'Shaukat Apa' without charging any money. Seeing us, Mujeeb and Habbu also began to address her the same way, but Shamim continued to call her by her name. Chunnu wouldn't talk to her at all; his satyagrah was still on.

Then one day Abba Mian left home to work as a judge in Sambhar. The whole house was in disarray. We could not live without him even for a moment. There was no other way besides leaving Jasim, Shamim, Mujib and Habib in the care of Nanhe Bhai and Shaukat Apa. With Abba's departure, Munne Bhai also left for Jodhpur. Abba Mian would send the money for everyone to Nanhe Bhai, but the money was not enough to run the house.

Jasim Bhai had a volatile temper. Shamim and Chunnu were naughty and ill-behaved. If Mujib was gentle like Jugnu, Habib was roguish like Chunnu. After doing his FSC, Jugnu had left for Bombay for his medical studies. Naiyer and I left for Sambhar with Amma. No one gave a thought to our studies.

Nanhe Bhai and Shaukat Apa could not control the boys. They made life hell for them. They tried to teach them a lesson by rationing their food. Both the parties would lodge their complaints with Abba Mian, but there was no remedy. No one knew who was telling the truth.

After completing his BSc Jasim Bhai left for Agra University to do his MSc. Chunnu was down with typhoid and it took such a bad turn that he had to be sent to Jodhpur for treatment. There was no good hospital in Sambhar. Apa made arrangements for Mujib to stay with Mumani Jaan and sent Habib to Bareilly. Everything was a mess.

~

My pen stops when I want to write about leaving Aligarh. The entire scene comes alive to my mind vividly. It was vacation time for school. All the doors of my education closed suddenly. I begged and pleaded to be allowed to stay in the boarding house but met with a stern refusal. Girls who stayed in boarding houses were thought to go astray. No one listened to my pleas. Naiyer was with me. However, once school reopened, Apa would call her from Sambhar.

Ugh! What a terrible place Sambhar was! As we got off the train there was no platform to be seen. There were some bullock carts standing there; there were some chariots too, with tassels and bells, but sheets were wrapped on all sides so tightly that we felt breathless. Surrounding the chariot were stately Rajputs, with their moustaches curled up and holding swords in their hands, on tall horses. Their eyes were like hot embers, as those of robbers. If the curtains moved a little they would immediately straighten them.

It was like a pageant. The bumpy journey on the mud track finally got over and we could see the gates of the mansion. The compound was large—on one side there were prisoners who were talking in Marwari behind bars. The chariots stood before a door and a passage was made with curtains hanging on all sides. The camel riders who were passing by the compound wall were stopped to maintain purdah.

It was a three-storeyed mansion, old and crumbling. Downstairs, there were the kitchen and the servants' quarters. Right above were the women's quarters where we were shoved into. There were two small and dark rooms with a long corridor and a narrow courtyard, and then halls and halls. Abba's quarters were on the top floor where there were three rooms with a veranda, a small terrace and an attic. Abba's room opened to a wide terrace that had the courtrooms at the other end. The doors remained closed throughout the day when the terrace remained crowded with the police and the criminals. The prisoners with handcuffs on would climb up or down the stairs through the day.

In Aligarh we lived in bungalows with thatched roofs. The rooms were spacious and the courtyards wide. Close by was Lal Diggi, the celebrated pond, where one usually saw buffaloes popping their heads above water as though they were taking a bath; it was a soothing sight of water nonetheless. There were shady trees all around. With all this, Aligarh seemed like a paradise compared to Sambhar. One could see green harvest fields spreading far and wide. Majestic tamarind trees stood here and there. The moment new buds sprouted we would begin raiding the trees. First we ate the flowers, then the raw tamarind and finally the ripened ones. There was a jamun tree near the well. There was also a neem tree right in the centre of the courtyard. We had mounted a swing on the tree and Naiyer and I used to swing on it till late in the evening.

Aligarh! Dear, dear Aligarh. I cried my heart out while leaving Aligarh. In the house in Sambhar sand flakes fell off the crumbly walls. The floor was paved with stones. But the people who had lived in the house before us were very orthodox. There was cow dung everywhere. The figures of the Hindu gods and goddesses that adorned the walls had been drawn by a finger dipped in ochre. The male quarters were very neat and clean. The floor was smooth and the walls symmetrical. As opposed to this, the women's quarters had numerous ugly shelves, the walls were uneven. The doors had such heavy and thick nails stuck on them that when you opened them they groaned like jail gates.

Amma had the floor scraped and washed. The floor began to leak and soon the water rained down on the ground floor. The servants began to yell and complain. The stench of cow dung was unbearable. When the floor dried up it was scraped again and then paved. Still, we felt as though we were living in a buffalo shed.

Naiyer and I occupied one room the window of which opened on the street behind. People were strong believers in untouchability. The men would, of necessity, come to meet Abba Mian, but never a woman. Sometimes, women from the families of carpenters, tailors, blacksmiths and dyers would come but they spoke such a stiff Marwari dialect that we barely understood anything.

What a lonely place it was! Amma placed a settee on the veranda and draped it with a bed sheet. She propped a pillow on one side and then began to crack betel nuts into fine shreds and thus spent her time. We mounted a chulha close by so that we could cook whatever we wanted. While we were in Aligarh, our cook Wali Muhammad, seeing our dwindling family economy, had left us. He was now called back. Ali Bakhsh, the chief among the servants, never left us, whatever the circumstances. Besides them, when Amma reached, people from the neighbourhood began to arrive with boys in tow—uncouth lads ten to twelve years old. Apart from food and stay, their monthly salary was eight annas. Four of them were employed. There was not much work for them, they stayed on just for the food and clothing. They would keep fighting among themselves and often ate so much that they would make themselves sick.

Abba soon got four dogs and a brood of chicken. He had got so used to children in the house that he looked after the boys with as much care as he did his brood of chicken. All the boys had defective teeth, eyes and ears. He would have them open their mouth for inspection and then make them gargle with potassium permanganate, brush their teeth, wash their eyes with boric powder and apply balm on them. The wretched brats had dirt accumulated on their bodies and when they were given rigorous rubs with a pumice stone, their skin came off from places, leaving raw wounds. There were many rooms on the ground floor. When Bade Abba came from Agra, he stayed there in one of the rooms, as he could not manage without a bathroom and a water closet.

What terrible desolation! For Naiyer and me, crying was a daily ritual. She had to spend just a couple of months after which Apa would come to take her back. What would happen to me? No one would come to rescue me. The greatest deprivation we suffered from was of books. Naiyer had books that were in her course in the eighth grade; I had them for the ninth and tenth grades. I do not know what hope for the future made me hold them close to my heart, because there was none. We would receive *Tahzeeb-i-Niswan*, in which the romantic stories by Miss Hijab Ismail (who had only recently become Hijab Imtiaz Ali) were published. We read those stories together and got lost in the exotic world filled with the aroma of orange buds, the maddening music of the unearthly *arghanoon* (only later in life did I come to know that this was nothing but the ordinary organ), tapering fingers and heavenly dresses. Naiyer would really get lost in them. I was not the one for such exotic stuff, it would leave me cold. The stench of the salt lakes, crumbly walls, leaking roofs, heavy nails—this was our world. There was no way out, not even for death.

Then I realized why women chose to become sati. On our way from the station, while passing by the burning ghat, we had seen the gate that had imprints of hands in red. Before climbing on the pyre of their dead husbands the women would dip their hands in red colour and leave their marks on the gate. How many hands were there? Some of them were so tiny that they seemed to have belonged to milk-sipping babies who had turned themselves to ashes on the pyres of their husbands. Even now when I remember those hands, my mind goes numb.

However, the more the environment oppressed me the more I felt the urge to fight superstitions and do something with my life. In the storeroom I ran into a box which was full of books collected by

Apa with great effort. They were old and tattered and their pages were stuck together because of seepage. There were old volumes of *Tahzeeb-i-Niswan* and copies of other magazines such as *Saheli*, *Asmat* and *Makhzan*, books written by Maulvi Nazir Ahmad and Allama Rashidul Khairi. Naiyer and I began to devour them. Naiyer would sleep early, but I would go on reading as long as there was oil in the lantern. When the oil finished I would go to the terrace and read in the moonlight. The moonlight in Rajputana was extraordinarily bright, without the foggy blur brought on by moisture. My eyesight was already weak; now it became weaker.

In my enthusiasm I soon finished reading all the stuff and then there was the same emptiness. When I read that women were the weaker sex and that they were easily corruptible, it had a strange impact on me. I felt angrier with myself rather than the society, thinking there must be something lacking in me. I felt pity, not anger, for my parents. They were trapped in their limited world. They did not hate me. My mother worried about my marriage. How would she find a groom for me in Marwar? She loved me as much as she loved her other children. She loved her daughters as much as she loved her sons. She never thought of living off the earnings of her sons. Abba was her only support. She gave generous dowries to her daughters. Apa's children were dearer to her than her sons' children. She thought she was protecting me from the morally corrupt environment of the boarding house. Intellectually, she was a child; I was older than her.

During those days Chunnu was afflicted with repeated bouts of typhoid. Abba had him taken to Jodhpur for treatment. He received good medical attention there. Left alone in Aligarh, Shamim felt nervous and left the university without appearing for the exams. He had not even paid the fees for the exam and placed the blame squarely on Shaukat Apa and Nanhe Bhai. When Nanhe Bhai came over, he exposed him, saying that Shamim had taken the fees from him but did not deposit it.

What irony! Shamim did not want to study; I did but there were so many hurdles. Shamim had the right to spoil his life by not paying attention to his studies, but I had no right to improve my life by hard work. Who decides what is right in this world? Who were the makers of my life? If it is my parents then why did God endow me with intelligence? What can I do with it?

Bade Abba taught me and Naiyer English, but at the same time compelled us to listen to his poetry. I was not a great lover of poetry and listening to his verses made me hate them. But because he taught me I had to listen to them.

Naiyer left Sambhar, and my mental balance began to go awry. I had been through all the books. Now when I felt panic I would begin reading Abba's law books. I could barely understand them and drove myself crazy poring over the dictionary all the time. At that age the thought of suicide comes easily. I too made plans to commit suicide. Through the nights I would wonder whether I should jump upside down from the terrace of the third floor, or whether I should go and jump into the salt lake. In a few hours my whole body would turn into a lump of dough. But those hours! Uff, salt would slowly eat into my flesh; first the skin would peel off, then the flesh. While sleeping, if a part of the body got insensate I felt as though I was drowning in the salt lake. I would wake up with a scream.

Then one day I heard Amma saying to someone, 'Ai hai, I am not so stupid. I have married off three daughters and two sons. Everything is available in Jodhpur. I have spoken to the cloth merchant here. He promised to supply promptly whatever stuff is needed. There are many big seths in Sambhar. Each one of them has several kilos of gold jewellery in his shop. And the inlay work of Jaipur . . .'

The salt now turned into acid and began to corrode my brain. Pretending that she did not know anything about it Amma gave me a letter and asked to leave it on Abba's table. The letter contained a marriage proposal for me and a photograph of the groom, a handsome young man with newly sprouting moustaches. He was sitting with his hands placed over his knees and staring at the lens of the camera.

I wrote to Munne Bhai immediately, saying that I would not marry and that he should have the marriage stopped. He replied, saying that the proposal was sent through him. The boy was the younger brother of his friend. He was from Moradabad and was a deputy collector, and that he was from a big family. They had seen me in my childhood. Munne Bhai suggested that if I wanted to continue my studies I could do so as a private student.

Instead of being disheartened my blood began to boil. Now, I played the trump. I wrote an impassioned letter to Jugnu: 'I swear by God I will not insist on marrying you, but only you can stop my marriage now. Write a letter to Mamu saying that you want to marry me. He should come to Sambhar immediately and stop the marriage. If you do not help me you will regret it.' After this I began to make plans for suicide. I was scared of death, but life was closing in. The fear of marriage was more potent than the desire to get an education. From my childhood I had heard from everyone that I had no merits, that I would ruin the family to which I would go, that I was outspoken and stubborn and that in two days my husband would divorce me and turn me out of his house. I had very low self-esteem—I did not have a good physique or a beautiful face. Which stupid fellow would fall for me? Not pining for something I could not have, I thought it was better to reject it. If I did not marry, no stupid fellow would have the chance to divorce me. I would rather get an education and become independent. Divorced by my husband, I did not want to spend my life rearing the children of my brothers' wives.

In a few days Bade Mamu reached Sambhar. He talked to Amma and Abba. I knew that Jugnu was regarded as a golden swan. Everyone in the family with a marriageable daughter had an eye for him. My trump was not going to fail. I cannot express how emboldened I felt, coming out of the crisis unscathed. From that day I decided that I was going to be the sole navigator of my own lifeboat.

The whole family was involved in the project. I did not inflict pain on anyone, nor was there any question of family honour being sullied. Even today no one, except Jugnu and me, know what trick I played.

The trump did its work, but now I was going to need the joker. I had to go to Aligarh to study. I had to brace myself for the fight.

Chewing on Iron

Amma was now very generous to me, assured as she was of my future. She had bought some pink and blue sarees of thick artificial silk. There were some blouses with collars to go with the sarees. She had bought some Banarasi thaan too. She had now stopped all purchases. She had also got the goldsmith to make bracelets, armbands and ear tops weighing eight tolas of gold. I did not want any of these. What I needed were several pairs of shalwar–qamis and dupatta, sheets, pillowcases, towels and bedcovers. I needed dresses to last me a year. We had white lengths of cloth in our house. I got eight shalwars made though I told Amma that I had only three made. She had no idea. I also had qamises made from the lengths of cloth. What I needed now were dupattas. I wondered how I could have the necessary things organized without telling Amma. In those days students had to bring a lantern and a lota each with them. I hid the two good dupattas that I had and started wearing the tattered ones. Amma did not take any notice. Who cared? One could take away the entire bed.

I would dream about the boarding school for entire nights. It was a strange feeling that felt as if it was suffocating me. The marriage of which Amma was so sure was not to take place, as I had promised Jugnu. I was not in the mood to marry even a king. The date for the opening of school was approaching and I had not yet got the admission form.

Then one day I gathered all my courage and descended on the arena. It was a Sunday. Abba had finished his breakfast and was reading the newspaper. Amma was sitting on the chauki and cracking betel nuts with a nutcracker. It was a scene that was etched in my memory from childhood. The old, suffocating atmosphere was making me lose my courage. A strange feeling of loneliness sat on me like a heavy burden. In such a large family I stood alone in my battle. There was no hope for support from any quarter. For several days I had a strange nightmare—I was dead and the whole family was in mourning. I seemed to hear the wailings of those millions of women who were mourning someone or the other.

Then I would open my eyes. The oil in the lantern would finish and the lamp would go out with a flicker. I would be drenched in sweat. From the small terrace I would look up at the sky to see that the stars were getting dim. The voice of the tubercular muezzin coming from afar would distress rather than reassure me.

One more day passed, and my destination did not seem any nearer. The following day I did wazu, sitting by the water drum, and said the morning prayers. I sent up my wordless prayer to God but could not ask for anything. God knew the state of my mind. I felt as though He had come to dwell in my heart. It created a tumult in me that seemed to destroy my being altogether. In the midst of hopelessness, some unknown force would come and grip my hand and lead me towards my future.

I sat on the moorha for a while. Amma was looking mournfully at the rotten portion of the betel nuts. Abba's eyes were flitting through the newspaper. I sized them up, by turns, with my eyes. The force of my stare probably compelled Abba to raise his eyes and look at me. For a while his big heavy-lidded eyes stared at mine. I did not blink. This had never happened earlier. It was no joke to be able to look at Abba's eyes. It was said that hardened criminals cringed under his glare and began to confess right away.

'I want to go to Aligarh to study,' I blurted out. There was no tremor in my voice.

'You're studying here with your Bade Abba, aren't you?'

'I want to take the matriculation exam.'

'What's the use? Jugnu has just two years of study left . . . And then . . .'

'I want to do matric.'

'Why? What's the use? It is better that you learn how to cook and sew dresses. Your three sisters are efficient in housekeeping, and you . . .'

'I have no interest in housekeeping. I want to study.'

'No. It's of no use . . .'

'Then I'll run away.'

'Where will you go?' Abba Mian put away the newspaper.

'To school . . .'

'School? . . . Which school?'

'Any school . . .'

'We aren't going to send you to any school . . .' said my mother.

'I have to go. There is just one week left for the school at Aligarh . . .'

'We can't send you to Aligarh. Shaukat is such an inept housekeeper. You are stubborn, you wouldn't listen to her. If something happens, the whole family will face dishonour.'

'Then I will run away,' I repeated. I was like one possessed.

Abba's blood-spewing eyes were now wide open but I didn't burn in their fire. In my imagination I had gripped the rope hanging from the eastern tower of the Taj Mahal. The rope was weak and my palms were bleeding. The rope would snap any moment, I would tumble down on the white marble floor, and my body would be crushed.

'Where will you run away?'

'Anywhere . . .'

'Just like that . . .'

'Yes. I'll take a tonga to go to the station. There I'll get into any coach in the train.'

'Then . . .'

'I'll get off at any station and ask people about the mission school. Once I reach there I'll become a Christian. Then I can study as much as I want.'

The world had come to a standstill. Amma's hand, holding the nutcracker, lay paralysed.

'Did you hear her, Begum? What is all this she is babbling . . .?'

'God's curse on the wretch! She is bent on sullying the name of the family.'

'But there are no tongas in Sambhar!' Abba's eyes had a twinkle of mischief. 'And you can't have my chariot or the camels of the government without my permission.'

'I will walk.' I had gripped the rope hanging from the eastern tower.

Again everything was quiet for a few moments. Amma wiped her tears in her pallu. 'How will I show my face to Zafar?'

'Well, it was Zafar who landed himself in the middle of such a good proposal. If he had not intervened we would have been free of the burden of this brat by now.'

'So, it's my brother who is to blame? Arrey, he would get princesses for his son! He wanted to lighten my burden out of love for me. He grabbed my feet and said, "I am not going to let go as long as you do not say yes."' Amma began to cry in earnest.

'Go to hell, kalmohi!' She hurled her shoe which missed me and hit the chicken which was foraging for grain. I could not stop my laughter and left the spot.

I drank two–three glasses of water from the pitcher and went to the room inside. I closed the door and the windows and kept sitting on the floor.

I was not embarrassed by my brazen conduct; on the contrary, I felt a strange peace. I picked up a book that bore the title 'The White Hair of the Sorceress'. I was so peeved that I flung the book at the wall where it lay upside down. I had not slept well the earlier night; now I was enveloped by sleep undisturbed by any dreams.

I woke up in the evening but pretended to be asleep. Once or twice someone came to see me. Shekhani Bua called out to me but I lay still. She was bent on feeding me. I heard Amma telling her, 'You need not carry the platter for the princess. She will eat if she feels hungry.' I had dozed off again and woke up at eleven at night, feeling ravenous. I had not performed any prayers after the dawn prayer. It was as though I had a pact with Allah Mian that only if He listened to my morning prayers would I pray to compensate for the missed prayers. If not, no one knew which church I would say my next prayers in!

~

The Congress was gaining popularity by the day. But in the princely states, to mention Gandhiji's name was considered a sin. We were the subjects of the maharaja of Jodhpur and owed our livelihood to his generosity. The previous November, the birthday of the prince was celebrated in all towns with great pomp and show. Abba Mian had also arranged for celebrations and lighting. The nautch girls and jugglers danced through the night. We witnessed the spectacle from the terrace of the court. Naiyer was still there.

Abba Mian was unhappy about the celebrations. Many people in the state were abjectly poor. There were no decent schools or hospitals. The rich would go to either Jodhpur or Jaipur for treatment, or they would call doctors to their homes. The poor would either spend whatever they had to survive or die. Abba's department had nothing to do with this. But he did not believe in the worship of Shitala Devi and would have the doctor inoculate all the children loitering in the street. The children would wail and their parents would raise a racket. But it made no difference to Abba. He was consumed with having people vaccinated against smallpox. Mamu had no faith in the smallpox vaccine. When Amma got Mamu married and his first daughter was born in our house, Abba had her vaccinated promptly. It is said that there was quite a scene. Mumani Jaan was so angry that she left for her parents' house. None of the other three children was allowed to take the vaccine. All of them got smallpox. They were small, so their spots were not very deep, though their skin sagged. Only Akhtar's complexion remained fair and unblemished.

Bade Mamu's children were given the vaccine in our house. When he had a daughter from his second marriage, she died of smallpox. The second daughter had ugly scars all over her body because of smallpox. The third child was a son, who also died of smallpox. After that, Bade Mamu had another son, Asghar, who had become so ugly after a bout of smallpox that he looked like a monkey. No wonder that Mamu developed a morbid fear of smallpox.

The vaccine issue reached even the Jodhpur court. There was a detailed investigation. But when Abba responded spiritedly, the matter was hushed up. At one time Abba had been associated with the Indian government and had threatened to take the matter to the higher echelons of the government. He had also sent in his resignation. The resignation was not accepted. On top of it, the medical department was also placed under his supervision, which he accepted, without caring for promotion.

He had the children of all the officials vaccinated. The clerks and the peons had also to take the vaccine. He did not even spare the prisoners.

'Sir, among the prisoners there are those who are accused of murder. Do they need vaccines?' An intelligent clerk raised the question.

'If they get smallpox, they will infect others. And if their lives are spared and they appear before Allah Mian on the day of judgement with their ugly faces, they would be thrown to hell right away, without reckoning.' There was so much uproar about the vaccine that people began to call Abba the 'smallpox judge'.

～

My stubbornness was part and parcel of my family lineage.

I felt hungry at night. Irked, Amma had the cupboard under lock and key. I raided the box of spices, got some gram powder made for kofta, and then munched on some poppy seeds. In the vegetable basket there were two shrunken carrots; the wilted cabbage was quite tasty. I found some pistachios, nuts and dried dates, gulped down two glasses of water and lay down on the terrace under the starry sky. I faced the situation with great spirit, and the silent battle continued for two days. The dream of the mission school was fading. The station was quite far. If I was found alone on the road, asking people for directions, there would be an uproar and I would be caught. My planning was weak, but I do not know why I had such hopes. Then I had a plan—I would ask Jugnu to ask my parents to send me to school, and if they did not he should threaten them by saying that he would not marry me.

I liked this new strategy immensely. And the siege began to seem insubstantial.

On the third day Abba called me to his room.

'What did you decide about going to the mission school?'

I kept quiet.

'You will become a Christian?' he asked again.

'Yes,' I said in a choking voice.

The Christians that I had encountered so far were from the lower strata of society. The women were pitch-dark, their black feet protruded from below their skirts; they wore dirty canvas boots and ungainly, crushed hats. They spoke an extremely distorted and raspy tongue. In childhood I had heard only paeans in praise of Islam. I developed a romantic view of Hinduism and its trappings: the bells and bhajans in temples, the gods in their fine attires, especially Krishna wearing the peacock crown, his antics commemorated in lyrics, his peccadilloes with the gopis, the lilting tune of the flute. However, I had no idea how one could become a Hindu. When I was small I had witnessed the rituals in my friend Sheila's house and had requested her mother to make me a Hindu. For a moment she was perplexed. Then she said, 'Are you crazy?' Everybody had laughed at me.

Amma would also give money secretly to Panditji for Satyanarayan Katha and would give offerings to the goddess Shitala. However, Christianity was considered the preserve of the English rulers, and to show any admiration for it was considered dishonourable. I do not know why.

'Crazy girl. You should not have such wild thoughts. I had no idea that you have such an urge for learning. You can stay with Nanhe and Shaukat,' Abba said, handing over a booklet to me.

'This is a passbook. With your signature, you can draw money from the post office. You have six thousand rupees in your account. You may consider this your dowry or your portion of inheritance. We want to be freed from your responsibility.'

I held the book in my hand but felt truly perplexed.

'We have also made over a house in Agra in your name. You could sell it or rent it, whatever you want.' He handed me the papers of the house.

I began to cry uncontrollably. It was as though a boatman, after seating me in a boat and handing me the oars, was leaving me alone to navigate in the sea.

'Crazy girl! Why are you crying? Send for the admission form immediately and make your preparations. Yes, and you needn't tell your mother now. Here are fifty rupees for your dress and fare.'

I let go of the rope hanging from the eastern tower and landed right on the white marble floor.

I do not know what Abba had said to Amma. She behaved as though nothing was the matter. She sent for a full thaan for dupatta. For three rupees one could get twenty yards of double-width velvet material. It was enough for eight dupattas.

Amma got all kinds of dyes and taught me how to dye dupattas. I still remember—there was one five-colour ensemble for the rainy season, one yellow one for the spring and one that had the colours of kites. First, Amma had the dupattas dipped in water, then, after wringing them, she spread them out and then folded them. The folds were tied tightly with ropes and starch was rubbed over them, then they were dipped in colour, half rose and half earth colour. When the rope was untied, the dupattas would have the beautiful colours of kites . . .

The prospectus and the admission form arrived in course of time. I filled out the form and sent it. It appeared that I would be admitted to the ninth and not the tenth grade as I had wanted. I proceeded to Aligarh. Amma was not at all unhappy. Abba would talk a lot about different things during the evenings.

'You never fall sick. Your teeth are quite clean. Open your mouth.' I opened my mouth and he began to examine my teeth one by one.

'Don't eat paan. Always brush your teeth with neem twigs. And bathe in cool water.'

'Ai hai, even in winter?' Amma asked.

'Yes, in winter too. Bathe in fresh water. And take part in sports, you've grown fat.'

I wondered what had happened to my parents! If children are

disobedient, their parents disown them, even throttle them. And here was I—my parents were treating me with genuine love for the first time.

Shaukat Apa was sleeping when I reached their house in Aligarh. When she woke up and saw me she said, 'There is no spare bed in the house. Where will you sleep?'

'I will buy a cot. Are there any lying in the attic?'

'There is one but the ropes are tattered.'

'We can get new ropes.'

'We have only two rooms. We are managing with great difficulty. We have rented out two rooms.'

'Well, there must be some space in the veranda.'

'We have got our kitchen there.'

'The veranda is quite long. We can put up a curtain.'

'It will block the bathroom. You will make a racket when people go to the bathroom.'

'I won't. And if I do, what difference will it make to you? Where does Naiyer sleep?'

'She has left for the boarding house.'

'Boarding house?'

'Yes, indeed. She had problems here. Naim used to make noise. Shall I stifle my own child for her?'

I did not unpack my stuff. I sent the sweeper woman to the hostel. 'Tomorrow is Sunday. Tell Naiyer that I have come.'

Naiyer arrived at noon. We clung to each other. It was as though we hadn't met for ages.

'I am famished, I'll die of hunger.'

'Haven't you had your meal?'

'No. It had not been cooked yet. Then I had to take permission for coming here. The moment I got permission I simply ran. Is there anything to eat?'

We looked around but found nothing. Soiled plates and pots were lying around. When did Shaukat Apa and Naim eat? Was it when I was poking through the odds and ends in the storeroom? I found a bed in perfectly good condition at the far end of the storeroom, knitted with new ropes. I dragged it out and placed it in the veranda, leaving the passage for the bathroom. I lay down on the cot and waited for Naiyer.

'Would you like to eat?' Shaukat Apa called me.

'Leave my food in the pot. I will eat later.'

What Shaukat Apa had forgotten was that while I could manage without eating, Naiyer was a frail creature and too young to go without food.

We searched the tins secretly. In one we found some coconut. Naiyer began to nibble at it. Then we raided the milk pan. A thick layer of cream had formed on the surface. Naiyer touched it with her finger.

'Shaukat Apa will kill us.'

'Eat it. You're hungry.'

'Well, she has invited me a couple of times as I was missing home-cooked food.'

'She probably had not cooked enough this time. Why did you leave for the hostel?'

'Don't ask me now. I'll tell you later.'

'No. Tell me now.'

'Come. We'll go over there and sit under the neem tree.'

'It'll be quite hot.'

'Oh no. A gentle breeze is blowing. If we talk here Shaukat Apa will wake up.'

We went over to the neem tree, gathered dry leaves and sat on them. Naiyer said, 'Listen to me. You should also come to the boarding.'

'Why?'

'What do you mean why? If I could not get along with Shaukat Apa, how will you with your fiery temperament? Besides, Naim does not allow you to read. He climbed on my back and punched me so hard that I could not bear it any more.'

'He won't do that to me. I'll give him such a thrashing that he wouldn't forget it in his whole life.'

'Just touch him and see! There will be hell to face.'

'You are a ninny. I am not going to be cowed down by anyone.'

'This is what I fear. But you have come here to study, not to fight.'

This made me think. It was good that Naiyer had not eaten the cream on the milk. When Shaukat Apa got up she promptly checked the tins, and when she saw that the piece of coconut had disappeared she flew off the handle.

'Naiyer was very hungry. You did not leave anything for me in the pot. I did not get anything to eat, neither daal nor bread.'

'We do not make daal in our house. There was some minced meat which Naim ate. I forgot about bread. There was some leftover bread there which I gave to the dogs. But why did you eat my piece of coconut?'

'Hey Shaukat Apa. It was only a piece of coconut. Why are you making such a fuss?'

'And why not? I like to munch something in the afternoon, you didn't think of that.'

In the meantime Nanhe Bhai arrived. Naiyer left for the hostel.

'Well, I was going to call a tonga and go.'

'Where?'

'Boarding.'

'No. You're not going to boarding.'

'I certainly am.'

'We wouldn't allow you to go to boarding.'

I felt an urge to laugh. I wanted to tell him—your revered father also used to say that.

'What is it to you, whether I live in the boarding or here?'

'It will be our loss.'

'What loss?'

'The money for your boarding, etc., would help us,' said Shaukat Apa.

'I see. So you people want to make money out of me?'

'Not really. On the contrary, it will be very uncomfortable for us to keep you here.'

'And what about the help that you will get?'

'Don't jabber too much,' said Nanhe Bhai. Shaukat Apa smiled wanly.

'Nanhe Bhai, I will pay you eight rupees for meals. For laundry, etc., I will pay myself. I do not know what profit you will make. Let me warn you that I will eat more than ten rupees' worth. If Naim disturbs me in my study I will give him a thrashing.'

'Don't you dare! How can you give him a thrashing?'

'Like this.' I gave Naim a smack. He laughed and started wrestling with me. 'And Shaukat Apa is quite frail. If she dares to raise her hand to hurt me I will beat her to a pulp. As a child I have given her a taste of my fists. But I am no longer a child.' Nanhe Bhai began to laugh.

'Shaukat, you want to have a bout of wrestling with Chunni?' he asked mischievously.

'My shoe will do the wrestling.'

'All right. I think it's better that she goes to the boarding. She is a banshee. If she gets into a rage she will really turn you into a pulp.'

'Come on! Let her touch even a finger of mine!'

'First thing, I will be in college. Second, if there is a fight between two wrestlers I do not like to intervene. I like to see the fun.' Saying this, Nanhe Bhai smacked me with such force that it would have been enough to send a delicate woman into her death throes.

Before leaving for the hostel I had made up with Shaukat Apa through much flattery. I asked her permission to come to her every week even though I had no desire to do so. I praised her cooking a lot and condemned the hostel food. As I was stepping out of the house she asked me in hushed tones, 'What about these rumours about you and Jugnu getting married?'

'I have no idea!' I feigned innocence.

'Looks like the doing of Bhai Sahib.' She called her father 'Bhai Sahib'.

'This marriage will never take place. I have written to Jugnu.'

'Then?'

'He did not reply. Look, doomsday may come, but this marriage can't come off.'

I felt like telling her not to make me too angry. I could yet pull off the marriage out of vengeance. Jugnu was very dear to me. I always wished him well.

'I would like to study up to BA.'

'Will you be studying even after marriage?'

'Insha Allah!' And I moved on.

I was given admission in the ninth grade, but I insisted that I should be taken in the tenth grade. Khatoon Apa was the newly appointed principal. She tried to argue that I would fail, and it would have a bad impact on the school result.

'I won't fail. And even if I fail it will be the same class!' I told her briefly what hurdles I had to cross to come to the school. 'I have antagonized my entire family. I have to succeed. I will study day and night. I will take tuitions, if needed. You have not tested me on my competence in Urdu. Please give me an opportunity, I will not disappoint you. I have lagged behind in studies. Naiyer's mother encouraged her to study. She is proud of her daughter. I have come here after waging a battle against my entire family.'

Right then, like an angel, Ala Bi arrived there. She was the wife of Shaikh Abdullah, founder of the Aligarh Girls' College. She would make daily rounds of the school and the hostel. She supported me to the hilt and said in her typical style, 'Ai, Bi Khatoon, to hell with the school result. The child is saying that she will work hard. Give her a chance.'

'If I am not given the chance I will appear in the exam as a private candidate. But I have to take the matric exam this year.'

'Yes, my girl. And you can stay with me. Khatoon Jahan, you cannot stop her from appearing in the exam. Give her admission; I will take responsibility for her.'

After admission as I was coming out of the room I heard her telling Khatoon Apa, 'God's curse, Khatoon, why were you discouraging the girl?'

In the hostel Naiyer and I stayed in the same room. Naiyer was very orderly in her habits and a stickler for tidiness. I would make a mess of the room and run away to study. She used to mutter complaints but make the room spick and span. She was both intelligent and beautiful. She always stood first in her class. I had always thought that she would acquire a good education and earn a name for herself. She had always been an obedient, gregarious and well-turned-out girl. Her mother and grandmother had arranged her marriage with a very suitable boy from her father's side of the family and she was very happy. She had always dreamt of becoming an ideal Eastern woman—a good daughter, an obedient wife and an exemplary mother. She held on to the old values. We had been together since our childhood. She did not like my ways and I had only contempt for her preferences in life. But we loved each other deeply. We were happy in each other's happiness.

She was really loveable—with her nice features and delicate hands and feet she looked very attractive. She had long, shiny golden hair. She loved chatting with friends and was mature beyond her years. From her childhood she had been better than me in everything. She had read the entire Quran at the age of six. She was an expert in sewing and knitting. She cooked well. When she was five she had stitched a shirt for a kochwan. Everyone watched in awe when she embroidered with her delicate fingers with such neatness that even the adults could not match her skill.

I was the opposite. I was always compared with her and considered a cipher. But she never considered me inferior to her. We were very good friends. Through her girlfriends in Bareilly she had come to know about things of which I had no knowledge. She was ahead of me in everything. Through desperate efforts I had gone one grade ahead of her, but she could teach me a few things.

Before Naiyer came to share my room, there was a girl of third grade who was my roommate. The girl was very poor, sick and ugly. She had no family. Her eyes were so big that her face looked terrifying. She would sit at one place for hours and try to mug up a sentence which she would forget the next moment. She stared at me so hard that it would drive me crazy. Like a servant she would fold my clothes, arrange my books or bring water for me to drink. She had widely separated protruding teeth that seemed to rest on her lower lip. When she talked, strings of saliva would make a web between her teeth and lips, and I would almost throw up. In the evenings, while I studied, she would drag my cot to the courtyard, make the bed and deck my pillow with jasmine flowers.

At night when I opened my eyes I often found her staring at me with her big, frightening eyes, and my hair would stand on end in unknown fear. I would scream at her and, frightened, she would huddle in her cot. Irritated, I would drag my cot far from hers, but when my eyes opened I would see her ice-cold fingers crawling over my body. I was so scared of this shrunken, dried-up girl, as though she would devour me. She would keep staring at me, but I did not have the courage to meet her stare.

I felt disturbed by the hatred and contempt that welled up in my heart for her. I could not even talk about her to anyone. I did not know why I felt such aversion for her.

The distractions in the hostel made me forget my life's objective for a few days, which was to pass the matric exam. Otherwise, life's door would close on me forever.

I participated in all games and lost weight quickly. In fact, I got obsessed with games. Then, Asmat Ali Khan from my class took me under her wing. We had the same name. There was always confusion at the time of roll call. The maths teacher Miss Ram, particularly, would feel annoyed. She would think we were up to some mischief. She would get furious, throw away the attendance register and order us out of the room. She felt that we two had assumed the same name just to annoy her. Sa'dat had been studying in the school for two years. She called her 'Asmat' as was recorded in the register. But everyone called her Sa'dat, which was her pet name. Since I was new, the teacher would be furious at me. As she called out the name I would respond and she would be upset. Seeing her like this we could not help laughing, and this would make her angrier. She would vent her anger on me.

In the playground too Miss Ram had serious reservations about me. I would start playing games that I had never played earlier, without any idea about their rules. I was healthy and strong. I could pick up any game easily. But there would be pandemonium on the ground. The teacher felt that I was breaking rules knowingly, just to tease her. As I had grown up with boys, I played better than more experienced girls, and they would like to have me in their teams.

Sa'dat knew that I was weak in several subjects. I was weakest in Urdu. While in Sambhar, I had read sundry books and magazines in Urdu, but I had worked more on maths, geography and history than on Urdu.

I had never read poetry. The atmosphere at our home was not conducive to poetry. I had to put up with Bade Abba's poetry, though, which made me hate it more. Seating behind the curtain, I would learn Urdu from Mubarak Ali, the teacher. He had no idea which girls he was teaching. He would normally teach us difficult subjects. It was Sa'dat mostly who followed the class seriously and understood the subjects. In the class there were six girls in all, excluding me. I can remember Zuhra Bhat, Mahmuda Umar, Mona Pierson and, perhaps, Saida Umaruddin.

As mentioned earlier, seeing me wrapped up in games Sa'dat would take me under her wing and compel me to study with her. She would prepare her own lessons by teaching me. If she were not there I might not have worked so hard. She took all the sap out of me. Many a time I had wanted to talk to her about my wretched roommate but I couldn't manage it.

When the exams came close I shifted to my aunt's house because now Sa'dat wanted to study alone. Ishrat Usmani, my uncle's son, was also taking the matric exam. So we could study together. Ishrat was extraordinarily intelligent. He also put me through a rigorous work schedule. Apaji, our teacher of religious studies, had taught us an incantation that was to be read at the time of entering the exam hall for sure success. During the exam season everyone would say their prayers regularly, particularly the early morning prayers. The advantage was that one could get up early, and after doing one's ablutions and saying the prayers, one did not feel sleepy at all. On top of it, the prayer was sure to bring benedictions and facilitate study.

When we entered the exam hall the girls would wish their friends by placing garlands of flowers on each other. However, my roommate would buy a garland from the market every day to present me with. I would feel like throwing it on her wretched face. One day, when I had to appear for the last paper, I got up early and thanked God that there was no garland on my pillow. While leaving the room I heard a gasp and turned back to see her big eyes burning like embers. When I went up close she did not blink. Her eyeballs began to roll like a frog's and threatened to grab me. Her bed and pyjamas were wet and her body was turning blue. I ran out from the room.

As I finished writing the last paper I seemed to grow wings. In my zest I entered my room singing scraps of Urdu and Hindi songs out of tune.

'Shhh!' the matron chided me.

'What's up?'

'Rasool Fatima is no more.'

My pen does not have the strength to describe the hatred and contempt I felt for myself at that moment. She must have been dying at the moment I had left her in the morning. I did not inform the matron and went away to take the last paper, which was Urdu. Had I informed her, perhaps Rasool Fatima could have been saved. For the past couple of days she had been writhing in pain but had not been ready to leave the room and go to the nursing home. She felt that I would be uncomfortable living alone in the room and would not do well in my exam.

Two wounded eyes began to chase me day and night. They would stare at me from the dark. She had no one to call her own and no one came to her funeral. Heaving her bier on their shoulders the girls cried volubly. I wish I could cry like others. My eyes began to sting. I had killed her. To this day, I have not told anyone that I am also a murderer.

No girl in the hostel had been prepared to have her as a roommate. She was very clingy. The girls would keep her at arm's length. How generous I was to have stayed with her peacefully all those days!

'We hope she did not bother you?'

'No,' I retorted.

'You have a heart of gold!' Everyone had words of praise for me.

But what about me? I had never allowed myself to question or reflect on her. I had to keep myself quiet to hold on to my mental balance.

I began to have the same dream that pursued me in my childhood, and in my sleep I would get up and search around for something. In the enveloping mist I could see someone looking like a bale of dirty, discoloured clothes, grinding something white on a stone slab. It was probably rice for kheer. The sound of lamentation would spread as my breathing got more and more difficult, and I would finally choke. I would get up with a start and light the lantern. And two big, wounded eyes would peer at me from the dark.

Lady Macbeth saw spots of blood in her hallucinations. She would keep washing her hands, but the spots would become deeper and deeper.

It was later learnt from the doctor's report that she had been lying dead for eight to ten hours. The gasp I had heard could have been from somewhere else.

They could not close her eyes despite all efforts.

~

Shamim lived in the hostel and received money for his expenses directly from Abba. Nanhe Bhai had kept him in his house for a few days. He would keep bothering Shaukat Apa and making Naim cry through the day. If he could lay his hands on food he would gobble it up without caring about whether it was cooked or not. He would tear the bread into shreds and feed crows. Shaukat Apa would be sleeping most of the time. When she got up and found that the food had disappeared and Shamim was not to be seen, she would curse him. He would disappear from home frequently. Slowly he shifted his things as well. But the day he landed there he would clean out everything; he would not spare even the milk and cream meant for Naim.

Nanhe Bhai wrote to Abba to save his family from Shamim's depredations, and Shamim shifted to the hostel. He knew that I had money and he wanted to get some by any means. As it is, he could lie through his teeth.

'Abba Mian has asked me to take some money from you. In any case, if I failed in the exams, you too would fail,' he said.

'Why's that?'

'Because you pass only because of me. I am chummy with most of the professors and spend a good deal of time with them. Come to think of it, I even assist them in setting the papers.'

I did not know at the time that most of the examiners were from outside the university. I would be a prey to his confidence trick and he was able to wangle money from me.

After the exam, when the parties and invitations were over, we thought about going back to Jodhpur. Shamim came to see me several times so that we could go together. His friend, the nawabzada, had left without taking the exam. When it started getting really hot he left for Mussoorie. At that time Shamim had gone in a group to Agra to attend a musical soirée where prostitutes sang. Otherwise he would have accompanied the nawabzada. If I asked him to study he would say, 'I have studied the course for the last three years. Only one booklet has been changed. That is no problem for me. I can help you if you have problems with any topic.'

'Which booklet are you talking of?'

'Don't remember. It's a thin one—by that wretched fellow, Shakespeare.'

'*Macbeth*?'

'Yes, of course. What's there in it after all? I have mugged up all of Shakespeare. You can ask me questions from anywhere you want.'

'But it's quite a thick book.'

'Pyare Mian—that worthless bloke—fed his dog half of it. In fact, I am left with less than half. But I remember everything.'

'All right. Do you remember Lady Macbeth's soliloquy?'

'Whose . . .? Oh, you mean that witch. What gibberish! I have dealt with her as she deserved. But you will see, I'll get full marks.'

I always sympathized with Lady Macbeth, thinking she was a victim of guilty conscience. How human beings are destroyed by their greed for power and wealth! Rashida had come two days earlier. I don't know what transpired between Shamim and her, but from then on Shamim insisted that he was going to get a first division. He might even be the topper in the class!

Shamim was a great one for bragging. If I had stayed in the same class for three years I could also obtain first class. What was so great about it? He was with Mujeeb who had appeared in his BSc exam this year. Shamim should also have appeared in the BA exam this year. But he did not want to waste more time here and was making plans to join films.

'In films, it is mainly fools who succeed.' Unwittingly, he designated himself as a fool.

'Absolutely wrong. Sundar is a BA. Motilal is also a BA.' I had not yet seen either in any film but had heard about them.

'Come on. They have added the degrees to their names just for publicity. Charlie and Dikshit.'

'I have heard that Charlie is a BA.'

'Not at all. He was a pickpocket. One day he picked Chandulal Shah's pocket with such skill that Chandulal had not the faintest idea that his pocket had been picked. He was impressed and employed Charlie at a monthly salary of five hundred rupees.'

'Five hundred rupees!'

I did not know even the names of these filmwallahs—Motilal, Surinder, Ashok Kumar, D. Billimoria and E. Billimoria. Indeed, Shamim knew quite a lot. I had seen just one film with any of these actors during the nomaish*—it featured Sulochona and Billimoria. On learning that we'd gone to see a movie, Abba had given Amma a good scolding. We were not allowed to go to the nomaish for the

---

* Fair and exhibition. The Aligarh nomaish had always been an occasion for the university students to have fun and indulge in little peccadilloes. It has had romantic associations in Urdu literature. Ismat Chughtai's novel *Terhi Lakeer* also has copious allusions to the nomaish.

remaining days. I wanted to go to nomaish this year, but Sa'dat did not allow me to because of the exams.

'Well, if you give my fare, I can take you home.'

'I came here alone. I will also go back alone.'

'No. I will not allow you to go alone.'

'You wouldn't even know which day I left on. I will wear a burqa and go in the company of other girls.'

'What meanness! Sister, please take me along with you. I do not have the fare. Give me the money for the ticket.'

After bandying words with him for a few moments more I gave him the money. He laughed heartily. 'Silly ass! See.' He took out money from his pocket and held it up. 'I have received the money order only today.'

'You scoundrel! Give me back my money.' Shamim left laughing all the way.

Shamim had fooled me hundreds of times. But I never learnt. He always managed to get the better of me.

On the platform he asked me for my ticket.

'Why?' I asked.

'Stupid. I will keep it safely. You will lose it.'

I did not give him the ticket. It would not be surprising if he returned the ticket even at this point and got the money back, and I would have been caught travelling without a ticket. I said to him, 'Don't worry. I will keep it safely.' Then I added, 'Look, the ice-cream vendor is standing there. Give me a treat.'

'Give me the money.'

'Treat me with your money.'

'Get lost. Don't talk rubbish.'

'If you don't give me a treat, I will let out a scream and tell people that you are teasing me.' I held him by his shirt front.

'Shut up, impudent girl. I am your brother.'

'The ticket collector does not know this.' Shamim was helpless.

'Filthy witch. Let go of my shirt. I'll get ice cream for you.'

I let go of his shirt. He stepped back and said, 'Want to eat ice cream? I will give you a shoe beating. You wanted to make a fool of me?'

'All right. You are not going to get anything from the tiffin box. Mumani Jaan has stuffed it with kebab, parantha, omelette, sweet potato halwa . . .'

'Come. Give my portion.'

'How about a shoe beating?'

'Cheat!' he muttered and went to get ice cream.

'Let worms grow in your gullet. Let God afflict you with diphtheria!'

'Yummy! The ice cream is very tasty.'

Shamim was a mischief monger, but he was good company. He would make one laugh so much that one's stomach would begin to ache. He could make a fool of everyone in the house and manage to get whatever he wanted. And the fellow never told the truth. Despite all this it seemed dull when he was not there. He would tease Shaukat Apa endlessly, but she also could not help laughing at his antics.

He would often eat up Naim's milk and cream. If Shaukat Apa confronted him he wouldn't deny it. He said, 'Yes, I ate it, so what? Don't you know I am the uncle of that doggy? It is obligatory for the young to look after the old. He could not do it so I told myself, "You're his uncle. If you do not care for him who will?" I have eaten the cream and he will receive God's blessings. To look after the old is an act of great merit!'

'To hell with merit! You shameless creature.'

'Well, it is for his good that I ate the cream. I have no fancy for it. By God, I hate all greasy stuff.'

'You pretend to be an elder reverend. Have you ever give any gift to your nephew?'

'How mean can you be, Shaukat? Naim, here you are.' He took out some money from his pocket and placed it in Naim's hand. Shaukat Apa felt embarrassed. 'Go son, enjoy yourself.'

Nanhe Bhai came out of the bathroom and began looking for something on the table.

'Shaukat, did you pick my money from here?' Then he saw the money in Naim's hand.

'Naim, this money . . .'

'M . . . m . . . money . . .' Naim stuttered a lot.

'You ass! How many times have I told you not to touch any of my things?' He snatched the money and gave him a whack.

'Un . . . Un-c-l-e,' Naim stuttered and cried.

'Wait a minute. Why hit him? Shamim gave him the money.'

'Would Shamim give money to anyone, and that too from his own pocket? Do you have your wits about yourself?'

Shaukat Apa was really hurt and began to curse Shamim. But Nanhe Bhai was smiling.

'Give the rascal a good drubbing.'

'I have got my money. I do not want to give a drubbing to anyone.'

Shaukat Apa told me this story and laughed.

ALIGARH

The holidays were coming to a close, and everyone was preparing to leave. Nanhe Bhai went to Jodhpur to fetch Shaukat Apa. She was staying at Ishaq Bhai's. Chunnu had been there for the past year getting treated for typhoid, but he was getting no relief. Nanhe Bhai took him to the hospital for examination. It emerged that he had contracted TB, which was in its second stage. Nanhe Bhai told him straight off that he had TB. He decided to take him to Sujat where Abba would decide on the future course of action.

When Chunnu arrived he was unrecognizable. I was seeing him after two years. He had grown tall as a bamboo pole. He was all skin and bone, no flesh. The whole house went into mourning. Amma began berating Nanhe Bhai as though he was responsible for Chunnu's TB.

Abba sent letters to sanatoriums but there was no vacancy anywhere. Apa was there, preparing to leave for Aligarh with her children. Abba said to her, 'You take Chunnu to Abu hill station. Your children can easily go to Aligarh by themselves.'

Chunnu was six feet and three inches. One day when he spat blood, he began to cry like a child. Amma also cried uncontrollably. She had not had the chance to demonstrate her affection for him. No one ever worried about him. He had been strong and as fit as a wild boar. Munne Bhai had also contracted TB, but he was better now. But no one had thought that Chunnu could ever have TB. From our childhood, Chunnu and I had been very close. Shamim was very naughty and ill-behaved. If he ever attacked either of us, the other would immediately rush to help. He could not match our combined assault. And Chunnu had TB! I felt desolate, and cried my heart out secretly. The house was in a state of shock.

Naiyer, Mujeeb, Habeeb and I left for Aligarh. There were only six girls in FA. Nowadays there are two sections in every class in Aligarh College. It is difficult to get admission there. In those days one could study only up to FA second year there. Muslims were against the education of girls. Sa'dat had shifted to IT College in Lucknow where she wanted to study medicine. During the holidays she would prefer coming to Aligarh than going to Bangalore, which was very far. At times, she would also sit in class with us.

Life in the hostel was limited but a zestful mind can find its own sources of pleasure. I took active part in all kinds of pursuits. There were many friends; there were also many with whom I fought. I had learnt all the games by that time and participated in them.

Girls studying in FA lived in special rooms that were located near the dining hall. We also had bathrooms at the back of the hostel rooms. There was no electricity, so we had to light lanterns. Every girl had to make her own arrangement for the bedstead. One day, when Shaukat Apa was sleeping, I pilfered the bed from the storeroom and brought it to the hostel. I never mentioned it to her. She must have looked for it, and not finding it anywhere must have blamed the sweeper.

My roommate was a girl named Qaiser, who was studying in the second year. She was very charming and of a pleasant temperament, and adept in games. She was very dear to me. She put up with my disorderly ways. If I wasted my time gossiping, she would catch hold of me and take me to my study table.

Mumtaz Abdullah taught us history. She was very young and of a nervous temperament, which is why she tried her best to establish her hold over us. Girls were scared of her. I was also somewhat scared of her and, as was my tendency, I could not go along with those who scared me. I could just not bear those who gave themselves airs. As opposed to her, I doted on her elder sister, Khatoon Abdullah. She was very soft-spoken and her face wore a smile when she talked. If she had to chide any girl she would look very uncomfortable, and break into a laugh while ticking anyone off. This would threaten to erode her authority. As she was so soft-hearted we were in real awe of her.

Miss Ram did not take any of our classes, and would come only during games. She had no interest in games but had to do her duties. She had known me from the fourth grade and blamed me for all trouble. Other girls would explain things on my behalf and I would provide her with proof of my innocence, but she would say demurely to me, 'Please sit down in the corner.' I would finally give up. After a while she would forget about her instruction and seeing me sitting on the stairs she would flare up, 'Why do you sit idle all the time and not take part in games?' I would not remind her that it was she who had devised the punishment and would promptly join the games. One day she was shepherding a crowd of girls to her class during a vacant period. I too had no class in that period.

'Come along with us. Why are you sitting here?'

'But . . .' I wanted to say something.

'Come . . .' she said sternly, and almost dragged me with her.

'Miss, please . . .' I made another attempt to say something, but she thundered, 'Silence!' Hiding their faces in their dupattas the girls were laughing. I was made to sit in the seat of another girl, who was puzzled and began to look around herself for some cue.

Seeing her standing by me Miss Ram said, 'No chatting in the class. Do this during the free period. Now get out, please.'

'But Miss Ram . . .'

'Please get out . . . Go to your class.' Miss Ram looked at the other girls who were standing and blurted out, 'Sit down, please,' and drew their attention to the blackboard.

The girl turned her face and began to cry. She had been newly admitted to the college.

Khatoon Apa would visit all the classes. She would come quietly and stand in the middle of the classroom. The girls would begin to rise to show her respect but she would ask them to sit down.

She was leaving the class when her eyes fell on me, and she flinched. 'You! . . . What are you doing in this class?' she snapped.

'Me? . . . It so happened . . .'

'Come to my office, please.'

I took Miss Ram's permission and went with her. She had also heard Khatoon Apa asking me to accompany her. Now she began to berate the girl who was standing and crying.

When I recounted the details, Khatoon Apa said, 'Don't talk nonsense!'

'I swear by God. You can ask the girls of the eighth grade. Miss Ram literally dragged me to the class.' Khatoon Apa broke into laughter.

'Miss Ram has been teaching for a long time. She's tired. When I ask her to take a vacation she gets annoyed.'

Miss Ram must have been very beautiful at one time. She had stately features, unblemished skin, her hair was curly and grey. I felt curious about her. Usually, question and answer sessions with teachers get dull and boring. But Rasheeda Apa would never give a dull answer. She told me that Miss Ram had fallen for an Englishman. He was in the police department and his fiancée was in England. Miss Ram was a stunner. Her grandma and great grandma were Indians. But she was an Anglo-Indian. She could not marry the Englishman and immersed herself in work in the department of education. When she had come to Aligarh she looked very attractive. Several professors showed an interest in her, but she did not pay heed. Arithmetic requires a lot of mental gymnastics. You do not generally get good maths teachers like her among women.

Akhter and Jamila were in the seventh grade. They would prepare sumptuous dishes at home and invite me over. Naiyer was preparing for her matric exams and wouldn't go over that often. But I would visit Usman Villa almost every month. After passing his matriculation, Ishrat was now studying in St Xavier's College in Bombay.

When Akhter's family repulsed Jasim Bhai's proposal for marriage, he was heartbroken. Abba sent him to England to study engineering. His proposal was rejected because Akhter's family had got an offer from Dawood Beg Bawa, nephew of Rafiuddin Beg. They were associated with films and had tons of money. When they returned home with pomp and show, Akhter was quickly engaged to him and Jasim Bhai's proposal was rejected.

Akhter showed me the ring and the expensive wristwatch that she had got as a gift. Shamim had been right—in the film line what counted was your acting skill rather than degrees. Dawood Beg was young, handsome and very successful. Till then I had seen just one movie, featuring Sulochana and Billimoria. I did not have the remotest connection with the film world. I had only heard about some actors from Shamim.

I used to take care of Khatoon Apa's office. I would get it opened half an hour before time to air it out. Mumtaz Apa gave herself airs but Khatoon Apa would chat informally about many things. I was the president of the debating society and participated most actively in hostel meetings. The food in hostels is usually bad; one gets fed up eating the same food day after day. One day, when a girl found a fly stuck to a roti, all the residents left the dining room and raised a ruckus. They went on a hunger strike. A meeting was held in the Common Room where heightened sentiments were expressed and earlier slip-ups were remembered. No one touched the food at night as well. Nuts and chickpeas were stealthily brought from the market and younger girls were fed. Khatoon Apa, along with some other teachers, came to talk to the girls. But all of us filed into the prayer room and after making the obligatory evening prayer kept ourselves busy in supererogatory prayers. I had thought of this strategy, which was quite successful. Akhter and Jamila had learnt about our hunger strike and brought several dog biscuit packets and pickles concealed in a bale of cloth. Zuhra Bhatt had managed to smuggle in a big pot of greasy food which was distributed in all the rooms like consecrated food. The higher-ups were worried that the girls were starving. Well, the girls always kept stuff in packets and tins. All that was brought out in the open now. But the administration was unaware of this. There were also raw mangoes hanging from the tree branches. As and when they fell to the ground, the young girls would gather and distribute them among everyone. We were tasting food of different flavours and having fun.

At night we did not adhere to the sleeping hour when the gong blared. We laid durries on the tennis court and sang qawwalis at the top of our voices. A satire was written parodying the teachers and we sang it in our croaking voices. The dining staff would lay the food on the table, the bell would ring and mice would gambol in the plates. But we stood steadfast in our resolve.

The delegation from the management came again and the girls pushed me forward to face them. I was the old sinner and everyone wanted to vent their anger on me.

'We would prefer death to eating this rotten food,' I said quite dramatically.

'The food is good enough,' said Mumtaz Apa.

'How much do you manage to eat, after all?' I made a jibe at her frail frame. She was fed up with me. She winced but remained quiet.

'And, you have pickles, chutney, butter, milk, eggs at home . . . and fruits and sweets are aplenty. They go waste.'

The girls did not budge. The delegation went back, terribly annoyed.

At about four in the afternoon Ala Bi appeared as though floating in the wind, dressed in a baggy skirt, white chikan kurta and white crinkly dupatta. The moment she arrived she called out: 'Girls, where on earth are you?'

Hearing her voice several girls began to cry and ran to hide in their own rooms. The smaller girls promptly surrounded her. We called them 'chicks'. She marched towards us accompanied by the crowd of chicks.

'So, are you devouring raw mangoes? You'll get a sore throat, it will kill you.' She slapped Hamida's hand and the mango dropped to the ground. Hamida clung to the neem tree and started crying.

'Why are you just standing there and looking at my face? Come with me.'

Immediately the warehouse was opened, and wheat was kneaded for puris. Some girls began to peel potatoes. There was great commotion.

'Chutney, girls! Where's chutney? Can you really enjoy puris without chutney?' Ala Bi interjected.

Several girls plundered the mango trees. They ate some and made a bowlful of chutney with the rest. Ala Bi sat down to fry puris. All the round objects available there were pressed into service. Besides the rolling pins, bottles were used, and pooris were churned out in all shapes and sizes. One girl was kneading on her slate! I can't describe how we enjoyed ourselves that day.

'Crazy girls, here are sweets for you!' Ala Bi screamed to the baffled girls.

'These are laddoos for Hamid Mian's engagement. Amma has sent your share.' Achchan Apa entered with a boy who was carrying the basket of sweets on his head. Right behind them was Pali Aunty, her mother, holding the burqa and panting for breath.

'So, you're having great fun!' This was Rasheeda Apa in her shalwar and qamis, without a dupatta, and her cropped mane. The girls surrounded her in a moment.

Mats were spread, gunny sacks were dragged for people to sit on and plates were placed before them. Uff, how much we ate! Namkeen, then sweets, then chutney, then namkeen again, then sweets . . .! After quite a while we saw Khatoon Apa standing on one side like a stranger and smiling.

'Ai hai, someone go and call Dulha Mian.' Ala Bi called her husband Dulha Mian. It was as though someone had rubbed Aladdin's lamp. Shahid lifted the sack curtain and Papa Mian* entered with his head lowered. Amidst thunderous clapping he was seated beside the pans and pots.

After the meal Ala Bi, Papa Mian and the staff members sat on chairs.

'Girls, one day this wide stretch of land,' Papa Mian swung his stick and said, 'was a big jungle. Jackals and hyenas would scream and

---

* Born Thakur Das, Papa Mian was a Kashmiri Brahmin born in a village near Poonch in 1874. On his conversion to Islam, he was given the name Shaikh Abdullah. He was educated at Aligarh and became a champion of women's education. He worked tirelessly to establish the Girls' School at Aligarh in 1906 and, with his wife, Wahid Jahan Begum, popularly known as Ala Bi, devoted his entire life to this mission. He also founded the journal *Khatoon* for the edification and uplift of women. Aligarh Girls' School

snakes spewed venom. Standing on the edges of this jungle I dreamt of a garden. Now flowers have bloomed in that jungle.' The face of even the darkest girl gleamed. Some habitual criers began to shed tears.

'You are the pride of this college. It is because of you that a house of learning stands on this ordinary piece of land. I wish and pray that you also dream beautiful dreams in your life and may those dreams turn into reality!'

When the clapping subsided a little, Khatoon Apa said, 'Papa suggests that every month four senior girls of the hostel will take up the responsibility of food. Next month another group of four girls will take up the responsibility.'

'We are ready,' yelled the girls. I was silent though everyone was looking at me.

'Before the month begins you have to prepare the budget for the groceries—wheat, pulses, oil, kerosene, etc.' Miss Jeremy said something in Khatoon Apa's ear, 'And, of course, breakfast in the morning and cookies with the afternoon tea.'

'We're done for,' I muttered.

She gave more details but my mind was wondering.

'Why? What do you think of the arrangement?' Mumtaz Apa asked me sarcastically.

'Me?' I was startled.

'Yes. I think Ismat should be given the responsibility for the first batch.'

---

became an intermediate college in 1925, and degree classes were started in 1937. Their three daughters, Khatoon Jahan, Mumtaz Jahan and Rasheed Jahan, were all educated in this school and stayed in the school hostel. Later, all of them taught in the college, as is evident from Ismat Chughtai's allusions. Ala Bi looked after the girls in the hostel as though they were her own daughters. For a wider perspective on Muslim women's education and the challenges Shaikh Abdullah faced in establishing the school and hostel for girls, see, 'Sharif Education for Girls at Aligarh' in Gail Minault, *Gender, Language and Learning: Essays in Indo-Muslim Cultural History* (Ranikhet Cantt: Permanent Black, 2009), pp. 116–34.

'Me and responsibility!' I thought.

'Through this, the girls will also learn housekeeping.'

'Housekeeping?' I felt giddy. 'If he is poor I'll make khichdi, if he is rich he will employ a cook.' I remembered my own words.

'Ismat, please stand up and answer,' Khatoon Apa said softly, and I stood up.

'I am too disorderly for the job,' I said proudly.

'Then you can join the second or third batch. In the first batch we can have Qaiser . . .'

'Please, no. This is my final year,' Qaiser intoned.

'Then let's have Mahmuda, Masuda, Ismat and Sultana.'

'Please do not include Ismat in our batch. She'll spoil everything. She will do nothing herself nor will she allow us to do anything,' Mahmuda said. She was extraordinarily beautiful and the girls doted on her. But we had had a tiff over something.

'You are making a false allegation!' I chided her.

'Ask Qaiser Apa. I can't get along with her even for a minute. She talks nonsense all the time.' All the girls began to giggle.

'You have never complained to me against her. What is the reason for your quarrel?' Khatoon Apa asked, looking at the girls.

The girls continued to laugh volubly. Mahmuda was silent.

'Ismat and Mahmuda, meet me in my office tomorrow during recess,' she continued. Mahmuda began to cry. I wore an innocent face. 'And think over the problems regarding food and let me know what we should do to address your complaints. Before resorting to a boycott and strike you submit your just complaints to the office.' Ala Bi and Papa Mian blessed everyone and started to leave.

'Ismat and Mahmuda, come with us up to Abdullah Lodge. The servants will bring you back,' Khatoon Apa said, looking worried. Her face was ashen and forehead wrinkled. We kept walking for a while. 'Now tell me, Mahmuda, what is this about?'

Mahmuda lowered her head.

'Ismat, you tell me.'

'Khatoon Apa, I have nothing against Mahmuda.'

'Still, surely you are aware of which words of yours offended her.'

'Khatoon Apa, in a day I say many things that might offend a lot of girls.'

'You are very ill-mannered.' I lowered my head in shame. 'You tease the girls a lot.'

'Has anyone complained about me? And why haven't you punished me?'

'You argue too much!' Khatoon Apa was annoyed.

'Sorry, Khatoon Apa. I am friendly with all the girls. The younger ones surround me to listen to stories. When they feel nostalgic for home they come to me. I love all the girls. None of my teachers is unhappy with me. I haven't been impolite to anyone.'

'Didn't you utter some nonsense about Munti?' She called Mumtaz Apa Munti.

'Shaheda and Khursheed must have reported it, the witches.'

'No, they didn't. Why do you make these comments?'

'Is Mumtaz Apa annoyed too? Khursheed is really wicked.'

'No. But she's your teacher. Should you talk such nonsense about her?'

'Khatoon Apa, all the girls talk about teachers behind their backs. But we do not go report them. Khursheed is a liar.'

'No. Don't say anything to Khursheed. I had promised her I would not tell you. And this way others also will get to know of this. But why do you say such crazy things?'

The crazy thing was this—one day Mumtaz Apa berated me for losing my history notebook. Later, she found that notebook in Miss Jeremy's room. She had taken the notebook with her and left it there. Miss Jeremy returned it to me directly. Mumtaz Apa had turned me out of the class for not having the notebook. I was piqued and had said, 'Just wait and see. I will marry her father-in-law and teach her such a lesson that she will remember it all her life.' Khursheed had laughed to her heart's content and said that it was indeed a novel way of taking revenge.

'Now Mahmuda, what is your complaint?'

'If she doesn't tell you let me,' I said. 'Khatoon Apa, I swear by God I had no evil in my heart. Mahmuda is very beautiful. I said to her that I would like to have her daughter married to my son. Tell me, don't girls make such romantic promises?'

'Of course, they do.'

'Then should this act of mine be taken as a crime? She replied that she wouldn't agree to it under any circumstances. I said if she didn't agree I would have her daughter kidnapped. Hearing this all the girls broke into laughter, but Mahmuda began to cry. Stupid, isn't she?'

Khatoon Apa began to laugh, so did Mahmuda.

'Mahmuda, don't you worry,' I said. 'If your daughter falls for my son, then I'll strangle him, that is, my son. Are you happy now?'

Two years ago, I met Mahmuda in Pakistan. Her moon-like daughter was with her. I said to her, 'Sweetheart, I have no son. If I had one, I would have broken all barriers to have you lifted across the border for him.' Hearing this, Mahmuda's daughter clasped herself to me.

What charming days I spent in the college! Every little detail is etched in my memory—not just the fun and laughter, but the time I spent with Ala Bi, and the moments I spent sitting at Papa Mian's feet.

~

The elders in the family never answered the questions that exercised my mind. Whenever I asked them anything they expressed annoyance or anger. I was scared of talking to Amma, she was always unhappy with me. I was not a 'proper' or a wise girl, I had no interest in housekeeping. Each of my three sisters was adept at sewing, embroidery and cooking. They proved to be successful wives. Apa had become a widow, but some very happy years of her married life and three smart children were proof enough of her being an exemplary woman of the East. Amma had passed on the responsibility of running the house to her and she did it very skilfully. She was greatly impressed by the way the Khwaja family of Aligarh conducted itself. She did much sewing and embroidery for them. Apa really worked like a machine.

She would get up at dawn and, after prayer and the reading of the Quran, would start preparing food. After that she would sit on the chauka with the sewing machine and a bale of cloth before her. As long as Chhoti Apa was not married she would help her with the chores. Amma would sit on one corner and cut betel nuts to fine shreds. She had virtually retired and Apa's commands reigned supreme. We, the younger ones, were like her subjects. As I did not take interest in sewing and cooking I was always found fault with. I tried my best to stay away from her shadow.

Under the circumstances, how could I have asked her to answer my questions?

Ala Bi treated us like friends. Her conversations had the flavour of stories and legends. She would tell us about how she and Papa Mian were maligned when they established the school. Her family was very enlightened. Even before her marriage she had dreamt of establishing a school for girls. She would collect the servants' children and would teach them the Quran, Urdu and some arithmetic. This was a time when the Muslim community was beginning to realize that it had lagged behind other communities. As far as women's education was concerned the situation was much worse.

The school that Ala bi had started before marriage became popular among the neighbours and they began to send their children to it. She was worried that after her marriage it would cease to exist. From an early age Papa Mian was moved by the plight of Indian women. He came from a Brahmin family of Jammu and was very sensitive from childhood. There was a man in his mohalla who would beat his wife after getting drunk. The wife's screams did not allow Papa to sleep. He would wait with trepidation for the hour when the beating and screaming would begin. On nights he did not hear screams he would wonder and keep awake. He seemed to have absorbed the pain of the woman in his own being. By dint of his own efforts he got an education and made a place for himself.

Ala Bi said, 'You know, on the night of the wedding, I could not help my tears from streaming down my face. I was on the threshold of something so momentous that I felt awed by it. How would the stranger who was going to be closest to me turn out to be?'

The stranger turned out to be the prince of her dreams, who was devoted to women's education. Such commonality of ideals was indeed rare!

'Hey girl, I am told that you are allergic to marriage. Are you?' Ala Bi suddenly changed tack in the middle of her narration.

'Ala Bi, I can't be a slave to someone else and obey his commands. I have spent my life resisting the oppression of the elders. I want to make my own way. I feel repulsed by the idea of a proper Eastern wife devoted to her husband.'

'Ai hai, why is that?'

'Everyone thinks I am somewhat crazy.'

'God forbid!'

'But I am happy in my madness, and want to be responsible for my own happiness or sorrow, reward or punishment.'

'And if you run into someone who is mad like you?'

'As you ran into . . .'

'Oh yes. I can't imagine anyone else except Papa would have fully understood me.'

'People say that you neglected your family and children. Your sisters brought up your children.'

'Ai hai, who rears children in the Khwaja family? Ayah, dada, dadi, nani, khala or phupi. Mothers hardly rear children in our families. The first child is for dadi, the second for nani, then comes the turns of khala and phupi. And one ayah for each child. That leaves cooking, which is done by the cook.'

'Begum Amma cooks something herself every day.'

'That's just to amuse herself—she cooks something really exotic or spicy. Her husband has diet restrictions. And the sewing is done by Mughliani. Now tailors have also begun to stitch women's dresses.'

'Well, I can stitch my own dress.'

'That's enough. Look, I am hand-stitching Mohsin's shirt. As a matter of fact, people make too much fuss about housekeeping for nothing.'

'Do you sew the buttons on Papa's shirts?'

'The dhobi does that and gets some additional rupees. His daughter Ramdei is studying in the fourth grade. I have told him if he sends her to her in-laws before passing the middle school I will sack him. The fellow says her mother-in-law is blind and her sister-in-law is like a beehive. Then I told him she would go to her in-laws' house only after matric. The wretched fellow got her married when she was barely six. I have been told that the boy is demanding a motorcycle. He has been employed by Papa as a washerman in the college. I have told him if he demands a motorcycle he will have to wash his hands of his job. Let him dare! Of course, I will have a bicycle given to him.'

'People say Ratiram beats his wife.'

'A lot. The bastard instigates Cheddha's son and daughter-in-law. I have sent for the mother-in-law and the daughter-in-law. They must be on their way.'

Meanwhile, Babu dhobi arrived. Babu was tall and dark but neat. He was wearing a clean shirt and pant and looked like a college student. He would let his newly-wed bride climb on the middle bar of the cycle and they would go to see films. The mother-in-law would burn with jealousy. According to her, the Abdullah family had spoiled the servant class in Aligarh. The servants of the college swaggered so much as if they were the offspring of the governor general. It was as though Begum Abdullah had taken up the mission of 'saving' the servants in Aligarh. If you reprimanded them or thrashed them a little they would run to her and she would give them employment either in the college or at the university. Only servants who were allowed to avail of discounts from the cloth merchant and earn commission from grocers and vegetable sellers stayed with families. In the mango season you had to give them mangoes, dresses for their brats.

'Bibi, more buttons for the pant are needed. Mohsin Bhai breaks too many buttons.'

Ala Bi gave him a strip of buttons.

When he left she said, 'He's a thief, but it is difficult to catch him out.'

'What does he steal?'

'Shawls, pillowcases. He uses them himself and gives you older ones instead. The girls hardly notice. The next year, when they get new ones, he does the same again. He keeps the new ones for his own use. But how do I catch him?' I remembered that I got six sheets from home and when I returned home at the end of the term they had been reduced to rags.

'Cunning fellow! Can't you catch him out?'

'How many will you catch? These gypsies lived on stealing. Pilfering is their second nature.'

I remembered another incident. Jasim Bhai was sleeping outside the house. He liked sleeping outside when there was a slight nip in the air. After Nanhe Bhai got married, a corner of the courtyard was earmarked for him. Boys had begun to sleep outside. Someone lifted the quilt and started running away with it. Jasim Bhai chased him but the fellow disappeared into the harvest field. When he returned he found that the mattress, the bed sheet and the pillow had also disappeared! There were watchmen stationed in every mansion, but things still disappeared like this. That is why Abba would let loose the dogs at night, and no pilfering took place in our thatched bungalow.

Ratiram's mother and Cheddha, his father, arrived. It appeared that the person from whom the controversy stemmed was Rasheeda Apa. She had handed her used pink shalwar suit to Ratiram's wife. She was shy and reluctant to take it but Apa got her to wear the dress and taught her how to tie the waistband. When her mother-in-law saw it she had flared up.

'This kind of dress won't be allowed at my place,' she said.

'Why not?' Ala Bi reprimanded her.

'The people of the community will make fun of us.'

'Let them.'

'No, Begum Sahib. This cannot be permitted.'

'But why did you beat your daughter-in-law? You could have come and told me if you had any problem with the dress.'

'My mistake, Begum Sahib. I got very angry. And the slut was looking at her face in the mirror and preening.'

'Look Bahu, Rati's bride will wear the shalwar suit. She will also preen herself before the mirror. And if Ratiram dares to lay a finger on her I will get him handcuffed. I hope you understand?'

'You can't do this to us, Begum Sahib.' She was visibly annoyed.

'Shut up, you slut.' Cheddha gave her a big slap.

'Hey Cheddha, you are hitting her again?'

Whenever I visited Ala Bi, I saw her arbitrating between servants. Not only this, servants' wives from the neighbourhood came to her with their complaints and Ala Bi resolved them with the help of their masters. It was the time when there were hordes of domestic servants in Aligarh. Every kothi had an outhouse where sweepers, dhobi, watchmen, chaprassi, watermen, drivers, cooks and odd-job boys lived with their families. There were nannies and ayahs who breastfed babies; both the husband and wife in the family would have their personal odd-job boys. They lived either in the storerooms inside the main house or in the servants' quarters.

~

During this time a storm broke out. Some footloose young men from Lucknow brought out a book with the title *Angarey*, in Urdu, which was thought to be the language of Muslims. A cleric by the name of Shahid Ahrarwi turned his attention to the Girls' College. He began to publish a rag in which he went about tarnishing the reputation of the Abdullah family. He stated that the Girls' College was a brothel and that it must be closed immediately. He also published obscene cartoons of Rasheeda Apa and other writers.

I had not read the book. Ahrarwi created a desire in my mind to read it. A day scholar fetched the book from somewhere and I devoured it through the night by the light of the lantern. We had hung quilts on the windows so that no one could see the light through the glass panes. The book was a revelation!

But it left us with strange feelings. We looked for obscenity and vulgarity but didn't find any. But no one had the courage to say that *Angarey* wasn't obscene. It would have been considered shameless for a girl not to call the book obscene. Other girls looked at me—they often agreed with my views but were not as wild as me. I had now realized that there were many things that they accepted in their hearts but could not bring them to their lips. They wanted to hear it from my mouth. I said, 'The book is really obscene—my hands, mind and heart all feel rotten. Let us all go to the prayer room and seek God's forgiveness. This book must have offended God greatly!'

'You should not make a joke of such serious things.'

'Who the hell is making a joke? If genteel people are calling the book obscene it must be so.'

'Nonsense!' Jamila Hamid blurted out. She was convent educated and from a high family. She was very blunt and outspoken and so we got along very well.

'Shame on you, Jamila!' some girls yelled.

'Have you read *Lady Chatterley's Lover*?'

'It must be there in the university library.'

'No! It has already been banned!'

'How did you get to read it, then?'

'One of my classmates studies in Loreto Convent. She gave it to me.'

We were consumed with jealousy. The girls who studied in government schools were in awe of those who studied in convents. Sa'dat was extraordinarily brainy. She had stood first in the university. She had also studied for a while in the convent. But the ease with which Mahmuda Umar, Jamila Hamid, Uzra Hyder spoke English left us speechless. Of course, Jamila Hamid's Urdu was weak which was considered to be a good sign. There was just one way to get even with her—speak high Urdu interspersed with Persian and speak it fast. She would say from her high pedestal, 'Nonsense! Speak slowly.'

Eventually, many girls, through their misgivings and hesitations,

came to the conclusion that the book might be obscene but it left a
deep impact on them and the facts described in it were true.

I had not read such an 'obscene' book before; such materials were
not available in colleges and universities. But, from my hiding place
under the bed, I have heard old women talking about even more
obscene things. I knew that same sex love existed but did not know
what exactly it was. Students would talk about some girls who were
so infatuated with one other that they could not bear the thought of
their favourite one even talking to anyone else. But it was considered
a sign of decency and good breeding to ignore such friendships.

After reading *Angarey*, I read Ahrarvi's rag. I felt deeply offended
and wrote an article in which I said, 'Muslim girls are backward and
deprived of many opportunities. On top of it, Mulla Ahrarvi has
become their mortal enemy. Let the college be closed, but only our
corpses would go from here. Who will come to close the college? We
will deal with him appropriately. We have six thousand brothers in the
university; will they see our corpses being defiled and remain quiet?
Whenever Mulla Ahrarvi comes to our mind we remember our six
thousand brothers in the university, and the venerable professors and
teachers, and we feel emboldened. As long as they are there, no son
of a mother can do any harm to us. The queen of Jhansi sent a rakhi
to Emperor Humayun. All the girls of the college are sending their
best wishes and rakhis of esteem and affection to thousands of our
brothers. We are sure they will take some steps for our protection.'

I read out the long and rather emotional article to the girls. There
was great commotion. Papa Mian got to know of it and came to
see me. When he heard the contents, he had the letter sealed in
an envelope and sent it to the *Aligarh Gazette*. It was published the
following day. The boys read the article, and on the same night gave
Mulla Ahrarvi a thrashing and vandalized his office. No one had
the courage to support him. We conveyed our gratitude to the boys
through the girls who were related to them. After that, Mulla Ahrarvi
disappeared from the scene.

We celebrated our victory in the hostel. We sang songs, many of them out of tune. Khursheed Abdullah danced on the tennis court. We sent for sherwanis from the university, dressed ourselves as famous contemporary poets and read from their verses. Khursheed Jahan, who was fair and bulky, became Josh Malihabadi. Misha, who was pitch-dark with sparkling teeth, sported a beard and played Jigar Moradabadi. Sufia Siraj was Majaz's sister. She brought her brother's outfit and when she dressed herself as Majaz girls began to scream. Fakhira played Saghar Nizami. The tennis court had turned into a dance floor. The mushaira left everyone spellbound. Khatoon Apa declared the following day a holiday.

Mulla Ahrarvi's funeral procession was taken around the hostel. His effigy was burnt at the centre of the courtyard and girls roasted peanuts in the flame and ate them with great relish. For months we were intoxicated with this victory. Rasheeda Apa appreciated us a lot. This was our own victory. It was the first occasion that the girls and boys of the college established a sacred relationship. It was mandatory for the boys in the college to wear black sherwani. If we went to Stratchey Hall for a mushaira or to the nomaish and the boys trooped behind us, we were berated for that. As a matter of fact, we were no more than a moving crowd of black achkans and white pyjamas and had no individual identity. The girls used to call the boys 'kodiale'* which was a venomous snake whose bite was fatal. It was a romantic word that represented the fear and romance hidden in the mind of many girls. In those days even dark, weak and shrivelled-up boys looked attractive from a distance. When I looked at them up close I was sorely disappointed. Most of them were dark and ugly.

Now the boys started coming to the Girls' College freely. On the occasions of 'Sales' girls would look after them well. They no longer looked venomous but ordinary, simple human beings. The girls of an older generation, who had now become professors and teachers, would longingly say that the boys used to be very handsome during their college days but now they were all rotten. Actually the purdah

---

* cf. Ismat Chughtai, *Terhi Lakeer*.

that stood between the sexes allowed for the imagination to weave romantic dreams that were now destroyed. Now, when girls saw boys, they did not feel weak-kneed, but considered them ordinary students like themselves. That did not mean that all romance came to an end with the lifting of the purdah. Love thrived even now and sometimes culminated in marriage too.

However, one thing is certain—once the purdah is lifted, some base emotions that thrive simply on imagination and become the cause of much mental confusion get resolved. One stands face to face with reality. One does not look at another simply as a member of the other sex but as an ordinary human being. The possibility of blind love gets reduced and life can be built on surer foundations.

After FA there was no provision for doing BA from Aligarh. My bank book had a substantial balance. Abba Mian gave me permission to do BA from IT College, Lucknow. Jugnu had to work for two years at the Habib Hospital, Bombay. He was given the scholarship on this condition.

The two years I spent in Lucknow turned out to be crucial in my life. My mind discovered new routes, and new doors opened before me.

SUJAT

Perhaps I've forgotten to mention that Abba Mian was transferred to Sujat. Instead of going to Sambhar, we changed trains at the Phalera junction and got on the train to Sujat.

In comparison with Sambhar, Sujat was a paradise. It rained well here, there were many deep wells too. It was lush green all around. In place of a rath we got a tonga here, one of the half-dozen tongas allocated for the judiciary. We had had the experience of the tattered tongas drawn by bony horses in Aligarh; the ones in Sujat seemed like phaetons in comparison. The horses here were fresh and strong. There were both camels and horses. In Sambhar, the kochwan was unhappy with the camels. Here he was very happy being the head syce, in charge of many horses. The servants' quarters had tiled roofs and were very clean. The bungalow was really beautiful and had many rooms. Abba Mian had laid out the courtyard. There were lawns in front as well as at the back. There was a staircase going to the roof but there was no room there. Sheds were erected on both sides of the wide roof so that the beds could be pulled under them during the rains.

Milk was very cheap. Farmers would bring their milch buffaloes and milk them before our eyes. Amma bought a buffalo immediately, saying that without a buffalo the compound looked desolate. There were goats and poultry as well. There were three new dogs, one of whom looked dangerous. A prince had come hunting. Abba, who was an expert hunter himself, became his friend and the prince had given him the English dog as a gift. Abba had given him a silver container, which had a pair of fighting pythons engraved on it, from Japan. We loved that box very much; it seemed as though the pythons were alive and moving. And the wretched dog looked really bloodthirsty.

He would place his paws on Abba's shoulders and lick his moustache. Amma wouldn't allow him into the house without the leash.

There were plenty of tailors, dyers and butchers among Muslims. Men would wear dhoti, kurta and bright-coloured turbans, and women wore tight pyjamas and baggy kurtas that went way below their knees. They also wore gold and silver jewellery on their arms, legs, neck and ears. The Muslims and the Hindus looked alike. Men who had beards would notch them up in a roll. Some Muslims kept goatees and wore Islamic pyjamas.

The women from the houses of the Agarwals and the Oswals would go out in large groups. At the head of the group would be a maid, called Daodi, wearing a large shawl that would be draped over the other women of the group. At the tail end of the group would be another maid holding the shawl in her grip. One could see only the embroidered lower parts of the women's baggy skirts and their ankles that were laden with heavy anklets. On marriages and other social occasions women would wear jewellery weighing as much as four to five kilos.

Seeing them, we also started wearing shawls over our sarees. If we met their caravan on the way we would join it. Mostly, young and beautiful women would go out in this fashion. Children accompanying them would leap and frolic.

The grown-up women would wear what they called *boor*, which looked like a crown, and they would drape their dupattas over it. There was a fine muslin dupatta, coloured light blue on one side and light golden on the other. I asked many people but could not find how this miracle materialized. How two sides of fine muslin could be coloured in different hues certainly seemed like a miracle.

The vacations had begun and all the family members had either arrived or were planning to arrive. Abba had had the word sent to everybody that all would be given return fare, reasonable pocket money, two white suits and a pair of shoes. Apa had finished her course on indigenous medicine in Delhi and had arrived. Baaji was to arrive the following day. Chhoti Apa could not come, as she was heavily pregnant. Ishaq Bhai was to come, along with Zakia and others. It was also rumoured that Bade Mamu and Jugnu were planning to come.

We were waiting for the exam results. Amma was preparing for a grand party to celebrate. Tins of ghee had arrived from Pipad. About a dozen young goats had been bought at the price of eight annas each. On top of it, there was electricity in Sujat. We blessed the benevolent British government that had arranged such amenities for us. After a while we received a telegram from Nanhe Bhai, saying, 'Chunni has passed in second division.'

'Ai hai, didn't he write about Shanna's result?' Amma asked, peeved. 'This Nanhe is so mean!'

'He must be jealous seeing me pass in the first division!' Shamim said. A reply-paid telegram was sent forthwith, asking for Shamim's result. Nanhe Bhai's laconic reply came on the third day, 'I am reaching in a week.' There was no mention of the result. I felt let down. I could not celebrate thinking of Shamim. He was very upset. Amma would feed him and reassure him, 'Nanhe is coming in two days. The results can't remain unknown forever.'

When Nanhe Bhai arrived, there were curses and jibes from all sides. As usual he was smiling shamelessly.

'You ignored the reply-paid telegram?'

'No. I informed you about my arrival.'

'Who cared about your arrival? Why didn't you write about his result in the telegram?'

'There was no space for so many words.'

'Couldn't you pay for the additional words with your own money?'

'But everyone knew about Shamim's result. Even he knew that he was going to fail.'

'Ai hai, God forbid!'

'Why do you blame God for it?'

'So, has he really failed?' Amma asked wistfully.

'How could he not fail? He wandered aimlessly day and night, was more interested in dancing and singing, spent his time in the company of the scions of Jawra, then the musical soirées in Agra . . .'

'He's telling lies!' Shamim muttered.

'Anyway, Chunni and I have passed.'

'God's curse! What's the use of her passing? She could have failed, for all I care! If only Shamim had passed!'

'How can you say that?' I landed on the arena.

'Unh! What do women need degrees for? Men need them for jobs, otherwise their lives are ruined.'

The celebrations were postponed. No one insisted on having them. Shamim's failure had dampened our spirits. Seeing his quiet and sad face I forgot about the joy of my success.

The house gradually filled up with guests. Mamu arrived with Ishaq Bhai and some of his other children in tow. He had seven children at the time. Three had come with him, along with Mazhar Bhai, his wife and their daughter. The atmosphere changed from gloom to one of joy and commotion. Then Baaji came along with Midhat, Azim Bhai's daughter whom she had adopted. She was healthy and smart. Right after she came, she flew at her elder sister Nuzhat for some reason. I gave her two mighty slaps to bring her to her senses.

At mealtimes a long dastarkhwan was spread. Dinners would be organized for every new arrival. Three days after Mamu came, Jugnu also arrived from Bombay. Mamu had written to him to come. Jugnu and I carefully avoided each other which was not difficult in the crowd. One day, somehow, we came face to face with each other.

'So, you have passed?' Jugnu asked. When Jugnu laughs his small eyes disappear.

'Yes,' I said with great confidence. 'I had filled out the form for FA. The condition was that I must pass, so it is fulfilled now.'

'Hoon.' He let out a guffaw needlessly.

After that I wandered about in the room and when he took his seat I sat among others at some distance from him. Once or twice he glanced at me but the glances were not romantic. They were normal glances but he seemed to be suppressing his laughter with some effort. It was as though he wanted to convey that the secret only he and I were privy to was a ridiculous one. Well, no one had ever thrown romantic glances at me as one reads in stories, so how would I know?

Gradually Shamim got back his sangfroid and laughed at his failure. 'Some of the questions were so silly that I knew the examiner was making a fool of me. Even a five-year-old could have answered them. I wrote, "Mister, you can't make a fool of me! You know the answer very well, then why ask me?"'

'Did you really write that?'

'Of course. What do you think? There was another absurd question. What was it, bhutni?' I was stuck with the name 'bhutni', and I had passed the stage of being teased. I would not remember that it was a tease. Earlier, when anyone called me 'bhutni' I would scratch their faces. Now no one except Shamim called me by that name.

'Which question?'

'You don't remember the question? How did you pass? It was a fluke. Take the exam again.'

'Well, you have failed the exam.'

'I prefer failing honestly and fairly than passing by fluke like you!'

One day he said, 'Abba Mian, do not send Chunni for FA this year.'

'Why?'

'When I pass next year we will be able to study together. We can save money on books.'

'Sounds reasonable. But she studies in the girls' school and you stay in the boys' hostel.'

'She can keep the books. I can study from the books of my friends.' He said this in all seriousness though everyone knew that he was in a playful mood. However, Abba was in a mournful mood.

'Worthless boy. All my money has gone down the drain.'

'Wah Abbia, don't be so niggardly towards your own offspring,' Shamim said in such a plaintive tone that everyone started laughing. Abba Mian also could not remain serious.

'Begum, what will this worthless boy do?'

'Look, Abbia,' he would sometimes shorten Abba Mian to Abbia. 'Help me get a high position and then see how I impress people. Help me to be a governor.'

'You and governor!' Everyone began to laugh.

'Why are you grinning? What does the governor do after all except attending dinners and parties, unveiling statues and taking a spin in a car? By God, I can do full justice to dinners and parties. Bhut, if I get to be a governor I will make you the headmistress of some school. And this dim-sighted vet is breaking his head doing medicine. Don't worry, Jugnu, the moment I become a governor I will employ you as chief vet for my horses. You will enjoy life!' Then he turned towards Mamu and said, 'But people should do something for me first. You know such a lot of people. You're making your imp of a son a doctor. You do not have a thought for the real son of your real sister—you could make me a military commander or a landlord if you care for your blood relation! See, Zafar Husainji is not even listening to me. This is the problem!'

'Yes, my Lord, what is your command?' Mamu said with mock reverence.

'Make me a governor or ask the maharaja to adopt me. He can disown the stupid prince, how clumsily he plays polo.'

'Good idea. But, my Lord, you will have to wait a while. Apa is bringing out food, the aroma of pasanda is quite irresistible. Let me take a few morsels and then make you a governor.'

'Where to? Are you leaving, Mamu?' Baaji, who was busy whispering something in the ears of Dulhan Bhabi, gave a start and asked him.

'Yes, I have to make Shanna Mian the heir apparent. Apa, hurry up, it's a question of your son's future.'

'I *am* taking out food, can't you see? Lay the food cloth.' Everyone got up from their seats; some helped in spreading the food cloth.

'Hey Shanna Mian,' Mamu said.

'Yes, Mamu.'

'Why don't you come to Jodhpur with me? I'll pay the fare.'

'I'm ready, Mamu. Imagine that I have reached already, what then?'

'I'll look for a job for you.'

'Job!' Shamim let out a scream.

'Why, how about your Abba Mian? Doesn't he work at a job?'

'Yes, indeed. He has done one job or another throughout his life, poor fellow!'

'Then why do you object to it? Do you consider yourself superior to him?'

'Well, I am taller than him, and since the head is at the top of my physique and the brain resides in the head, I must deduce I have to be superior to him in intelligence.'

'So, you are superior to him in intelligence too?'

'I know it is impudence on my part. But intelligence is Allah's gift and to find fault with Allah is a sin. But hush!' Shamim said. Abba Mian was listening.

'Why?'

'Well, when people get old they can't bear such home truths. Abba will be heartbroken.'

Mamu could not continue further with this mock-serious dialogue and laughed out. Then he said, 'So, it's settled.'

'Of course, boss. But let me know what position you are going to offer me?'

'The same one, that of a peon!'

Shamim stared at him for a while, then suddenly picked up a plate and began to fan him with it. 'Mamu, you lie down.' Mamu was splitting his sides with laughter. He took the plate from Shamim's hand.

'Oh my sweet Mamu, dearer than my life!' Shamim sent up a cry of lamentation.

'Oh God, what happened?' Amma, disconcerted, dropped some of the kofta curry she was carrying. Sheera jumped to taste it and yelped as the hot gravy scalded his tongue. He ran to some distance, then looked back at the kofta and started barking. He had never tasted anything so hot.

'If you make me a peon, the entire family will be disgraced and you will regret it. It won't make any difference to me. You will hold your head and cry. Come on, don't appropriate the entire bowl. My Lord, at least give me the bowl.'

Mamu kept laughing. He held his plate before Amma and said, 'Apa if you want your son to obtain a high position, give me two koftas.'

'Why two? Take four. If you eat, it is as though I have eaten.'

How much Amma loved her two brothers!

What a difference there was between the two sons of Bade Mamu. The elder son, Mazhar Bhai, was always with his father. Mamu had a strange temperament. He had friends in high positions; he was also friendly with tailors, dyers and butchers. If he was chummy with the well-known artists and musicians in the royal court, he would also patronize vegetable vendors, jugglers and snake charmers. There was no special lane for the whores. Usually when a child widow grew into a woman, she would get attached to a wealthy landlord. No one would dare point a finger at him because of the position he held in the society. Moreover, this was something that had been going on for centuries. Sati had been abolished but widow remarriage was still a far cry.

In general, the Brahmin women were very beautiful. They all wore forty-yard baggy skirts of the same print, very short blouses in different colours that left half the body bare, and black dupattas made of fine velvet. As they went to draw water with one corner of their veil pressed between their teeth, men would stop on their tracks to have an eyeful. The dupatta descended to the ankle from the back, but there was no veil in the front. The circular navel, delicate feet sheathed in dust and moon-like face peeping out of the black dupatta! Balancing three or four pitchers on their heads, they would move in a group. But no one would dare make a pass at them as they knew that they were under the protection of big officers.

Their children were called 'rajgola'. The lady doctors in the palace would help in their delivery and they would be brought up inside the palace. There was no need to kill illegitimate children, nor would the girl's parents or in-laws find fault with her. Anyone could take these children to the palace and would get some reward in return. The police did not meddle in this. These children were looked after very well. There was a separate school for them, and after army training they would be inducted into the royal troupe. This troupe could be seen on some occasions like the birth anniversary of the king or on weddings. Every soldier in the troupe looked handsome and manly. English staff was in service to train them. 'Rajgola' meant that they were the adopted sons of the maharaja.

Girls so born were also brought up in the palace with great care and were called the 'queen's daudi', i.e. entourage. People said that they could not marry among themselves as, who knew, they could be brothers and sisters. I have never heard of a marriage between a rajgola and a daudi. However, I have heard of widowed girls being kidnapped or eloping with someone. It was said that there was a thriving market of such girls in Karachi. The zamindars there would eagerly buy young and healthy maidens, who would stay with them till death.

The royal corpse-burning place in Jodhpur was very grand. It had a tall gate. On the adjoining wall one could see thousands of palm impressions, some of them very small and possibly of girls four or five years old. They looked pale. When the king was burnt, the queens and the daudis were also burnt. Before entering the enclosure they would dip their hands in red dye and leave impression of their palms on the wall.

Mazhar Bhai grew up in the free and colourful environs of Jodhpur. He was well-endowed, had fine features and a ruddy face of beetroot hue. He had romantic eyes and fine, symmetrical teeth like pearls. But he was a positive terror. Before marriage he would pass no chance to grab girls, he would grope even small, tiny girls. Girls were mortally scared of him. Even after marriage he continued his old habit of heaving deep sighs, staring at girls and kneading their hands. His wife would often get furious because of his behaviour. She was very religious, spent her time in prayer and fasting. She was delicate and beautiful. She was Bade Mamu's sister-in-law and two years younger than her elder sister. In other words, Badi Mumani was quite young. She was a pretty woman except for a permanent mark of fear and anxiety on her face. Both the sisters had yards-long hair, but both remained rather mournful. They read the Quran for hours in the morning. The children would howl and scream but they remained unmoved.

Jugnu looked quite different from his elder brother. He was lanky, had ugly, small eyes, jaws with thick lips and curly hair like blacks have. He was exactly the opposite in temperament too. He never took a romantic interest in girls. If girls were scared of Mazhar Bhai, Jugnu would run away from them and could be found holding forth or sitting among 'safe' girls.

For two weeks we had great fun. The court was held in the bungalow. The men's part was very large. The drawing room was turned into a courtroom with a fenced enclosure for criminals. A durrie was spread on the floor. On the dais there was a grand chair for the judge. In the storeroom there were dozens of rope-strung beds, pillows and bed sheets because the guards who came with the criminals had to stay overnight. The charpais and the beds were comfortably laid out on the floor. Every family had its own little corner; then if one wanted to join a particular group they could just drag their charpais to that group. Some settled down on the chauka. Those who could not be accommodated here slept in the outer compound. Abba and Amma slept on the roof. Their daughters-in-law envied their privacy, saying that the oldies were enjoying themselves while the offspring were thrown into the open. Mazhar Bhai's wife was really worried as he was not accustomed to sexual abstinence.

After the meal at night we all assembled in the courtroom. Electric fans hung from the ceiling there. Nights in the desert were usually quite cool. Shamim had got over the sadness of his failure. He would drape his head with a towel, sit on the judge's chair and pretend to conduct the trial.

'Order! Order!' he would bawl, hitting the table with the hammer. 'I will sentence everybody to saza-e-kalapani, i.e. exile beyond the seas. Accused number 1, Bade Mamu, aka Zafar Husain, should be informed that His Highness is very pleased with him because he has promised to make me the heir apparent of the king. If the king has the impudence to refuse this good luck, let it be known that some other befitting position will be made available to me. To reward this self-sacrifice I am pleased to make over the chattar palace [under construction] to him.

Once I am adopted by the king I would take the reins of the kingdom of Jodhpur in my hand.'

'Long live the king, our saviour!' Mamu joined his palms and raised them over his head.

'But His Highness is very angry with the stupid and unworthy son of Mamu, i.e. Athar Husain, aka Jugnu. This horse doctor tells me that overeating causes indigestion. The fool does not know that if we under-eat then our mother, who has paradise beneath her feet, will be grief-stricken. She is a devoted wife and her sorrow will affect our esteemed father. We would prefer dying from indigestion than breaking the hearts of our parents. The rascal is throwing his fist at me. Soldiers, sever his head from his body immediately and . . .' Jugnu was threatening to get up and make a go for him but others were restraining him.

'Soldiers, catch him! Or else, on charge of the contempt of court, I will . . . All right, I forgive you. If you don't want to be punished then go to hell! However, I will not leave Munne Bhai, aka Azim Beg Chughtai who is a well-known humorist. His profession is law practice and his vocation is procreating. His wife, aka Dulhan Bhabi, brings forth a new brat every two years. I can deign to forgive him on one condition—that he file a suit against Aligarh Muslim University for the perfidy done to me, i.e. failing me while I passed in first division. The university should compensate me for the insult and tender an apology to me.'

What days they were! We laughed heartily about everything. Shamim would parody Abba's voice and we would go crazy laughing.

'Now, it is the turn of Madame Chunni, aka Ismat Khanum Chughtai, who has gobbled up her middle name. She is a disobedient, impudent and shameless girl. She stole the exam numbers of her elder brother and added them to her own to pass the exam and levelled the charge of failure on His Highness. This command is being given that she forget about the loans she had given me earlier and lend me ten rupees more now. Inshallah, on the Day of Judgement I will be able to reward her with thousand times more money. The luckless girl is so imprudent, she does not think about the future at all. The elder brother is almost like the father.' Shamim was older than me by one and a half years. 'I am her guardian and soon I will find a blind, stupid but rich fellow to yoke her in marriage and thus blacken her face.'

I threw my shoe at him, directly hitting his chest.

'Impudent girl, you will burn in hell fire! Then, accused number . . .' he raised his finger and was stunned. Abba Mian was standing right there! His laugh always got lost in his moustache but the eyes would sparkle. 'Baap re!' Shamim took off the towel promptly and said in a dying voice, 'It is commanded that as His Highness can't find his voice . . . the court is adjourned.' Shamim leapt and disappeared from the back door.

'What will this rascal do with his life!' Abba looked worried and sat down. The assembly that was reverberating with laughter became silent like the grave. 'What will this drummer do?'

'Sir, do not worry. Send him to Jodhpur to stay with me. I will make him slog. He will certainly pass the exam,' Azim Bhai said.

'He is not going to pass,' said Bade Mamu. 'I will find him a job in some department.'

Mamu was not educated, but his uncle, Kale Mian, had become a risaladar in the military and that brought great fame to the family. We had become like the native Marwaris. Maharaj Umed Singhji would give a darshan to Mamu in the court once a month. It was also being said that he was soon to get gold anklets. In the state if anyone was given a gift of gold anklets by the maharaj then the women in his family could wear gold ornaments on the feet. Otherwise, it was considered a serious crime. He had got permission for law practice for Azim Bhai, a job in the secretariat for Wasim Bhai, employment for Mazhar Bhai in the police and the job of a sub-inspector for Ishaq Bhai. And yes, he had also got Chhote Mamu the job of an excise inspector. Jugnu had also got a scholarship to study medicine through his good offices.

In Jodhpur there was no conflict between the Hindu and the Muslim communities. Muslims held key positions. There were many Muslims in the army and the police. The Muslims of Jodhpur were known for their peace-loving nature and were called Mian Bhai. Muslims did not live in separate mohallas. Not only was there no conflict in times of festivals like Eid, Bakr-eid, Holi, Diwali and Muharram, they also participated enthusiastically in all of them. Amma would light diyas during Diwali. She firmly believed that she was in the good books of Goddess Lakshmi, and it was due to her blessings that our family was thriving. After Abba's pension we had to rough it out in Agra and Aligarh. Now, in addition to the pension money, Abba's salary as judge had brought prosperity.

No one knew when the burqa disappeared. While going out, women from genteel families would wear shawls, as was the custom among the Hindu women. Among the tailors and dyers there was no purdah. They wore Kuchhi kurtas and tight pyjamas. They would wear jackets while going out. The older women did not observe ghunghat. If they draped dupattas over their chests their hands got tied, so even if they wore ghunghat they would place the dupatta over the head and the dupattas hung on their backs. One corner of the dupatta would be tucked in the waist so that it did not trail on the ground while the women walked. The dresses of Marwari women were always in bright colours. The colours would last for months. They would not change the pair as long as it was not tattered. The women would go to a pond and take off their clothes to wash them. Men would not look at them if they happened to pass them by, nor would the women care! A woman's body was not a source of wonder for men! Children up to the age of seven to eight years went around naked.

Bade Mamu, Mazhar Bhai, Badi Mumani, Bhabi Jaan and the children spoke Marwari better than Urdu. Slowly, everyone began to use more and more Marwari words. All the servants and chowkidars, except Ali Bakhsh and Shekhani Bua, spoke Marwari. Amma understood Marwari but did not speak it.

Marwari women were extremely musical. If four women assembled they would put their heads together, and, putting the veil over their faces, would begin singing. The women from the neighbourhood would gather around and what an orchestra it would be! We could not understand the words but the varying pitches of the tune made us restless. There was deep ache and sadness in the tune, and a strange intimation of loneliness. The tunes from Punjab are usually lively and conjure up images of lush green harvest fields, dense clusters of trees and singing rivulets. The tip-tap of rain invests the Punjabi tune with a dancing quality. However, in the desert you have only the shrubbery of thuhad, then only sand for miles and miles, and bare rocks. Occasionally, one scanned one or two slender trees of babool or bhat kataiya. And then sand and only sand. The paucity of water and the ruthlessness of drought had caused a permanent wound in people's minds. The lover is breaking stones while the beloved is sending her cries of longing to him. The real lover seems to be water and everyone, men, women, children, flora and fauna, seemed to yearn for her. There were lots of peacocks whose twitter had heart-rending pathos.

Snake charmers would go out in the sizzling midday sun, carrying the snake basket and the flute. When they showed the snakes they would tie a string of bells around their ankles and dance around the basket where the snake lay. The snake charmer's wife beat the drum. The cobra god would sway his head. The beat of the drum, the magic of the flute and the sound of ghungroos created the effect of thundering clouds. It seemed as though the god would dissolve at any moment into tears and the earth would get soaked. But this rain enters through the ears and soaks every pore of the body. Nonetheless, the throat gets all the more parched.

The puppeteer came regularly every fortnight. One charpai and one lantern and the stage was ready. The play was the same old one, but Abba loved Marwari songs. He would put up a show that would soon be over, but the songs would continue. One could never have enough of them. Abba did not turn away any charmer—the monkey man, juggler and the women dancers dressed in tight pyjamas and short blouses. It seemed as though their bodies were made of rubber. The dancers twisted their bodies so that it looked as though their bones would break any minute.

The spectacle men would come once a month. They came in the morning to fix the deal and put up the stage in the evening. A five- or six-yard-long piece of thick cloth was propped up with bamboo poles on both sides. A veritable universe dwelt there—the king sitting on the throne, beautiful women drawing water, Lord Krishna playing on his flute and consorting with the gopis, merchants selling their wares, the bear man and the monkey man, bangle and dupatta sellers, vegetables, fruits, fountains, Lakshmanji with his bow and arrows, Lord Hanuman with his mace and his tail in flames, Goddess Kali with her garland of human skulls, her tongue dripping blood and trampling the demon under her feet, the boatman controlling his oars. In one corner one could see the British governor general with a cigar between his lips. You could see everything in that canvas which was six yards long and one and a quarter yard broad.

People from the neighbourhood would gather in the courtyard. Abba would sit on a moorha surrounded by his admirers—officers holding key positions in the town and the entire police fraternity. Women would watch the spectacle from the terrace. Abba would leave rather early, followed by other elderly gentlemen. No one in the assembly would notice. Those who left early did so quietly, stealthily. Through the night two youths, with ankle bells and flute, would keep dancing. It was always the woman who beat the drum, and through the night music would flow from inside the veil. They sang some narrative which was carried along through questions and answers.

Time was passing fast. I thought of going to Jodhpur for a couple of days. Munne Bhai had asked me to. Dulhan Bhabi looked after me very well. I also thought that I would buy some dresses. Munne Bhai worked hard as a lawyer throughout the day. His health had improved a little; the asthma that had bothered him had healed. He kept writing late into the night. By the time I would wake up in the morning, he would be gone to the court. Dulhan Bhabi would fix a quick breakfast for me, and then would ask me to read the story written by Munne Bhai at night. He was writing 'The Mischievous Wife' at the time in which he had drawn on some incidents from actual life and combined them with the world of imagination. Dulhan Bhabi would be livid and say 'all this is untrue'. One day she fought with Munne Bhai and threatened to burn the manuscript. He could not help laughing and tried to explain to her that it was only a 'story', but she was not convinced. The upshot was that he would take the manuscript with him to the court. If an episode was complete he would send it to Shahid Bhai in Delhi. Dulhan Bhabi was annoyed but could do little. She was advancing in her pregnancy but was active and full of life.

One morning Munne Bhai nudged me, saying, 'Wake up.'

'A little later, please.' I turned to the other side to get some more sleep.

'Won't you like to see our son?'

'Your naughty sons kept on kicking me throughout the night. This Tajju and Chabba are very restless. I won't allow them to sleep with me any more. They just come and tuck themselves in.'

'Oh no! I'm talking of our newborn.'

'Newborn? What are you saying? Is the baby born already?'

'Yes. Come along and take a look.'

'Bhabi slept at night as usual. And in the morning she gave birth to the baby, just like that?'

'No. She had pain at night. I had to send Chhote Khan to bring the nurse and . . .'

'I didn't hear a sound!'

'Well, my wife has become an expert! She didn't even wake me up.'

It was their third son and fifth child. Quite plump. Dulhan Bhabi lay there smiling.

As we had social interactions with the Rajputs, we talked about their valour and glory all the time. Munne Bhai named Tajju Mohan Singh and Chabba Suhan Singh, and the newborn was Makkhan Singh. Well, he was like makkhan, i.e. butter, fair and soft. He never called them by their real names but Mohan, Makkhan and Sohan. And if he felt particularly doting he would call them Mohnia, Sohania and Makhi, or Makkhu. Today, only the youngest one is called Makkhu, his elder brothers are known as Zaim and Najeem.

We were ten siblings, two of whom did not have any children. Thirty-nine children were born to eight brothers and sisters. Out of them, thirteen migrated to Pakistan and sixteen chose to stay back here in India. Azim Bhai had already died. Among the brothers, four migrated to Pakistan after Partition, one stayed in India. All the four sisters, including me, stayed back in India. Among the four brothers who went over to Pakistan, three have died and one, who is younger than I, is alive. The brother who lives in India is older than me.

But I do not mention the dead ones. It feels as though each one of us—six brothers and four sisters—is still alive. One sister, my dear Baaji Amma, who had brought me up since I was two years old, recently died. She was fair and I am dark, or else people would have thought I was her daughter.

THE GOLDEN SPITTOON

Munne Bhai had gone away from the family to Jawrah for the first time. He had written several letters inviting me to his home. I always spent my holidays with him. When Abba was a judge in Sambhar, I would stay there a few days after which I would leave for Jodhpur. This time Munne Bhai was insistent that I go to his place first. So I went straight to him. Meanwhile he had called Nanhe Bhai from Agra and got him appointed as revenue secretary. The nawab of Jawrah treated Azim Bhai with great respect. I do not know how it was impressed upon him in some convoluted way that we were somehow related to him through our maternal grandmother.

As soon as I got there, Munne Bhai began to complain about Nanhe Bhai, saying that he had got him such a good job but Nanhe Bhai was bent on spoiling his chances. First, he became stubborn on the question of bowing three times, as was the practice, while paying respects to the nawab. It was explained to him that the court had some conventions that could not be changed for him. When everyone, including Shaukat Apa, reasoned with him, he relented. They thought that he would probably change his attitude, thinking about his future. But when he reached the court he greeted the nawab by saying 'Assalamu alaikum' and then took his seat even before the nawab could give his permission. The nawab barely replied 'walaikum-as-salam' and managed to pronounce words of permission even though Nanhe Bhai had already taken his seat. Placing one leg on top of another he was shaking his knees as he was accustomed to do. A hush descended on the court as Munne Bhai's throat was getting parched.

Nawab Sahib was the ruler of a small state. It brought him eighteen lakhs as yearly revenue, out of which fourteen lakhs were spent on his family and the rest, which was a pittance, was spent on the welfare of the state. Apart from the palace and the bungalows of the princes, all the other houses had thatched or tiled roofs. The nawab's elder brother, who was the chief minister, had an impressive bungalow.

The nawab was called Shah. The palace and its enclosure looked like another world. There were well-paved roads, electric poles, five swimming pools and an exhibition hall. In fact, there was no dearth of anything. The nawab had a passion for dogs. There was a British doctor and a trainer who lived in great style in the bungalows. In the parade ground troupes would put up spectacles on royal birthdays and other occasions. A gun salute would declare the arrival and departure of the nawab.

The railway train would stop there twice—once during the day and then at night. There was a rundown platform which was dark except for a dimly lit lantern. The special train that carried the nawab would go right up to his palace for which a separate line was laid. This train was one of the wonders of the state and it was one of the sights guests were shown along with Hasan Tikri and old mansions. It was an extremely beautiful train, white with golden flowers. It looked as though it had flown straight out of Buckingham Palace. Inside, there were plush chairs and sofas taken from the palace.

Two of the nawab's sons were studying in England. More than studying, they were having a good time there. He had also sent his twin sons to Aligarh. The year I was taking my matric exams, Shamim too was taking them for the third time, having failed twice before. He would go to dance parties and musical soirées with the sons of the nawab.

They were hardly interested in studies. They lived in great luxury in a large mansion with their entourage. The nawab had made a hefty donation to the university, so no one dared ask his sons any question. At that time wearing the university uniform was compulsory, but not for them. The princes, Munne Mian and Pyare Mian as they were called, wore georgette kurtas with fine embroidery work of zardozi and silk pyjamas and shoes with inlay work, and would occasionally show up in class. Musicians also lived in their quarters with them. Every other day there were some music or dance programmes that were attended by like-minded students who were their sycophants.

As his two older sons were in England, the older among the twins, who was older by a couple of minutes, was named as the heir apparent. This made his eldest son angry and frustrated. He had married an Englishwoman and had two children by her. The twin princes were rather odd. They were not interested in women. They liked dressing up and wearing make-up. The nawab was quite worried about them.

The English wife of the eldest son pulled some strings and the nawab was pressured to revoke his earlier declaration about the heir apparent and issue a new one making the eldest son the heir apparent. When his position as the heir apparent got established he returned from England with his wife and children. His younger brother had returned to India before him. He had married and had two children. He was a gentle person and doted on his wife. He was given a mansion, a car and some position, probably in the army, with office staff. He lived peacefully with his small family. However, the people in the court were scared of the heir apparent. Soon after his arrival he undertook a detailed investigation of many departments. He was very successful as the commander-in-chief of the army.

My arrival at Jawra created a veritable stir. A woman who had passed BA and that too a Muslim woman! Such a beast was never seen in the state. Nawab Sahib promptly offered me the post of the headmistress in the girls' school on a salary of one hundred rupees a month. An old bungalow was turned into a school. Some benches and desks were brought from the boys' school. A blackboard was mounted and an old map of India was hung from the wall.

I felt annoyed at the extraordinary turn of events and threatened to leave for Jodhpur. But Munne Bhai was very persuasive.

'Nawab Sahib has issued orders. You have already been appointed. You will receive the order in a day or two. If you refuse now there will be hell to face. To disrespect the order of Nawab Sahib is . . .'

'Come! I do not want to do such a job.'

'You have already been appointed,' Nanhe Bhai teased me.

Sarfaraz Ali Khan who was our distant maternal grandpa came to tackle the crisis. One of his granddaughters was betrothed to Nawab Sahib's son. In fact, the marriage had already taken place. The nawab had gone for a dinner and seen the six-year-old girl and taken a fancy for her. On the following day he got her married to his twelve-year-old son. The girl's destiny changed overnight—she was draped in a gorgeous trousseau and made to wear heavy jewellery. Nawab Sahib was like an ascetic. His first marriage was into a reputed family of Delhi who were related to the family of the Mughal prince, Sikandar Bakht. The lineage was explained to me a couple of times but it has slipped my mind. This wife of his was very beautiful and had a fair complexion. She was fourteen or fifteen years old when she was married. Nawab Sahib had lifted her veil and then dropped it abruptly. He felt nauseated when he saw the pale complexion. He never turned to her again. She had come a virgin and remained a virgin throughout her life.

Grandpa advised me to take up the job for the time being. Then I could leave if I wanted to. There were about thirty girls of different shapes and sizes. Most of them were from the royal family. They just wanted to learn and speak English! Now, when I look back I can't help laughing at the enterprise. What a funny class it was! The girls came well dressed and had elegant manners. They looked endearing and sat in the most proper way. I taught them verbally and with the help of the blackboard how to write and speak English. You could not call anyone by her real name—they were Nanhi Bi, Gori Bi, Pyari Bi, Achchi Bi, Sachchi Bi . . . All of them were bibis. There was a very sharp girl with delicate features who would speak volubly. Her name was Shahzadi Begum. She was the cleverest of all, cultured and elegant.

I enjoyed myself thoroughly. The daughters of the chief minister were very naughty but adorable. Sometimes when I went over to their house I had great fun. Quite often, programmes for picnics were made, with dancing and singing. It was an unending series of entertainment. The wife of the younger brother of the heir apparent also had the whim to study English. Every day the car came from the palace to take me to the palace and I returned after having had my meal with them. However, very little actual study took place; it was mainly gossip, dancing and singing by girls. There was only some practice of speaking English. Monty Mian's love for his wife was exemplary. She had fine features, her well-endowed body looked transparent, her complexion was smooth and white without a trace of ruddiness. She had black, curly hair and black, sparkling eyes. She wore dresses of light colours and very sober jewellery. I also met Monty Mian a couple of times. He was amiable and soft-spoken. Despite being careful, I would sometimes blurt out something that could be construed as criticism of the nawabi lifestyle. At such moments a hush would fall on the assembly and the discussion would not go any further.

One day Monty Mian said longingly, 'I often feel like leaving this princely state and looking for some job.'

'What prevents you from doing so?' I asked.

'Nothing. It is the same world outside. The British government will give me some position. It will make no difference.'

'In England?'

'Why not?' he said cheerfully.

'Do you lack anything?'

'By the grace of God, no.'

'Then?'

'It is sheer sameness, boredom . . .'

'Did you ever go round the state?'

'No.'

'Simply confined in your shell . . .'

Monty Mian looked somewhat miffed. Meanwhile the food cloth was spread and the conversation stopped abruptly.

I had never seen such variety of food on the table. Even if I took a morsel from each bowl it would have caused indigestion. There were six or seven kinds of bread! And they heaped food on your plate!

During those days the birth anniversary of Nawab Sahib was celebrated.

'We have to give him gifts.'

'I am not going, then,' I said.

'Why?'

'He is the wealthiest person, and you have to give him more wealth! This is the end of the month, and as usual, I am broke.'

Munne Bhai gave Dulhan Bhabi one gold coin and eleven rupees to be presented on my behalf.

Nawab Sahib was wearing a white silk pyjama, an embroidered chiffon kurta and a glittering garland, and was seated on the throne. Carrying the presents, women first saluted him and then presented the gift on a kerchief. He would place his hands on the money and the courtier standing by him would grab the present. I placed the kerchief given to me by Dulhan Bhabi. Nawab Sahib stared at me silently and I felt so scared that he might put me into his harem right away. Then he placed his hand over the money and the courtier picked it promptly. The gold coin stayed there. But before I could grab it and run away the kite pounced again and I stood there discomfited!

The wives of Nawab Sahib, one uglier than the other, wearing sarees and drowned in jewellery, were making a lot of noise. Only Badi Begum, the Queen Mother, was sitting quietly. She was rather plump, extremely beautiful with a fair complexion. She probably looked fairer in comparison with her ugly co-wives. I was staring intently at the jewellery they wore.

I don't know how the servant guessed when Nawab Sahib wanted to spit and promptly held the gold spittoon for him to spit the betel juice into. Several maids accompanied each one of his wives, holding spittoons and perfume dispensers. I marvelled at how they knew when their mistresses were going to spit and placed spittoons before their mouths!

Meanwhile the heir apparent appeared with his English wife in tow. He was dark but looked young. She was draped in a long silk gown and wearing a real diamond necklace. Her diamond eartops were sparkling. With her hair that was the colour of burning embers and green eyes she looked old and horrible. Everyone present there became self-conscious. Nawab Sahib also got up and started talking to his son and his wife and then left. With his departure the assembly fell in disarray. Only Badi Begum seemed lost in her own world.

The compatriots of the rulers of India also had the aura of rulers! There was a time when Englishmen would marry Indian women and the big nawabs and the rajas gave their women in marriage to British generals. Even Englishmen of lower stratas would consort with Indian women, if not actually marry them. That meant that the unmarried women of England were having a hard time. The young men of the country were leaving to capture and control new colonies. Even if married, they struck up liaisons with native women. The white women decided to have it out with the native women, and the wives and husband-hunting maids started pouring into the colonies. They agitated against the native women and compelled the rulers to put in place laws against such interracial liaisons. Hybrid children were looked down upon in both countries. They considered themselves English, but English society was not ready to accept them. They considered themselves superior to the natives who, in their turn, treated them with contempt. These Eurasians or Anglo-Indians became an intellectually paralysed community. They were given a position somewhat superior to the black Christians but inferior to the whites.

Both the blacks and the whites treated them as strange creatures. India was free from the prejudice against the blacks. A dark complexion was appreciated here. However, even this society found it difficult to accept them.

The English wife was a strong support for the heir apparent. And he began to make efforts to consolidate his position.

There were military parades on the nawab's birthday. A polo match was arranged in which Nanhe Bhai, who was an accomplished polo player, became a pain in the neck. He did not pass the ball to the heir apparent and continued kicking the ball to the goalpost himself. Munne Bhai was in a cold sweat. The courtiers were all puzzled, and the nawab had a thin smile playing on his lips. Nanhe Bhai was striding across the field. His playmates tried to explain to him the delicate situation but he felt puzzled. Instead of appreciating his skill, why were they asking him to behave himself? No one appreciated Nanhe Bhai's feats. Quiet had descended on the field and the heir apparent was getting angrier and angrier. Miffed, he attacked Nanhe Bhai a couple of times but Nanhe Bhai manoeuvred to escape unhurt. Nawab Sahib ordered the game closed.

For Nanhe Bhai his success did not matter much and he did not notice the absence of clapping at the end of the game. The next game started. An earthen pot containing five gold coins was held aloft at one end of a bamboo pole and the marksmen were standing in a row. If my brother had done anything worthwhile in his life it was target practice. He has been hunting game since he was ten years old.

The heir apparent could not hit the target. As a strategy all others missed the target as well. Nanhe Bhai did not care about the courtly ploys. He directly hit the target, the pot broke and the gold coins lay scattered on the ground. No one said anything and the competition began again. The pot was held aloft. Again, Nanhe Bhai shot it to pieces. The heir apparent was furious and shaking all over. After he had missed the target twice, Nanhe Bhai broke the pot to smithereens once again. The pot was replaced one more time.

Someone came and whispered in Nanhe Bhai's ear, 'What the hell are you doing, Chughtai Sahib?'

'What have I done?'

'Do you think we are lesser marksmen than you are?'

'Why aren't you hitting the bullseye, then?'

'Don't talk like a child. Every year only the heir apparent breaks the pot.'

'Let him do it this year too. Who is preventing him?'

'Oh my God, you do not want to understand. Listen . . . let the heir apparent try as many times as he needs. When your turn comes even if you fire let it not hit the target.'

'Oh, come on! Why should I do that?'

'Look, Chughtai Sahib, this "why" of yours will cost you dear,' the person growled.

The heir apparent made three attempts. The pot still stood intact.

In his life Nanhe Bhai never showed any trace of prudence. He was not one to stand on ceremony. He kept breaking the pot to pieces. Munne Bhai panicked and fell from his chair. Nanhe Bhai forgot about the competition and leapt and picked him up as though he were a child and brought him home without caring for anyone's permission. Someone from the nawab's entourage followed him saying, 'Nawab Sahib has ordered that Judge Sahib should be taken home forthwith.' Nanhe Bhai did not listen to anything and brought him home. And then one cannot describe the hilarious scene in which everyone laughed to their heart's content.

Usually, after dinner, Munne Bhai broached a controversial topic that would raise a fierce debate. Munne Bhai would throw in his mischievous comments and the war of words would begin. Bade Mamu designated these battles as 'jang-e-azeem' (world war) as Azim Bhai would initiate and conduct these battles. He would describe these battles as 'digestive' as the debates caused so much heat that our food would get digested and we'd feel hungry for more. On days we did not have this digestive it seemed as if our food was not properly washed down the gullet. On occasion, when we had to forgo this session in honour of a guest, we would feel as if there was a burden on our chest. These battles provided children the occasion to sharpen their tongue and if a child came out with a telling repartee or an attractive turn of phrase it would be much appreciated. The sons-in-law and daughters-in-law of the family were nonplussed at this spectacle and would take quite some time to get accustomed to it.

'Nanhe Bhai, you will have both Chunni and me sacked from our jobs,' Munne Bhai complained one day.

'It may be a good idea for all of us to return to Agra,' retorted Nanhe Bhai.

'No way. I'm not going to go back to Agra even if I have to die here.' This was Shaukat Apa.

'Nanhe Bhai, the nawab is looking after us very well. He says when Jaseem comes back from England with his engineering degree he will be made the chief engineer of the state. All of us will prosper here.'

I did not know why Munne Bhai was such an admirer of the nawab. He was the author of 'Khurpa Bahadur' in which he had taken digs at the nawab of Rampur and the nawab of Jawra. Even then the nawab was not displeased with him. Of course, the nawab could not be expected to have known about 'Khurpa Bahadur'. The book that Munne Bhai had written while at Jawra—I forget the title—was dedicated to the nawab.

'Let no one worry about my future!' I snapped. 'I am not going to return after the holidays are over.'

'Stupid. They hold you in great esteem. You hardly have to do anything, and get a salary. You go for a spin in the car. The princesses dote on you. Our nawab is an angel. Don't be so ungrateful.' I thought if I had to earn money without work it would be far better to get married to a rich fellow. People would then no longer pity me and say that the poor woman could not get a husband and had to work to earn her keep.

Everyone would try to reason with Nanhe Bhai, who would not pay any heed. He wouldn't listen to anyone except Shaukat Apa. But in this case she too seemed helpless.

Before the incident about the heir apparent cooled down, Nanhe Bhai sprang another surprise on us. Hunting tigers and crocodiles was banned in the state. It was a heinous crime. Nanhe Bhai went out on a Sunday and brought in a fairly big croc. Munne Bhai was horrified. Shaukat Apa began to howl and lament. Dulhan Bhabi began to worry about her husband's job and argued with Nanhe Bhai.

'Tell me if I got an opportunity to shoot a croc, could I let it go?' Nanhe Bhai countered. 'Did you expect me to run to Nawab Sahib and invite him to shoot the croc?'

'For God's sake, Nanhe Mian!' Shaukat Apa said, beginning to cry. This seemed to have some effect on him. Nanhe Bhai promptly went to Nawab Sahib with the croc and reported that he had to kill the croc to save his own life, otherwise he would not have broken the law. Nawab Sahib was pleased to see him repentant and forgave him.

On the following day, however, when the heir apparent was making his rounds he appeared in Nanhe Bhai's office. He had received reports of many irregularities.

'I have joined only recently. I had told Nawab Sahib that I have no expertise in revenue collection. He did not listen and gave me the job. The more I try to control these irregularities the more complicated they get. I do not have the power to take decisions on my own. I carry out the orders of the chief minister.'

The heir apparent left, fuming. Immediately Nanhe Bhai received an order asking him to leave the state within twenty-four hours if he wanted to escape penalty. Shaukat Apa was in a terrible state. But Nanhe Bhai packed up in two hours. There were not too many household things. They had borrowed some stuff and were getting along. Despite Shaukat Apa's protestations, he had not even got a four-poster bed made.

After Nanhe Bhai left, the nawab became even more benevolent towards Munne Bhai. He offered the services of the royal medic for his treatment. Munne Bhai had become bedridden after the shock. He would cough away the entire night. He became so weak that it was an effort for him to speak. The medic's potion worsened his condition. The moment he took it he would break into a sweat and lose his senses. Dulhan Bhabi would keep vigil, sometimes me. But I could not help falling asleep, and would sometimes go to sleep sitting there. Driven by thirst, Munne Bhai would try to call us but would not be able to utter a sound and would become breathless. Dulhan Bhabi would feel restless and get up. If she gave him the medicine he would begin to writhe like a slaughtered animal.

One night, at about two, there was a light knock on the door. The old grandpa rushed in and said, 'Put out the lamp.' For some moments he took deep breaths in the dark. Then he said in a tremulous whisper, 'Listen to what I say and do not ask questions. Dulhan, take permission from Nawab Sahib in the morning and take Munne to the sanatorium at Miraj.'

'What about the children?' Dulhan Bhabi asked.

'She will look after them.' He pointed at me. 'There's nothing to worry.'

'Munne Bhai, you should go. I will look after the children,' I said, though I was a little overwhelmed.

'But why do you have to come stealthily at night to say this?' Dulhan Bhabi asked.

'He told us not to ask questions, just go.' I was puzzled. We were a worried lot. As usual, I went to school in the morning. At night, I was waiting to go to Monty Mian's house but the car did not come. This increased our worry. Munne Bhai had sent his application to Nawab Sahib asking permission to go to Miraj. 'I am leaving my sister and two children in your care,' he had written.

Nawab Sahib gave permission and he started for Miraj that evening. He also carried a recommendation from Nawab Sahib. The following day I went to the school as usual. Monty Mian's wife's car came there to pick me. She met me cordially though she was rather quiet. The girls were looking at me and smiling. Why?

On returning home I felt quite uneasy. I had never been so alone. The servant was also new and very stupid. I gathered the children in one room and stayed awake till late at night. Grandpa came to see how we were doing and said to me, 'The children are sleeping. I want to talk to you about something.' Both of us got up and went to the big room where Munne Bhai's empty bed was still there. The room was filled with the odour of medicine.

'Daughter, you are very lucky. I have brought good news for you.' I do not know why my heart began to pound faster. But I controlled myself and asked him in a level tone, 'What good news, Grandpa?'

'Nawab Sahib wants to make you his daughter-in-law.' I had some premonition that it must be something like this. I kept quiet.

'His son is studying in England. After marriage Nawab Sahib will send you also to England for higher education.' I continued to be quiet, because if I spoke he would have been offended.

'His Majesty has decided that the event would take place after two days, on the auspicious day of Friday.'

'My mother and brothers . . .'

'They must be proud of this relationship. Nawab Sahib says that they will be informed by wire. Don't you worry, daughter. I am here. The prince has arrived. After marriage . . .' I clenched my teeth and kept quiet.

'In fact, we can make optimum use of the occasion. Nawab Sahib thinks that if Nuzhat is also given in marriage to the young prince Shabbu Mian . . .'

'What about her parents?'

'His Majesty is both father and mother to us. He has the right to get his subjects married.'

'Think about it, daughter. Your father is no more. You can do so much for your family. Nawab Sahib is very generous. Both of you— aunt and niece—will lord over the palace. You can go for higher education after which you can do a lot for Jawra's development. You would know that His Majesty, in his extreme kindness, had accepted my granddaughter for Baley Sahib and the nikah was read. You must have seen the jewellery given to her. Many big princely states cannot compare with Jawra in its cache of gems and jewels. There are pearls the size of a pigeon's egg. After marriage His Majesty will forgive your elder brother and reinstate him. Munne will be given a raise in his salary and will be allowed to live inside the palace. Nawab Sahib is not happy with the heir apparent. His English wife is getting too ambitious. Your father was a government servant, and the fact that you are highly educated will strengthen His Majesty's position. Your family will be granted jagirs. I hope you are happy?'

Like an obedient daughter, I lowered my head.

Grandpa left. I do not know for how long I sat there like a statue in that room filled with the odour of medicines. The royal palace, gold and silver spittoons, perfume dispensers and real pearls as big as pigeons' eggs were chasing one another on the floor. And the opportunity for higher education in England. But all these came with a prince who was a stranger to me! Uff!

We felt so uneasy in Azim Bhai's room that all of us huddled together in two beds and went to sleep. Every child insisted on sleeping by my side. After their parents had left they were looking for refuge in my care. If I went to the bathroom they would begin crying and follow me there. I felt both angry and sad—angry at the situation and sad at the helplessness of the children.

Only two days later, on the auspicious Friday, we would leave this ramshackle house and shift to the palace. There, what a sweet sleep would embrace me on the soft mattresses over the ganga–jamuni bedstead hidden behind the most elegant silk canopy. I had never spat in a gold spittoon. The moment I stepped into the palace I would command the slaves to fetch the gold spittoon promptly and then I would spit into it with great style.

And then? What would I do?

Then the wedding party would come with great pomp and show . . . I would be a bride . . . my heart would miss a beat hearing the footsteps of the groom . . . the groom would then lift the veil . . . Uff! My imagination reached a stumbling block. I had not read any authentic book on sex. I had cut my teeth on politics, economics, history, geography, drama, poetry . . . But our college library had no book on the practice of sex, nor could I gather any delightful account of it from my conversation with others.

Mongia, our kochwan's daughter, had told me that marriage was an obnoxious thing. The husband acted like a bastard and continued to do so for the rest of your life. Once Azim Bhai had gone to Bombay to look for a job. I or Naiyer had to read the letter out to Dulhan Bhabi because Chhoti Apa, who was her confidante, had left after marriage. These letters contained some sentences that would redden Dulhan Bhabi's face. If we asked anything she would simply say, 'Go on'. Sometimes one would hear wives whispering among themselves. One day I heard one of them telling another, 'He does not have any interest in anything except dirty things. He is after me all the time.'

The walls of the palace began to close over me and I felt suffocated. The nawabs were not in favour of divorce. If a woman appeared to be obtrusive they just poisoned her. I could not get along with anyone for a second. How could I accept anyone as my spiritual god? For years I had stopped even the obligatory prayers. I prayed and fasted as long as I stayed in Aligarh. In IT College, Christianity was predominant. We went to the chapel regularly. My spiritual god, and that too a prince—how would I digest that? And Nuzhat? She was a simple girl who was easily frightened. Even the sound of a cricket scared her.

I woke up the servant and asked him to go tell Munne Bhai's tongawalla to come with his tonga at five in the morning. I would give him twice the normal fare. Then I stuffed things into two trunks. My trunk was ready. We did not keep our clothes in cupboards there. I took as many dresses of Nuzhat, Makkhan and Minu as I could lay my hands on. Thank God the dhobi had brought the laundry that day. I did not have enough money either. My fare and Nuzhat's half fare; Makhu was four years old but looked smaller than his age. I could manage without paying his fare. And Minu was only eleven months old. She could not even stand on her feet. I could not have left the two behind. They were very attached to me.

Tajju and Chabba were in deep sleep. I woke up Nuzhat quietly. I did not tell her where we were going. At five in the morning we reached the station and bought tickets. I took care of Makkhan, Nuzhat and Minu and we got on the train. My heart was pounding. When we reached Ratlam station I breathed easily. Nuzhat was staring at me strangely but I could not meet her gaze. What could I tell her and how?

'Phupi Jaan, Tajju and Chabba?' she eventually asked me nervously.

'I have told grandpa to take them with him,' I lied. She became quiet. It seemed as though I was on a boat with a hole at the bottom and that had no sails either. I felt suffocated. I came to know later that someone had reported to grandpa that the house was empty and two children were sitting on the threshold and crying. The servant had cleared the house and fled. Grandpa took the children home and sent a wire to Amma in Jodhpur.

For long I could not decide whether I had any other option, and what could I do with these three children. But I do not know why my stubborn heart always told me that everything would turn around, that there was no calamity in the world that had no solution.

RETURN TO BAREILLY

When I reached Bareilly from Jawra there was no one in the station to receive us. In the circumstances in which we had to flee from Jawra there was no time to send a wire. Naiyer's marriage was close at hand. Among the guests, only Baaji had arrived from Rampur. Apa was to come from Hyderabad but her husband was not allowed leave of absence from his office. She was not coming. No one had arrived as yet from Jodhpur. There was a week left for the marriage. Naiyer had already gone into seclusion.* They were waiting for everyone to come to hold the final ceremony.

I did not tell anyone that Azim Bhai and Dulhan Bhabi were in the TB Hospital at Miraj and that I had left the other two children uncared for while they were asleep. I was very worried about the children. I did not want to spoil the joy of marriage for Apa by talking about Azim Bhai's ailment, but whenever I thought of the children I felt a big lump in my throat. I was so restless that at some moments I felt that I must return to them, but the horror of returning was even more blood-curdling.

When Naiyer saw me lost in thought she felt pity. 'Hey sister, you're acting crazy. Why don't you marry Jugnu Bhai?'

'Forget it. You want to get me married, and my worry is how to look after these three children.'

'Why did you bring them along? Particularly Minu, who is still learning how to crawl?'

---

* The original, *mayoon baithna*, is the period of one to two weeks before marriage during which the would-be bride was not allowed to go in public and was given all kinds of beauty treatment and coaching related to married life.

'You already know that I am a little crazy.'

'Why didn't Mamu Jaan and Dulhan Mumani come?'

Uff! I felt like punching her, but I controlled myself. 'He was not granted leave. And how about your groom? Has he arrived?'

'Yes.' Naiyer became bashful. 'He says that he will take me to London with him,' she said, as she stitched salma flowers on the velvet waistcoat, tears streaming down her cheeks.

'Why cry? Don't you want to go to London?'

'Well, it is not in my hands.'

'If you do not want to go, just tell him. He is coming back after two years anyway.'

'He finds it lonely there. That is why he wanted to marry while still studying.'

'I see. So you want to go with him? Have fun.'

'I am not going there to have fun.'

'Then do your BA. The girls in your in-laws' house are educated.'

'It is his cousin who has done BA and BT. His own sisters were educated at home. He does not like girls who are highly educated.'

'Why?'

'Well, he just says that they do not have to find jobs.'

'But how about Badrunnisa Baaji and . . .'

'They are from his paternal grandfather's side. On the maternal side, women are taught at home and then they learn housekeeping, sewing, etc.'

'Hey witch, you're so brainy. You came third in matriculation in the entire university. Razi should be proud of you. He might not have got even a first class. Don't marry the fellow.'

'There you go! You and your bragging! For God's sake, do not say such things. He is studying in England, and is the only son of his parents. He is the sole heir to such a large property. He is one in a million. And what is so special about me? There are many girls in the family who have their eyes on him.'

Naiyer was extremely attractive. She had a fair complexion and fine features. She was innocence personified. She was slim and could carry off gracefully any kind of dress. She was all that I had desired to be. On top of it she was very respectful to her elders and an expert cook. No one sewed or embroidered better than her. Her inlay work and embroidery were the envy of the most accomplished connoisseurs. Whoever saw her work appreciated it. Everyone in the neighbourhood admitted that she would make an ideal housewife. Looking at her I felt an inferiority complex eating into me.

As she looked at my mournful face she asked softly, 'When will you marry?' I felt like telling her that if I did not have worms in my brain, I might have now been dressed in a red suit, wearing a necklace of pearls as big as pigeons' eggs and a drawing veil over my face, waiting to hear the footsteps of the groom. But I broke into a laugh—I and a veil? It seemed like an anomaly. I changed track.

'Abba had written to me that there's a girls' school here that requires a headmistress.'

'Come on. You're obsessed with a job again! Don't you want to marry?'

'I will, sweetheart.'

'When?'

'Let us discharge the responsibility of marrying you off. Then I will quickly have my own marriage party.'

Naiyer's face fell. Amma rightly said that I was like a bull on the loose. She looked at her watch and got up to say her evening prayers. I began to measure the velvet waistcoat with my forefinger. How slender Naiyer's waist was . . .!

The following day Baaji arrived with her husband and Midhat. Three days later Mumani Jaan arrived with Akhter and Jamila. The same evening Amma came along with Wasim Bhai, Bhabi and their son, Hakeem. Amma glared at me and I was in jitters.

'You rogue, why did you leave Tajju and Chabba alone?' she asked me when we were alone.

'Amma, don't tell anyone. If Sarfaraz Uncle comes he will tell you. Nawab Sahib was after Munne Bhai's life.'

'What are you saying?'

'I swear. Sarfaraz Uncle told me in confidence. And the nawab was going to have Nuzhat in his harem, me too.'

'To hell with the nawab! Has he been bitten by a mad dog that he should invite trouble by having you in his harem? Mark my words, you will ruin your future.'

'Well, the future will be mine and I'll tackle it.'

'You will bring dishonour to the family.'

'Abba is gone, Bade Abba too is no more. We are at loggerheads with Badshahi Phupi. Who is left in the family to feel dishonoured?'

'You think Mamu is of no consequence?'

'Well, Mamu is several hundred miles away, in Jodhpur. He won't get to know my infamy. Well Amma, do not tell Apa about Munne Bhai.'

'Do you think I've lost my senses?'

Naiyer's marriage was solemnized in great style. Apa stitched new dresses for Nuzhat, Makkhan and Minu overnight. I bought a white chiffon saree and Naiyer promptly stamped it with prints of tappa and kiran. We had great fun during the marriage. I was not at all in the mood to be treated as a mother-in-law.* Akhter and Jamila too were mothers-in-law. Among the sisters-in-law were the rickety Nuzhat and the red-hot-pepper Midhat, who was all of eight years. That is why we gladly took on the role of sisters-in-law and teased the groom's party no end. We also gave Razi a very hard time. To samdhans we were samdhans but to the groom and his sisters we assumed the role of sisters-in-law and gave them a tough time. Mujeeb, Naiyer's brother, had fallen for Jamila some time ago. In the rush, we also called the boys inside, telling them the lie that they were permitted to come in. Of course, it was all within the family, so there was no strict purdah. Many boys took the chance to come in. Ubtan was applied with great gusto. On the Chauthi it was as though we had grown wings. We had no time nor the inclination to listen to the admonition of elders. The older women were furious but the younger generation did not care.

---

* As Naiyer was Ismat Chughtai's niece, Ismat became a mother-in-law to
  Naiyer's husband.

When everything cooled down and the guests left, I was sought to be accused as the main culprit. However, the past few days had been so hectic that I was tired to the bone, and the admonitions served as a balm. I had just reclined on the bolster to take a deep breath and the next moment I was lost to the world.

During the marriage I also got to meet the wife of the manager of the girls' school. She reported that the school had been open for about a month, but no headmistress had been appointed so far. People were demanding that the headmistress be a Muslim woman. The manager's wife requested me to take over as soon as the marriage was over. The manager himself arrived on the third day and the terms were settled. The salary was one hundred rupees per month. For accommodation I could take as many rooms as I wanted. The school was close to the residence, there was only a wall in between. I took over the charge on the same day. It was very different from the school at Jawra. Regular classes were held here up to the eighth grade. I got Nuzhat admitted in the seventh grade and Makkhu in the first.

There was a sudden development in the family. A day after the Chauthi, Bhabi gave birth to a baby. We got up in the morning to see a new baby! Bhabi did not so much as make a sound. She was calmer than a cow; even a cow kicks or makes some noise. From school I returned straight home.

Nuzhat and Makkhu did not ask even once about their parents. And Minu had not started speaking yet. I would spend my holidays with Azim Bhai. The children would sleep beside me. They had done the same while they were in Jawra. Their father was always sick and their mother stayed busy looking after him. The children were closer to me than to their parents. In his sleep sometimes Makkhan called out 'Du Ammi'—he called his mother Dulhan Ammi—and my heart would sink. But what could I do? Amma wanted to take Nuzhat along with her, but I refused, lying that Munne Bhai had said that she should not miss school.

'Can you manage three children?' I asked, thinking that she would like to take away Makkhan and Minu.

'Yes.'

'Then don't complain later. I won't send anyone to fetch them.'

'That won't be necessary. If needed, I can bring them along. Let Munne Bhai first come back cured.'

The marriage was over and the guests left one by one. Mujeeb and Habib left for Aligarh. Naiyer was invited everywhere, after which she left for England with her husband.

Apa offered me a boy to cook meals. Poverty was widespread in Bareilly. Servants were a dime a dozen. Many of them wanted to work as nannies or cooks and would come to my office. There was a poor woman in the school. I gave her a place in the kothi. There were sweepers and other sundry work hands. There was also a peon.

I asked Apa to come and stay with me. 'Here you have only Munna [her mother-in-law] who wears her burqa in the morning and roams around the neighbourhood. You stay alone through the day.' She did not pay heed in the beginning. I engaged Nuzhat to work on her. Apa doted on her. Dulhan Bhabi was a novice, Amma and Apa had brought Nuzhat up. Eventually she agreed to come. I wanted to buy some household goods, but Apa had tons of mattresses and sheets. She also gave me all the crockery I needed. I would hand over my salary to her. If I needed money I would ask her. She must have spent money from her kitty too. At the end of the month when I handed her the salary, she would give me back whatever was saved from the previous month, which was quite a lot. I spent that money on sundry things. I was not extravagant by nature, and one hundred rupees was a lot of money during those days. There was a good cinema hall close by. The daughter of the manager studied in the school. Despite my protests, the manager would send me tickets for every new movie.

The woman who was headmistress of the school before me was older and more experienced than I was even though she had passed only the intermediate exam. She had laid the foundation of the school and the manager did not allow her to leave. Mrs Marks was very strict and successful. I had to be made headmistress because of the insistence of those who donated money to the school. The manager had told me all this.

'Mrs Marks is furious. Beware of her. Miss Phillips, inspector of schools, is her close friend, as both are Christians.'

I cannot take it if anyone discriminates against someone on the basis of religion. For the real good of the school Mrs Marks should have been made headmistress. The problem was that she was a Christian. Contrary to the manager's advice, I was very cordial with Mrs Marks when she came to visit. I stood up to show respect, but she thought I did so because I was angry and wanted to let off steam. 'Please take your seat,' I said. She sat with a glum face.

'Mrs Marks, I do not have sufficient experience for a headmistress, nor do I understand office routine. But our salary is the same, which is unfair. Anyway, your money is safe in the fund. I am not going to stay here permanently. I have wheels fitted in my feet. Next year I want to go abroad for training. The school is yours, you have given it life. I don't know much and I have no pretensions. If you do not help me I cannot run the school. I will resign and leave. My family is in Jodhpur, they will provide me support. And if all the doors are closed then I can marry some fellow. However, for the present I want to live life on my terms. If I leave, another Muslim headmistress will join. It won't matter to you.'

Mrs Marks was stupefied. My tone was not at all conciliatory or flattering. In fact, it was somewhat aggressive.

'Someone must have told you things against me,' she said in an intransigent tone.

'Mrs Marks, if I acted on what people tell me I would not have been here today. I am accustomed to forming my own opinions.'

'I have been told that you have a lot of experience and a hot temper. And you were a headmistress in a princely state.'

'Yes, I was a headmistress in a girls' school, but for less than a year.'

'I am attached to this school . . . I am also a strong supporter of women's education.'

'And you must have a strong sympathy for Muslim girls because they are the most backward among all communities.'

'Some Christian girls also study in this school.'

'Mrs Marks, we women should be free from sectarian considerations. What does it matter if the students are Hindu, Muslim or Christian? I received what education I have from Christian teachers. Most schools in our country have been founded by Christian teachers. My teachers never made any distinction between me and students from other communities. While imparting knowledge they regarded me as just a student. Most of the teachers in this school are also Christians. There are only two Hindu teachers. Among the Muslim teachers there are only Razia Begum, who teaches sewing, etc., and me.'

Meanwhile the bell for recess went off. The manager had introduced me to the other teachers. All of us had our lunch together that day. I had not brought my lunch and shared others'.

'You do not look like a headmistress at all!' Miss Lal, the youngest and the sharpest, said.

'I look like a perfect headmistress before the manager and the peon. Of course, I do not make an effort to appear so before the girls.'

'Are the girls scared of you?'

'To tell you the truth I am scared of them and wear the mask of authority in self-defence. It is different here. Before the public I would wear the mask of self-importance lest I be exposed. Be careful when I come to observe your class. If you smile as you are doing now then God help you!' Miss Lal, who had been laughing non-stop, became quiet.

Mrs Marks then began to explain to me the entries in different registers. Other teachers could figure them out better than I could. In Jawra I had maintained just one register in which I wrote the names of the girls. There were only two rooms, one for girls of all ages from royal families and the daughters of high officials. The girls sat on the benches, and I on a chair behind a table. The other room was for the girls from poorer families who were taught how to read the Quran by an old woman.

The way they were taught was ridiculous. Some knew the English alphabet, others knew how to write, and still others had a smattering of it. There was a Hindu girl in the sixth grade. There were two Christian girls who would come holding the primer for the third and fourth grades. I was stupefied to see that they did not know how to count. But everyone wanted to be able to speak English, so I taught them how to speak. The girls were quite blunt and had poor taste, except for one, Shahzadi Begum, who was extraordinarily sharp and intelligent. Decked in her finery, she wore a smile on her face and looked like a flower in full bloom. Most of them were engaged, several of them were married, and waiting to join their husbands. Thank God they held me in high esteem.

The girls in Bareilly were way beyond them in intelligence. They had a real love of learning, and I had a genuine love for teaching. The manager helped me a lot. The headmaster of the adjoining boys' school was very helpful. He gave me many books on education to read. One day the manager reported that Miss Phillips, the inspector of schools, was coming for a visit. When I did not show much reaction, he flared up.

'Did you hear what I said?'

'I am thinking about what I have to do,' I said nonchalantly.

'My dear ma'am, the inspector is coming and you . . .' He turned pale in anger.

'Let her come.'

'I must say, you are the limit!'

'Take it easy.'

'How can I take it easy? If the grant is stopped . . .'

'Manager Sahib, have you seen any mismanagement in the school? Noise in classrooms or general uncleanliness? The number of girls has increased. Two of them sit on one bench. I get the water changed daily in the jars myself.'

'This wretched office . . .'

'What is wrong with the office?'

'You do not understand. Do you have some photographs?'

'I had some photos taken in the fair.'

'Oho! I am not talking of the eight-anna and four-by-two-inch photo. What I meant was some scenery or calendar. Anyway, do not worry. I will have some sent. Vases too.'

'There are many flowers here. They can be arranged in a vase. I had talked to you about a gardener . . .'

'Gardener? You mean a real gardener? Do you know how I am running this school? My law practice is at a dead end because of this. Should I go begging from door to door or should I rack my brains with my clients? On top of it, there's my wife who makes my life miserable.'

'Then why did you employ Razia Begum in the school? What does she do? She sits there all the time holding her head.'

'You! . . . You're also blaming me for Razia Begum! I didn't expect you to do that. I had thought educated women should . . . All right, forget it. Say what you want. I have committed a crime. Razia's husband divorced her because they had no children. Should I have allowed her to become a whore? Tell me where she could have gone? She lives in one corner of the kothi . . . I pay thirty rupees per month out of my own pocket. My wife badmouths her, my neighbours are after her life. Poor woman, what can she do?' Tears sparkled in his big, frightening eyes. 'And people say she is a loose woman. She stays close to you. You can say whether she entertains men. I come to see her on the sly.'

I felt suffocated.

'Manager Sahib, rely on me for once. Let Miss Phillips come. And then this contract for one year,' I took out the appointment letter from the drawer and placed it before him, 'keep it with you. You can tear it to shreds . . .'

After the manager left I kept thinking about Razia Begum. All the Razia Begums of India passed before my eyes. My blood began to boil. I was angry with everything around me.

Why were lawyers obsessed with women's education? Papa Mian [Shaikh Abdullah, founder, Aligarh Girls' College] invested his entire life in the girls' school. Here, Mister Abdus Shukoor was bitten by the same bug. What did they get in return except abuses and curses? The community knew only this way to reward these pioneers!

I wrote a note to the headmaster requesting him to come over for ten minutes. Since it was Friday, the school was open for only half the day. The gentleman came promptly. He called the gardener and said to him, 'Fetch twenty pots of nice plants and flowers and arrange them in two rows. Make six or seven bouquets, put them in vases and send them to classrooms in the morning. And get some drawings and pictures of landscapes from the store and decorate the office right now. Oh yes, get a good pen-stand and a green tablecloth and drape it over the table. This you do right now.'

When the gardener and the peon left he said, 'Please get a ream of brown paper and drape the registers in it. They are looking pretty battered. Don't worry, everything will be all right.'

All the teachers gave a hand. Mrs Marks began to check the entries in the registers to see if there were any errors. The office looked quite impressive. The classrooms too looked brighter. The flower pots had created a veritable riot of colours!

Miss Phillips was dark but looked extremely sexy with her well-endowed body, her fine, stately features and her exceptionally intelligent eyes. She reminded me of the black princess of Ajanta. My heart was full and I opened it up to her. I gave her an account of the poor condition of the school, Manager Sahib's struggle, the absolute dedication of Mrs Marks and other teachers, the love of learning in the girls and their dire circumstances. I had not started writing yet but had a way with words.

When Miss Phillips started to leave she called me to her side and said, 'There is a party at my place this evening. Would you like to come over?'

'Sure . . .'

'I will send Syeed to fetch you, at about five.' Syeed Sahib lived close to my house. One day I had asked Headmaster Sahib for a book. He did not have the book but told me it was available in the library. 'I am not a library member. Syeed Sahib, who is your neighbour, is a member. If you tell him he will make you a member too.' I sent the peon with a note to Syeed Sahib. He came over himself.

He had quite romantic features. England-returned, he held a good position. His wife, Chhoti Bi, had an innocent face and was very amiable. After two or three meetings, Syeed Sahib became a regular visitor. He was an engaging conversationalist. We also used to go for walks in the nearby park. While in England he had fallen in love with an English girl who broke his heart. He remembered a lot of sad couplets. He would recite the couplets with such feeling and threw such glances at me, it seemed as though he was addressing me. Sometimes he would affix terms such as 'tormentor', etc., to his couplets. But I never took any notice. For one, I was not interested in having a romantic affair with him; and second, I simply detested lover boys who recited couplets and threw wistful glances at their beloveds. In my family, whenever two persons fell in love they would try their best to pull each other's leg. And I have never heard uncles or brothers reciting couplets. Well, Bade Abba was a poet. We could not understand his poetry. Abba Mian would listen to him out of politeness and breathe a sigh of relief when he'd leave. 'He is so boring, and reads couplets out of measure!' Abba said one day, and after that he put all poets on the same footing.

'Have you ever fallen in love?' Syeed Sahib asked me one day.

'Hundreds of times!' I replied boastfully.

'What do you mean?'

'Why? Shouldn't I have? Just because you have?'

'I fell for one girl. Just once in my life.'

'Just once? And you didn't ever again?'

'Strange! Madame, one falls in love, genuinely, only once in life.'

'Can you tell the truth only once in life?'

'You start arguing from the wrong end and spoil one's mood!'

'Sorry!'

Meanwhile, the servant announced that the meal was ready and the mistress had sent for Syeed Sahib.

'Why don't you have your meal with us? I think there is your favourite dish gobi–gosht this evening.'

'No. Apa would be waiting for me.'

'Bhola will go tell her that you're having dinner with us.' Bhola walked towards our house.

'I too had a kind of bizarre love.'

'Really? When?'

'It was when I was ten or eleven years old.'

'Oh, puppy love!'

'Oh no! It went on for thirteen or fourteen years.'

'Tell me how you felt at the time?'

'Don't ask me. I am not one for poetry. But I felt exactly the way you've described in the couplet you have just recited.'

'And how about your lover?'

'He was twenty-two or twenty-three years old. A Mughal prince and very handsome. He had a shock of golden hair, blue eyes so deep that anyone who gazed into them drowned. The stately way in which he sat on the horse! And you skipped a heartbeat when he leapt over the hurdle. Let me tell you something, but you must promise not to tell anyone . . .'

'I won't.'

'Seeing him I would cry my heart out for hours. My heart pounded uncontrollably.'

'And how did he feel?'

'He had no idea!'

'Oh hell! Curse on you! Why didn't you tell him?'

'He had a hot temper. He was twelve or fifteen years older than me and slapped me right and left.'

'My good woman, you should still have expressed your love.'

'You don't know, he had such a devilish temperament. We children used to tremble before him. Express love! He would have punched me so hard that my teeth would have broken and stuck to my gullet. But in my dream he always appeared loving and tender—he would heave deep sighs, lift my veil. Many times during 'mirror viewing'* his blue eyes would smile at me in the mirror. Uff! My whole body would be soaked in sweat.'

'And then?'

---

* In traditional Muslim marriages the bride and the groom are shown each other through their reflections in a mirror.

'Then he failed in the matric exam for the fourth time and fled to Bombay. I got to know that he married a film heroine.'

'What was his name?'

'Shahzada Mirza Daud Beg Barlos.'

'Did you meet him again?'

'No. Not yet. But my heart says that I will meet him at least once before death—those deep blue eyes, that silky hair, that broad chest. Just once I want to place my head on his shoulders and shed two drops of tears and say . . . Well, what can I say?'

'Dear Bhai Sahib, the meal must be getting cold.' From that day Syeed Sahib began to address me as Bhai Sahib.

When we reached his house Syeed Sahib sat in the drawing room. I went straight to the kitchen though he tried to stop me. Chhoti Bi was sitting hunched near the chulha doing something. When she saw me she felt uneasy. She was holding something in the tongs that she tried to hide from me. When I greeted her she replied nonchalantly and turned her face to the other side.

'Chhoti Bi,' I called her as I sat on the pirhi beside her. 'Oho! Today you are treating me with extreme formality.'

She kept quiet.

'What was there in the grip of the tongs that you were burning?'

'No . . . nothing.'

'Chhoti Bi, I have to tell you a secret. Promise me that you won't tell anyone.'

'Secret? What secret?'

'Your husband has fallen in love.' She stared at my face.

'And you do not say anything?'

'What can I say? I have told him he can marry a second time. It was not my fate to have children.'

'But you did have a child. If it did not survive it was not your fault. You are not barren. I just hate those women who, in their devotion to their husbands, acquiesce to their second marriage. My elder sister too did not have any children. She adopted her niece. Why don't you adopt a child?'

'But if he likes another woman . . .'

'Then you get a divorce from him.'

'Oh God! Have you gone crazy?'

'If a woman cannot have more than one man, then it is not permissible for a man also to have more than one woman.'

'You are talking like an ignoramus. Men are permitted to have four . . .'

'I certainly won't allow my husband to have four. I will get a divorce from him.'

'His first wife . . .' she stuttered.

'To marry a man who already has a wife is deeply offensive to me.'

'But he loves her. I can't see him unhappy.'

'Come on! I feel like breaking your head. What an obscurantist idea! If you have fallen for another man then get a divorce from him.'

Chhoti Bi's face was red hot with anger.

'So that he can marry without a hitch!'

'Uff! What did I say?' I leapt to pick the tongs and taking the amulet threw it to the fire. 'The cleric must have told you that as the amulet burns to ashes, so will your rival, hasn't he? See, the amulet has burnt and I haven't. Chhoti Bi, those who sell amulets are liars and cheats.'

'But this one seemed to be a really godly soul.'

'Chhoti Bi, do you think I am so stupid and blind that I can't see things. You treat me with such affection and prepare fruit punch for me. Today you have prepared my favourite dish, pasanda. Tell me the truth—do you do all this as a favour to your husband . . .?' I felt angry. 'If I meet with men with an open mind or share a hearty laugh with them why do they think that I am . . . How can I tell you that I do not feel ill at ease interacting with men? I have such a large family that there are any number of young men there. We have fights and arguments all the time. I am accustomed to it. I like intelligent men who are sharp at repartee. I also hit it off well with clever and outspoken women. I love pitting my wits against Prithvi Singh who is Miss Phillip's boyfriend. He teases me no end and Miss Phillips and I laugh to our hearts' content. One day I got to talk to her about Prithvi

Singh. She said, 'His wife is an illiterate, boring woman devoted to her husband. She does not seem to have a tongue in her head. Prithvi is an interesting fellow, and we are great friends. I don't care what other people think.'

'Miss Phillips sleeps with that man.'

'What is that to you? She does not sleep with you. And Chhoti Bi, what proof can you provide that when Sayeed Sahib is out of the way you and Chhote Khan do not . . .'

She picked up the wood from the chulha and we began to laugh.

'Hey, are we going to starve today?' Syeed Sahib hollered from the drawing room. The meal was truly delicious. The nasty worm, my family trait, crawled in my head.

'Oh Syeed Sahib, you don't know about poor Principal Sahib! Tch . . . tch.'

'What happened to him?'

'He is a family man with children. His wife is again in the family way. And the poor fellow . . . tch . . . tch. I do not know what is he up to. He comes to me every day to shed tears.

'Which Siddiqi? What are you talking about? . . . And why does he cry?'

'Don't you know? Really? . . . And even if you knew, what could you do?'

'What are you bragging about? Let me have some sense of it.'

'Don't pretend as though you do not know anything. Love and musk can never remain hidden. But this madam looks such an angel but has a stone in her heart.' I looked at Chhoti Bi with disapproving eyes and she was stunned.

'You! . . . Are you in your senses?' Chhoti Bi was furious.

'Oho, what could you do? If someone has lost his heart to your angelic face you are not to blame for it. And you don't even know that Siddiqi Sahib is going half-mad.'

'Who said that?' Syeed Sahib had difficulty swallowing the food in his mouth.

'The poor fellow comes every day to open his heart to me. Look

Syeed Sahib, he is a gentleman. He did not give himself away through his words or gestures. He did not want to defame a genteel and chaste woman.'

'Did Siddiqi tell you himself?'

'Yes, he comes every evening. He used to come to give me notes on education.'

'Yes, I have seen him a couple of times . . . but . . . '

'Look, Syeed Sahib, he's a gentleman. If you use some rough measures against him, things might get out of hand.'

'But you are a witness, aren't you?'

'Me? . . . I will deny the whole thing. If you are stupid enough to make inquiries, there will be hell. I will leave the place as soon as the holidays begin. If words get about then you will be defamed.'

Syeed Sahib had turned pale. But instead of displeasure, Chhoti Bi's face showed strange emotions. A measure of surprise tinged with assumed annoyance.

It so happened that after that day all three of us, Syeed Sahib, Chhoti Bi and I, spent our time together. We two bandied words while she plied us with tea and snacks. Apa also changed her attitude towards Syeed Sahib. Earlier, whenever he visited us, Apa would be quite rude to him. Now that he had begun to come with Chhoti Bi, Apa warmed up to them.

When I was leaving Bareilly for Aligarh many people invited me over to their homes. Syeed Sahib and Chhoti Bi also joined me on some occasions.

UNDER LOCK AND KEY

My meeting with Zafar Quraishi Zia was quite romantic though I was well past that sort of thing. I had met him cursorily at Shahid Ahmad Dehalvi's place. On my way to Jodhpur I had stopped at Aligarh, then at Delhi, where I stayed for two or three days before proceeding to Jodhpur. Shahid knew that I was studying in Lucknow and would send me books and clippings of articles. He'd had my address published in an English magazine after which I'd begun to receive letters filled with obscene remarks and photographs. I reprimanded him sharply and asked him to change the address. Not content with this, I sent another complicated fake address to the magazine myself. The letters stopped; so did those from Zafar Quraishi.

All this had happened more than a year ago. Meanwhile I'd moved from Jawra to Bareilly. One day, I received a beautiful letter from Zia, elegantly typed and enclosed in a nice envelope. I didn't reply. Then came a volume of *Sho'la-e-Toor*. I wrote a letter thanking him. Now Zia's letters began to arrive every day. They were about poets, especially Jigar Moradabadi and Majaz. If Majaz was his close friend, Jigar was his mentor and guide. We also exchanged views on *Angarey*.

I began to write to him twice a week. We wrote to each other in English. After a few days, he wrote saying he had some business in Bareilly and would stay there for a few days. If I met him at the station we could have lunch together. But how would we recognize each other?

Zia had written that he would reach by train at eleven in the morning and get off the first-class coach wearing a grey suit and holding a newspaper in his hand. And if I wore a blue sari and held a rose in my hand, we would have no difficulty recognizing each other.

I had written my first play, 'Fasadi', that year. It was prominently displayed in the annual number of *Saaqi*. Earlier, I had sent another story, 'Neera', to the journal. A third story, 'Gainda', was almost complete. I don't know why I had begun writing. In the beginning I thought Shahid Ahmad Dehalvi published me for personal reasons; he was a friend of Azim Bhai. But I was disabused of this thought when he sent me letters asking for my compositions. I began to write more regularly for his journal. I had sent 'Gainda' to *Naye Adab*, which was perhaps published from Lucknow in those days.

The duties at school, parties, invitations, cinema—my days were really crammed. Then there was this passion for reading. At night I couldn't go to sleep unless I held a book in my hands. Even today, no matter how late it is in the night, and even if I am busy with some composition—I brush my teeth and open a book before going to bed. It could even be one of my grandson's comics.

I began to experience the same thrill in writing as I did in reading. I was counted among the chatterboxes in our talkative family. When I wrote, I imagined my readers sitting before me. I talked and they listened. Some agreed with me. Some didn't; some smiled while others got angry, and some felt jealous. Even now, I experience the same feelings. I narrate stories to my audience like a traditional storyteller. And just as a storyteller inserts personal opinions in the telling of a story, I do too.

Look how far I have digressed. To come back, I didn't have a blue sari and it seemed silly to buy one merely to facilitate someone's recognition of me. As for the rose, some inferior specimens grew in the school garden. However, even Queen Noor Jahan would have looked foolish holding a rose. And the smell of marigolds gave me a headache. Apa had some flowerbeds where, after much hard work, two sickly looking flowers of some English breed had bloomed. However, to pluck them was to risk one's life. Apa drenched them in sacred ablution water every morning and evening. And, if one didn't immerse the flowers immediately after plucking them in a vase filled with water, they would droop and wilt away. I was not so drunk in love as to scour the station platform looking for my hero, holding the vase aloft.

When I saw the man who stepped off the first-class coach holding a newspaper in his hand, I stopped in my tracks. He was a replica of my cousin Jugnu. A luxuriant shock of hair, chink eyes, broad shoulders, fair complexion. The last time I had seen Jugnu, he had filled out.

I was still in a trance when Zia approached, smiling.

'Adaab arz.'

'Adaab arz.' No, he was not Jugnu, for his smile exuded confidence, not nervousness. Soon we began to talk quite informally and walked towards the waiting room. When I told him the story of the rose and the blue sari, Zia broke into a loud guffaw that reverberated through the platform and made people turn around and stare at us. I had heard such full-throated laugher only in Abba Mian's mehfils. Many years later, I heard a similar guffaw while cooking in my kitchen. It came from 5, Indus Court, the apartment opposite to mine. The laughter brought back memories of my past. In Bombay, people do not laugh so heartily. Consumed with curiosity I had gone up to apartment number 5 where Raj Bedi lived.

'Raj Bhai, who's laughing so heartily in your house?' I had asked in a hushed tone.

And the laughter was standing before me. Fair complexion, dark hair, a well-built body.

'This is Mohan Rakesh, editor of *Sarika*.'

'Great! So you advertise your arrival to others in this way.' Mohan Rakesh broke into another of his heart-warming guffaws. I had felt as if I had known him for years.

Why, oh why, do I digress and hedge when I begin to write about Zia?

We lunched at the restaurant at the station. Then we hired a tonga and went around the town. We went to the library and sat there. Zia knew thousands of shairs by heart—verses from Mir, Zauq, Ghalib, Sauda, Iqbal, Josh, Jigar, Akhter Shirani, Majaz. I can remember ordinary things to their last detail, I can also remember conversations, but I just cannot remember verse, though I do remember the content.

During poetry competitions in school and college, no team would agree to take me on . . .

'Have you ever been in love?' He threw me a trump! I felt like answering candidly—a thousand times! I'm very susceptible to the emotion. It invades me with all its intensity. After spending a few hours together, I felt as though I had known Zia for a long time and would continue to know him for the rest of my life. One could not rely on the next life. The people in my family and their friends are of the opinion that, given my ways and attitudes, I would be born a monkey or a cat in my next life, something about which I have no reservations. I have always liked both these creatures. Some of their qualities—the cleverness of the monkey and the defensive ways of the cat—do help one face the challenges of life.

I mentioned Dawood Bhai.

'He's ugly as a yam,' Zia said scornfully.

'Absolutely. Syeed Sahib has the same opinion.'

'Which Syeed Sahib? The deputy secretary in the education department?'

'You know him?'

'Of course. He sings very well.'

'Then we'll have dinner at his place tonight.'

'No way. Not a moment can be spared today. Well, any other passionate love, heartbreak, heartache? That cousin of yours who is a doctor in Bombay, whom you mentioned in a couple of your letters . . .?'

'You mean Jugnu.'

'Ah, yes. Yours must have been the love of Laila and Majnun from childhood.'

'Forget it.'

'Grabbing each other in dark corners, sweet kisses?'

'Never.'

'The blush on your face is proof that you're lying.'

'Oh no. I'm not in a mood for lies now. On the contrary, I've complaints against him.'

'What a funny fellow! And you're still in love with him?'

'I don't know. I'm studying psychology nowadays and analysing myself.'

'Any discoveries?'

'From childhood it has been drilled into my head that physical love is dirty.'

'But now you're past childhood. And . . .'

'Then came another obsession. Everyone says that educated girls go astray. I want to prove them wrong.'

'So you've employed guards to watch over your intellect?'

'Yes. And I'm paying them a good salary.'

'And no one has ever kissed you?'

'Only once. A mischievous cousin of mine.'

'On the cheek?'

'No. On the lips.'

'How did you feel?'

'I was stunned. My hands and legs started trembling. I was scared stiff.'

'I've caught you out. Shake hands.'

'Caught me?'

'Don't pretend. You can't backtrack now.'

'Backtrack from what?'

'Do you still think physical love is dirty?'

'No. I think it's a sort of mental disease bred by the environment. After reading about it I asked many women to collect first-hand accounts. I haven't yet met any woman who will admit that physical love has brought her pleasure. Everyone said that they did it because of the persistence of their husbands.'

'Poor husbands!' Zia's face fell. 'They can't be blamed then if they fall for other women. Prostitutes are better than such wives.'

'But a prostitute told me that she absolutely detests the act. She just cheats the customers to eke out a living.'

Zia stood up and began to pace up and down restlessly.

'Let's go out. Otherwise I'll go mad.'

As we moved out, his mood changed dramatically. On the pavement a juggler was performing his tricks holding a doll in each hand. Zia took out a five-rupee note and handed it to him. He pulled me away and we hopped onto a tonga.

The juggler could not believe his luck—he kept looking back and forth, from the banknote to Zia.

We entered a cinema hall. An English film was playing, I forget the name. Zia's hand frequently brushed mine on the arm of the seat and at that moment the silver screen would blur. His hands were very beautiful, with soft, long, rounded fingers and brown nails. I knew just one more person with such beautiful hands—Jugnu.

'Why didn't you become a doctor?' I asked Zia.

'I almost became one. I fell in love with poetry and shifted from science to the arts.'

'Doctors should have long fingers, for performing surgery.'

'Does Jugnu have long fingers?'

'How do you know?'

'From you . . .'

'How? I didn't even mention him.'

'Then why did my hand remind you of a doctor's? You're obsessed with Jugnu.'

'Not at all. We grew up together. When I was a child I thought he was my seventh brother. It was only several years later that I learnt he was the son of my maternal uncle.'

'This custom of calling men "brothers" is so convenient. Women who address men as 'brothers' are actually quite disreputable.'

'I haven't called you brother.'

'Just try it!' Zia placed his palm on my neck and gently pressed it. Then his hand slowly moved to my cheeks.

'Shhh . . .' someone warned, disturbed by our whispers, and we began to watch the film like two chastised children. Of course, we didn't follow a word.

After the film we went to a hotel for dinner—the best hotel in Bareilly. I forget its name. During the dinner we began to discuss politics. Zia was a strong supporter of Pakistan, I was a pucca Congressite. There was a tinge of pink in my make-up, Resheeda Apa's influence. I was certain that as the country got its independence, the Congress would try to implement the principles of communism. This was because Gandhiji was a leader of the masses. He would secure the right to respectable lives for Harijans. I had heard that he had eaten with sweepers in their basti, with other leaders who had accompanied him there. After the British leave, India would become a paradise. Mr Jinnah wanted to divide the country. The Muslim League was increasing its support base. After I had had darshan of Bapuji in Lucknow, I had given up using imported products. The homespun khaddar saris that I wore looked like silk, but were comfortable only in winter. The partition of the country seemed a ludicrous idea. Nothing could have convinced us that it would really come about. Zia was smiling and looking at me strangely.

'What is it?' I asked.

'It won't be wrong to say that I have known you a long time.'

'Why?'

'Majaz told me about you. You had gone to see him and he was greatly impressed.'

'Oh yes. Three years ago. When I was studying in Aligarh, I had gone with Safiya to see him.'

'You like him a lot?'

'Of course.'

'Do you want to marry him?'

'Is it necessary to marry everyone that one likes? I also like Jigar Sahib. I admire Niaz Fatehpuri too. And Patras is my life.'

'And Jugnu?'

'Jugnu too.'

'Life?'

'It'll be an insult to his honour. No! For Jugnu, there's a separate niche in my heart.'

'Heart or dovecot?'

'Every heart is a dovecot. Father, mother, sister, brothers, relatives, friends, favourite poets and writers, all stay side by side in their own niches. In my heart, there is also a niche for Adda, our old cook. When I was small I would enter the kitchen and sit, nestling against him. He would stir the pan and feed me bits of kidney. He would cook salty snacks for me and secretly feed me, away from the watchful eyes of the other children. There are separate niches for all my brothers, sisters and relatives, some on the upper shelf, some on the lower. On one of the upper shelves was a niche reserved for my saheli, Mangu, the daughter of our coachman.'

'There was . . . what do you mean?'

'She got married and went away. After marriage she began to consider me too inexperienced to be her equal. She would whisper into the ears of my sisters. To me she would swagger, "You're a virgin, what can one talk to you about?"'

Zia began to smile.

'Now tell me, can I marry all of them? God knows how many new niches I will have and who will be enshrined in them.'

'That means there's some space vacant still?'

'Of course.'

'Should one apply formally?'

'No. The application may be rejected. Neither recommendation nor bribe will help you.'

'Well, it's good to know that there is some vacant space left. So one needn't despair. Where can you put me, in an upper shelf or a lower one?'

'Maybe somewhere in-between. So, what did Majaz say about me?'

'Well, besides him I also knew you through your brother, Azim Beg Chughtai.'

'Have you already met him? In Delhi?'

'No, we haven't met. It was like this—a couple of months ago my father had put out an advertisement for my marriage. Chughtai Sahib had written to him in response to that. You were staying with him then.'

'So it was you! Oh yes, he mentioned a deputy collector. But he didn't tell me your name.'

'How could he know my name from the advertisement? Many proposals came from zamindar families.'

'There's such an awful lack of suitable boys in Hindustan and a deputy collector is like a king. And if he takes bribes, so much the better. Do you take bribes?'

'I haven't had a chance so far.'

'Don't take bribes.'

'If I get married to a princess, how would I manage the expenses?'

'Stay with your in-laws.'

'Well, the in-laws have their own sons.'

'Just employ some police officer or a dacoit and get rid of them?'

'Your father was a deputy collector too.'

'According to Shamim, my father was quite useless in this regard.'

'Who is this Shamim Sahib?'

'He's no sahib. My fifth brother, older to me by a year and a half. He's a funny fellow. He has taken the matric exam four times but has not passed because of the perfidy of the education department. He often makes plans to kidnap the only daughter of some millionaire. So far he has not met with any success in this mission. So, Munne Bhai had written to you?'

'Yes. He introduced himself as a judge at Jawra Estate and his elder brother as the revenue secretary. He also wrote that your family was distantly related to Nawab Sahib, who would continue to be benevolent towards you.'

'I was lucky to escape Nawab Sahib's benevolence and run away from Jawra. In the last few months of our stay there, the tables had turned. Nanhe Bhai was ordered to leave the estate within twenty-four hours. And we got to know from a reliable source that Munne Bhai was being given the wrong medicine by the doctor. He took refuge in the Meraj TB Hospital. He has resigned from his job at Jawra and gone back to Jodhpur. Now he is bedridden.'

'To stay there under such circumstances!'

'The circumstances were terrible. Nawab Sahib had decided to make me and my eleven-year-old niece his daughters-in-law.'

'Ah, what a grandiose prospect! But . . . Nawab Sahib's daughters-in-law?'

'Yes, indeed. Nuzhat and I, the would-be daughters-in-law, ran away from there on the same day and attained our swargvaas* here in Bareilly. I don't know why people use the term swargvaas for death. The fact is, one gets many chances for swargvaas right in this life.'

'You've started using many Hindi words.'

'Nowadays a venerable well-wisher, Onkarnath Sharma, is teaching me Hindu mythology.'

'The old fellow must be trying to make you a Hindu.'

'He's not an old fellow. Quite handsome, in fact. My fear is that rather than making me a Hindu, he may embrace Islam. You know, he's quite liberal and doesn't object to eating food prepared by me. He doesn't eat meat, but if there is meat on the dastarkhwan, he doesn't mind . . .'

'There's something fishy.'

'Just speak a few words with a man and he thinks that the woman is up to something. I don't know why men have such a limited view of women.'

'You mean sex.'

'Yes. It always comes to that, eventually.'

'Have you studied Freud?'

'Of course. But I don't believe him completely. Somehow Freud seems a fraud. There's something in me that militates against putting faith in anyone uncritically, however great an intellectual he may be. Such a bad habit! I first look for loopholes in his theory. One should first examine all points of disagreement before coming to a consensus. I can't believe in anything instantaneously, can't take it at its face value. I think the first word articulated by me after birth was "Why?" This "why?" has been the cause of many a chastisement.'

'Is the ritual of nikah so important?'

'Not at all. My own father, who was crazy about my mother, got

---

* Literally, abode in heaven, used as a euphemism for death.

married to another woman through some strange circumstances. The other woman was quite different from my mother. For centuries, man has been seen to be seeking change. My illiterate and simple mother proved to be a hard nut to crack and incited everyone in the family. So the whole family teamed up against my father, and my gem of a father was prevailed upon to divorce his new wife in a couple of months.

'However, my wayward chacha had brought home a washerwoman. She was not allowed to take her rightful place in the family. She was always made to sit either on the floor or on a pirhi, a little away from the others. Besides Chacha Mian, she would attend to everyone else in the family as well. He had made over his ancestral house in her son's name. After bringing her home he never chased another woman. One day, after a particularly delicious meal, he was in a generous mood and said, "Budhya, tell me what you want. My munificence is just overflowing at the moment." Budhya said bashfully, "Mirzaji, please perform the nikah with me. I can't live in sin any more." She had hardly finished when Chacha Mian took off his shoes and began to beat her right and left. "Bastard woman, I'm a Chughtai. You think I'll marry a washerwoman and spoil the good name of my family?" I certainly don't approve of his narrow-mindedness, but I do appreciate the way he treated Budhya. Even after marriage, many men think it their right to run after other women. It is actually considered a sign of their manhood.'

'If someone offers you such love . . .'

'Life will overflow with happiness.'

Zia was looking at me strangely, as though I was extending an open invitation to him. God knew what it meant. I can't control my tongue.

'We have three days off for Diwali,' he said.

'Yes. I'm thinking of applying for two more days of leave. And then it'll be a Sunday. I intend to go around to Aligarh for six days. I have been wanting to go there for a long time.'

'Why don't you come to Lucknow?'

'Lucknow?' I hadn't been to Lucknow since I left college.

'For two days only.'

'It's not a bad idea. The memory of IT College haunts me.'

'So it's settled. I'll come by the twelve o'clock train.'

'I'll reach the station. We'll put the luggage away somewhere and go loafing around.'

'And then we'll proceed to Lucknow by the afternoon train. On my way back I'll have to stop over at Bareilly for a day.'

We dined at a hotel. We were so engrossed in talking that we hadn't realized the clock had struck ten.

'It's very late. Apa will be upset.' I got up hurriedly from my seat.

'Come on. The night's still young.'

'You don't know Apa. She'll get panicky and send word to Syeed Sahib and Manager Sahib. The whole town will be alerted. In any case, people have seen me going around with you and the gossip must already have started.'

'Do you care about silly gossip?'

'I'm the headmistress of the only Muslim girls' school in the town. I may be half-mad but I detest irresponsibility of any kind. I know what struggles Muslim schools have to face. I know what expectations the members of the community have from us. Take a wrong step and they'll cut the ground under your feet. I can't change the attitude of the community in a day. It'll require a lifetime.'

'You consider Rasheed Jahan your guru, don't you?'

'I do. But I don't imitate the guru blindly. I take my decisions based on my own understanding. And I don't consider it irreverence to my guru. I don't feel any deep aversion to the illiterate and the orthodox. Every human being is a product of his environment. He is like a prisoner of his environment. You can't change him by pushing him around.'

'You support Russian communism. You also support the forceful suppression of religion and putting your tongue under lock and key. There's so much contradiction in your views.'

'Contradiction is the sign of life. I'm not a Taj Mahal made of stone—all symmetry and proportion. Questions trouble my mind. They have to be engaged with, deliberated upon and resolved. Such is life. I've no worry for food or clothing. Apa is very skilful. She can manage all that. When I was a child, she would punch me because of my clumsiness. She complains even now. Once, I felt hatred for her and prayed for her death. Now I feel that had she not been here with me in Bareilly, I would have been lost. My esteem for her increases by the day. One day she said, 'When I see the way you behave my blood begins to boil. But I restrain myself thinking that you are a venerable teacher now. If I tick you off before the girls, you'll lose face. Yet you haven't given up those habits that deserve a spanking.'

Zia came to see me home. We sat on the chairs in the veranda. I heard Apa clear her throat and realized that she was signalling to me that she had noted my arrival and would now go off to sleep.

We talked till two. Suddenly lights were switched on inside. Apa may have been checking that the chidren were sleeping well. Zia got up quickly.

'People are waking up. I should be on my way. Tomorrow morn . . .'

'Don't come here. On seeing you, the curtains of the nearby houses begin to flutter.'

The next day came and passed by as quickly.

Zia left innumerable dreams around me. When he boarded the train, I sat beside him. Both of us were silent. It was suffocating. The past two days had passed in a flash. Now it was as though our tongues were sealed and placed under lock and key.

When the guard fluttered his flag, we got up with a start and, in an instant, our two bodies became one. My clumsy, inexperienced lips soared towards heaven.

'Hello, Bhai Sahib!' Syeed Sahib's face appeared. 'Are you all right?'

After breaking all the locks that day, for the first time, my tongue was tied. I could not retort as quickly as I usually did. Syeed Sahib grabbed my arm and I walked away with him, fuming within.

'A most suitable boy!' he said sagaciously.

'So, you were spying on me?' My colour was beginning to return.

'Why, Bhai Sahib, isn't this humble creature allowed to keep a watch on you? Now tell me, what have you been up to for the last two days? You could not be traced in school. What's the matter?'

'But who has employed you to watch over me?'

'Arrey, half of Bareilly has been busy watching over you. This romance is on everybody's lips, in any gathering. After the Muslim League, you and your handsome suitor are the most discussed item in town. Yesterday, at Miss Phillips' . . .'

'So, the news has reached Miss Phillips as well?'

'She's the inspector of the school. If someone so much as sneezes, she comes to know of it. And this is meningitis! Tell me yaar, how deep is the affair?'

I burst out laughing, in spite of myself.

However, the lock that had sealed my lips earlier now shifted its position, and sealed my heart and the sensitive windows of my mind.

WOMEN'S EDUCATION

I would spend the first hour in administrative work in the office after which I taught English to the eighth grade. Then I taught mathematics in the third period and handed the students over to Razia Begum for the Quran and religious studies. After that, I stayed in the office where most of my time was spent in dictating replies to letters to the clerk.

That day when I entered the office the manager was right there and my heart missed a beat. Then I felt a rising tide of anger within me. He had no right to interfere in my private life. I was in a fighting mood.

'Greetings!' I said with mock cheeriness. There was no reply. I threw the books on the table. Startled, Manager Sahib looked at me. His face looked ashen, his eyes indicated panic, his mouth was contorted as though he was rolling a quinine pill under his tongue.

'Manager Sahib, you can terminate the contract whenever you want. I won't protest.'

'I see,' he said, freeing his tongue from under the quinine pill.

'I had told you that I was inexperienced. The school . . .'

'Uff! . . . well . . . I did not expect this from you. I thought you were different . . .'

'Different? What do you mean?'

'Look, I am extremely worried. I had come to request you to keep Zahida and Abida with you if it is not too inconvenient.'

'But . . . why? What's up, Manager Sahib?' I was disconcerted. I had declared war on him even before hearing his comments on my behaviour.

'The entire city knows. My wife must have shared her sob story with you too.'

219

'Manager Sahib, the fact is that I've got so accustomed to domestic quarrels that after hearing about them once or twice, I just switch off if anyone reels off the same story again. Outwardly it appears that I'm listening; I utter the usual "tch", "tch", "God forbid!", etc., but it does not mean anything. Begum Sahib goes on with her litany of woes while I think about something else. But I do not understand why you want the girls to stay with me.'

'I want my daughters to get higher education.'

'Both your daughters are extremely intelligent and love reading. Who is preventing them from studying?'

'My wife knows that if she throws spanners in the way of their education it would hurt me.'

'Oh, I understand now. She's trying to blackmail you.'

'She is dead against their education.'

'I am sure she's doing it to tease you. I explained Razia Begum's position to her in great detail. I think she brings in her name just to embarrass you. Her real object is something else.'

'The real object is money, or rather the lack of it. Her real grouse is that I have ruined my career on account of the school.'

'But you do not spend all your time for the school. You need not worry so much about it.'

'You ask me not to worry? Do you know people are threatening that they will burn the school? I have taken this building and the adjacent school on lease. I am still paying the instalments for the furniture. Do you know how?'

I did not ask him how. He continued, 'I applied for a grant to the department of education after giving full details of the expenses. I did not make any mention of the loan. I took receipts from the furniture shop and attached them with the application. I also took advance receipts from the teachers for three months.'

'You mean, without paying them a penny?'

'Of course. You may call it a crime or a fraudulent act. But Mrs Marks helped me a lot. She appointed all the teachers and made them agree to work without salaries. After that we begged from door to door for public contribution. Somehow we received the grant and the school took off. But we could not settle all the accounts shown in the accounts register. I cannot explain to you all the complications. You won't understand.'

I really did not understand why the manager had to take recourse to unfair means. The accounts and the receipts were all false! People said that he had collected money through public donation and embezzled it. I began to feel uncomfortable.

'But will your wife allow her daughters to stay here?'

'If they can't stay here, I do not see where else I can send them. She badgers them all the time and does not allow them to study. We have a small house. Our daughters feel disturbed by our domestic squabbles.'

'You can send the girls to me today.'

'I'll do it right now. And I'll pay you three rupees per girl a month.'

'Only three rupees per girl? You mean, three rupees for a month's boarding?' In Aligarh, the fee per student was seventeen rupees, and in Lucknow's IT College, it was twenty rupees.

'Why? Isn't that enough?'

'Manager Sahib, three rupees!'

'Let's work it out—twenty kilos of atta can be bought for one rupee. Ten kilos per girl should be enough. And then buffalo meat can be had for six paisa a kilo. Even if both eat a quarter kilo per day, then . . .

'One and a half paisa per day . . .'

'What remains is ghee. My daughters are accustomed to cooking oil. Even if they consume two kilos a month it should not come to much.'

'Twelve annas.' I knew the rates of ghee and oil.

'You could give them a quart of milk, even half. With tea you could give them two biscuits that can be had for one paisa. They are quite filling. You could give them leftover rotis too.'

'Right. I will earn such a lot of profit.'

'Oh no! You'll have to spend on oil for the lantern, fodder wood and coals. I will raise the payment from next month. Here you are, keep these five rupees. I will send the remaining one rupee in the evening.'

'There is no need for additional fodder wood for them, same with the oil for the lantern.'

'Still . . .'

'Keep your money, Manager Sahib. The girls are very intelligent and loving.'

'Anyway, I will send the money either in the evening or tomorrow. Please call them here, I want to talk to them. Let them stay with you right from today. I will have their stuff sent—bedding, dresses, etc.'

'There's one condition, Manager Sahib.'

'What! Are there more . . .'

'Yes. I will keep the girls but will not take the money.'

'You must. I can't thrust the burden of my daughters' responsibility on you.'

'Manager Sahib, no child in the world can be a burden on anyone.'

'No. I . . .'

'Manager Sahib, you pay me a good salary even though I am not a trained teacher. One hundred rupees is a lot of money, and you pay me regularly. So it's decided.'

'But . . .'

'Look, there is no point in this useless debate. Six rupees will be too much for their maintenance and I am not ready to earn a profit from you.'

'I feel embarrassed.' His face showed pain. I also felt a lump in my throat. I rang the bell and the maid appeared. I said to her, 'Send Zahida and Abida here. Then go and ask Apa to send a kettle of tea and some biscuits.'

The girls arrived. Abida seemed somewhat bold but Zahida would cringe at the sight of me. Each looked like a frightened dormouse.

'I'll be back in a moment.' I got up and went for a round of the classrooms. I did not want to hear the conversation between father and daughters. The girls were probably crying. I saw Zahida still hiccupping.

As the maid brought the tea I entered the office with her. The girls were laughing cheerfully. When they saw me they became quiet.

'Go to your classes now.' Manager Sahib pointed them affectionately to the door and the two slunk away from the office.

'They are scared of you. For God's sake dispel this fear from their hearts.' Manager Sahib seemed to roll quinine pills in his tongue again.

'The fear will go away when they begin to stay with me.'

'I am told that all the girls are scared of you.'

'I see! I don't know. In the class they work hard, particularly Abida. By God's grace she's very intelligent. She is not scared of me at all. Even if I reprimand her, she continues answering questions one by one and doesn't give anyone else a chance.'

'Zahida was shaking all over. It hurt me to see this.'

'What can I do if my face is so horrifying?'

'Well, if it has to do with looks then they would suffer heart attacks at the sight of Mrs Das. She is truly horrifying. She does not teach well and beats the children.'

'Students laugh to their hearts' content in her class.'

'But when you enter the class, a hush descends like the silence of the grave.'

'I don't know why.'

'You probably seem grim?'

'Probably.'

'Haseeb too has complaints against you.'

'Really?' I had almost forgotten that Haseeb was his younger brother. His young wife had died leaving behind a one-year-old daughter.

'He's a handsome boy. Doesn't look like my brother. His complexion is fair like my mother's.'

Manager Sahib had already alluded to Haseeb's handsomeness and to his late wife a couple of times. He took a deep sigh and said, 'I had thought you would like him. But you were rather cold when he met you.'

'Manager Sahib, try to remember. When I had arrived here you had said that it's a Muslim school and people were narrow-minded.'

'But Haseeb is a thorough gentleman.'

'I haven't met anyone here who is not—Siddiqi Sahib, Shankarji, Sharmaji, Mr Jacob. Mr Marks had come the other day; he seemed a perfect gentleman.'

'He's a missionary. Didn't he try to make you a Christian? He goes around converting all the sweepers and cobblers to Christianity.'

'Unfortunately I am neither a sweeper nor a cobbler.'

'Come on, I didn't mean that. You come from a good family. God forbid, why should you . . .?

'What does religion have to do with good or bad families?'

'Quite a lot. I am told that Sharmaji is reading out the Gita and the Ramayana to you these days!'

'Yes. He probably wants to make me a Hindu.'

'He certainly does. He is a rabid Arya Samajist.'

'You are a rabid Muslim.'

'God be praised!'

'You must be trying to make me a Muslim.'

'What? What do you mean? You *are* one.'

'But I have great interest in Christianity. And now that I am delving deep into Hinduism . . . But do not worry. Islam would not be proud of an adherent like me, neither would any other religion. Manager Sahib, sloganeering is different. It is very difficult to become a true Muslim, Hindu or Christian. I haven't met any so far, except one or two. Do you say your prayers—I mean, besides on Eid and on Fridays?'

'You're right. I do not say my prayers.'

'How about fasting?'

'Well, that does not mean that I don't believe in God's existence, that I am an atheist or that I believe in many gods.'

'You are a genuine Muslim, you are running a Muslim girls' school. Don't worry, you will be rewarded with an emerald palace in paradise.'

'God help us! I am not running this girls' school in expectation of any reward. You . . . I mean . . .'

I started laughing. 'I know you are genuinely interested in the education of girls. And I truly believe, and it's no joke, that God will be pleased with you. Miss Phillips told me that if I can make the journey to Allahabad then . . . The grant for the boarding house . . . But Manager Sahib, there is no boarding worth the name. Miss Phillips said that one day she would come to inspect the boarding.'

'Oh my God! It's been quite a while since I applied for the grant for the boarding separately. I forgot to tell you. That file is also lying in my house. You . . . I hope you've not told her anything?'

'Oh no! I guessed that you must have been up to something concerning the boarding. But you should have told me about this. If I had said something . . .'

'It would have ruined me. Anyway, I should be on my way. I will send the stuff needed by the girls. She will kick up a big row, I am sure. Well, Haseeb will carry the bundle here in the evening.' Then he said in an obsequious tone, 'Please talk to him nicely. The boy is very unhappy.'

'I am an unhappy girl too!'

'Don't say that, please,' he said somewhat bitterly. 'You have a blooming face.'

'Your spies must have kept you informed every minute about me.'

'You're unbelievable! Need I employ spies against you? This is Bareilly town; people here worry about everyone.'

'Except their own honour.'

'But I do not like that loafer at all. What's his name—Syeed? It will be good for you not to be too close to him.'

School was over. The maid had indicated twice that Apa was calling me. I promised hurriedly, 'I won't be close to him.' If I agreed to something without putting up an argument, I meant just the opposite. I should have said, 'Of course, I'll get closer to him. Let me see who dares stop me.' However, I learnt why he did not want me to be close to anyone.

'Zia Sahib has great influence there. He is a government servant. Please tell him to advance our case in Allahabad.'

'I'll certainly write to him,' I said, peeved, and began walking towards the house even before he left the office. When I reached my house I let out a scream, 'Baaji!'

'I have been calling you for a long time!' She punched me twice on my back. Oh, those sweet punches and teasing by Apa—how I miss them!

Midhat was peering through the door. She acted coy for a few moments, then came running and tumbled onto me.

At the dining table Zahida and Abida were sitting like frightened kittens and looking at me from the corner of their eyes. They were surprised to see Baaji punching me and seemed rather pleased. I seemed less frightening to them.

I had misgivings about what Midhat was learning from the maulvi and had written to Baaji to send her to me. Her husband first opposed the idea but finally gave in to the wishes of his wife, as was his wont. Baaji argued with him, 'I have adopted the daughter of my brother. Her elder sister is studying in school. If the younger one remains illiterate she will curse me. Her parents too will feel bad. If you do not allow her to be sent for study, I will give her back to her parents.'

Dulha Bhai doted on Midhat. She was not only the daughter of his brother-in-law but the daughter of his niece as well. In Rampur girls could study only up to the sixth grade in the school. After that she had been studying at home for the last two years. She was eleven but extraordinarily intelligent. Nuzhat suffered from ill health but Midhat was healthy and plump. Nuzhat was in the eighth grade; Midhat was admitted into the seventh grade. I had admitted Makkhan in the school as well.

Apa would also help out with the homework in the class of smaller girls. Now there were four girls, so we could start the boarding house in right earnest. I stuffed all of them into a big room. Baaji could not sleep without Midhat beside her, but Midhat was insistent that she would stay in the boarding. Baaji stayed with us for a week and then left.

Nuzhat was very timid. When she came to Bareilly with me she looked lost and was dumbstruck. She always seemed scared of something. She would give Apa a hand in household chores and keep an eye on her younger brother and sister.

Midhat, on the contrary, had been brought up with great care. She was outspoken and mischievous. In the beginning she would call me Khala Jaan, as she was the adopted daughter of my sister. When she came to Bareilly she began to call me Phupi Jaan. When I asked her the reason she said, 'You are my phupi and not khala. I do not like khalas.'

'Why?' I asked.

'She prevents me from doing things that I like to do and gives too much advice about how to conduct my life. She does not let me jump or even run. And she's always saying bad things.'

'What bad things?'

'She can't stop talking about marriage all the time.'

'What's wrong in marriage?'

'I won't marry. I have already told Ammi.'

'What did she say?'

'Nothing. She only beats me when I do not study.'

Nuzhat was our first niece, so everyone doted on her. Both Abba and Amma adored her. Apa also liked her a lot. But she always looked lost and sad and that is why everyone worried about her. Seeing her so lost I would sometimes ask her to sleep by my side which annoyed Midhat, who even hit her at times. I asked Nuzhat to hit her back but it was as though she did not know how to hit anybody. Constrained, I would have to give Midhat an occasional thrashing, but she was absolutely shameless. Instead of being unhappy she would throw herself into my arms. No one ever beat her, and she acted as though she longed for my beating. She was bored with everyone showering her with love.

The boarding house had a large courtyard for games. However, Zahida and Abida were too shy and Nuzhat was wobbly on her feet. Only Midhat would romp around the court and send everyone careening for their lives. I taught them gippal, and tip cat as well, which annoyed Manager Sahib quite a bit.

'The entire town is agog with the news that you are teaching boys' games to the girls.'

'Children can play all games. Games have no gender,' I argued. 'Which game should I teach them, then? I asked you to arrange for badminton, you did not oblige. Now tell me how long can the children go on playing hide-and-seek?'

Nuzhat lacked skill in any game besides tip cat, in which she fared better than Midhat. Midhat was not accustomed to defeat. She would get annoyed, and start beating Nuzhat. Trying to mediate between the two sisters was hell. Nuzhat wouldn't even complain, which infuriated me. There was a massive tamarind tree in the compound. I started teaching the girls how to climb the tree, creating quite a furore. But I egged the girls on, and they became unstoppable. On top of it, during recess the girls from school also began to come to play tip cat and climb the tree. As many considered these acts objectionable, the girls felt as though they were doing something heroic. They would engage themselves with a vengeance. This made the manager sad.

'For God's sake, what are you doing? All my efforts will go in vain.'

'You know that the enrolment in the school is increasing by the day. In fact, we cannot provide enough room. We have to seat two girls to a bench. Three girls have come from the government school, as their houses are close to our school. I had told them clearly that we have no space and that they will have to sit on the mat for some days.'

'But . . . Qadir Sahib tells me that the girls are given too much homework and if they don't do it they are told off.'

'Why should the parents interfere with the discipline of the school and the homework? You know very well that physical punishment was stopped the day a girl bled after being hit by a teacher and I had to take her to the hospital.'

'They feel that you made a lot of fuss for nothing. You could have asked me before taking her to the hospital.'

'If anything had happened to the girl, who would have taken responsibility? I will do whatever I think right. I cannot wait for your permission and risk a girl's life. Further, I do not support corporal punishment. Punishment can be of a different kind and degree. I have no patience with people who complain against teachers.'

'She was very upset on that day.'

'If the husband of a teacher falls for a female neighbour, the teacher lets off steam on the children.'

'Please speak softly. The poor woman is very unfortunate. Her husband does not give her a penny for domestic expenses. She has six children . . .'

'Who asked her to have six children? And now she is carrying the seventh one! I've told her a couple of times that I have a lady doctor friend who . . .'

'For God's sake, do not give people such dangerous advice. Abortion is a crime.'

'It is a greater crime to give birth to more children than necessary. You know the condition of her children. Her eldest daughter eloped with a stranger, and when she came back the mother wanted to throttle her. The girl came to me in a distraught state. Was it a crime to give her shelter?'

'Where's the need to interfere in other people's affairs? The rumour-mongers are spreading the canard that a girl of the boarding has become pregnant and . . .'

'Come on! Farzana is certainly not pregnant, nor have I had her operated on. As for interference, the affairs of the world are everybody's business. I have no sympathy with people who play with the life of a girl.'

'What's the use of taking on more worries for yourself?'

'I have no worries. I did not have to undergo any physical or mental discomfort. Manager Sahib, what more can the people do besides turning me out of here? In that case, I will say, in the words of the poet:

God's world is not a small one
And my feet are not tired yet.'

'Don't you fear slander?'

'I consider an act hateful only if my conscience does not approve. I have not yet been proved wrong in any decision I have taken in my life.'

'But what's the use of taking risks?'

'If every step in life is regarded as a risk then people will become just lumps of clay. Manager Sahib, I have told you earlier as well that you have drawn the contract. I do not attach any importance to a mere piece of registered paper. The paper can be deregistered. My father was a judge and two of my brothers are lawyers. I have not taken any steps that are outside the law. My appointment here was because of you and if you want . . .'

'You know very well what I want. I have given my daughters to your care. But what can I say to the world?'

'Do one thing. You can disown any responsibility by placing me in the forefront.'

'God forbid! What do you think of me? I am not such a coward.'

'I know very well that you founded this school and are running it. Besides you, I have also known Papa Mian who was the founder of Aligarh Girls' College. To open a girls' school, and that too for the girls of the Muslim community, is inviting trouble for oneself. Life becomes a hell. But the girls who pass out from here after acquiring an education will remember your sacrifices. Just think, in all their houses a little lamp of learning will be lit. And as for infamy, it boils down to this: you do not like those who want to fashion their lives according their own priorities rather than the expectations of the society. People like those who share their values. I don't care what others think of me. I won't allow anyone to interfere with my life.'

'You will find a lonely life unbearable.'

'I will go to jail, as I cannot make others responsible for my virtues and vices. As for loneliness, I am never lonely. There are a thousand memories and a thousand thoughts that crowd around me all the time.'

'Don't you need anyone?'

'I do. In fact, I need everyone. I cannot afford to lose anyone.'

'I see. That friend of yours, I mean the gentleman who writes you a letter every day, sometimes two letters a day, seems like a good fellow.'

The peon in school who brought in the mail was also the cook at the manager's house. After finishing his duties in school he would go over to the manager's house to do the chores. The mail was first brought to the manager, who looked over it and probably censored it. He thought that the loafers in town wrote obscene letters to the teachers and the students of the school, and he had to be vigilant.

I was stunned. If the manager had censored my letters then he would have to face hell. Zia's letters were beautiful—studded with nice couplets and dipped in the philosophy of love. They had a magnetic power. He had visited Bareilly twice after the first visit. He would arrive in the morning, we would spend the entire day together and then he would return in the evening. The last time he had brought his car and we wandered around a lot of spots.

I felt terribly annoyed by what the manager had done but did not allow it to show it on my face. I am truly a brazen creature.

Before things got worse Sayeed Sahib arrived.

'Bhai Sahib, the empress has sent for you. A parcel of guavas has arrived from her parents' house, and guava chutney has been made. The guavas have been sent for Apa and the children.'

'I should be on my way,' the manager said, standing up.

'He pulls such a long face at the sight of me, as though I've come to kidnap his daughters.'

'Even though you try to shield yourself behind the empress! Your intentions are also genuine.'

'Does he care much about what is genuine and what is fake?'

'If the money is fake, then one stands to lose. But if it is simply a question of intentions . . .'

'Can't I lead you astray?'

'Does leading a woman astray add to one's manliness?'

'Uff, Bhai Sahib, you do like making a mountain of a molehill. Moreover, I am not in a very cheerful mood at the moment.'

'Why so? Are there new amulets being burnt?'

'Could be. I have no idea. I have begun to fear these amulets.'

'Really? It is a proof of your honesty. You should be proud of the fact that you are turning out to be a devoted husband. May God bless you, my child!'

'This panda seems to have an influence on you. What a brazen story you have published in *Saaqi*!'

'Are you talking of "Kafir"? Is it so bad?'

'God help us! What vain thoughts! Thank God your manager has no time to read. Otherwise you'd be in real trouble.'

'What trouble? You mean I would be thrown out of the school? I don't care. In any case, I am leaving at the end of the year. It's just a question of two months. But I'd like to know what your objections are as a reader of the story. I have not said anything new there. You were bent upon marrying a Christian girl and you would have married her but for the fact that she imposed the condition that you should divorce Chhoti Bi. Many Hindu–Muslim marriages take place. Many stories have also been written on this theme. There was a time when every romantic story had a Parsi beauty as its heroine!'

'That's different.'

'How?'

'A Hindu, Parsi or a Christian girl can be a beloved.'

'And you mean that no Hindu, Parsi or Christian man can be a hero?'

'I am on my way. You really get on my nerves! How about the guava chutney?'

'To hell with guava chutney!'

'Look, I was saying all this for your own good. This is Bareilly. I hope you remember the Asghari Begum anecdote?'

'Of course. How can I forget it?'

'Then let's go.'

'Let me finish these two letters and I'll be on my way.'

Asghari Begum! The Murder of Swami Sharadanand! The Murderer is Sent to the Gallows! Asghari Begum had written a letter to Azim Bhai at Jawra. He was going through a bad patch at the time. Shahid Ahmad Dehlavi's father had written a book, *Ummat ki Maaein** (Mothers of the Prophet's Adherents). Muslims agitated against the

---

* *Ummat ki Maaein* (Delhi: Kohinoor Press, n.d.) written primarily for the edification of Muslim women, draws on the lives of the wives of the Prophet as exemplars of female virtues. In each life story, there is a lesson to be learnt and emulated.

book and it was banned. No one knew what prompted Shahid Sahib to bring out the book again to public view. The Muslims protested once again. Azim Bhai wrote to him to send copies of the book. The princely state of Jodhpur was an autonomous entity and British laws could not be invoked here. 'I will keep the book in safe custody. Let me see who can stop me!' This letter was published in the newspaper. Azim Bhai considered himself safe and published the news that he had received the parcel.

Azim Bhai used to go to the court in a horse-drawn tonga. One day he found that the tonga was there but the driver was new. When asked, the driver said that his brother had fallen ill and he had come to stand in for him. Azim Bhai sat on the tonga and it began to move. After a while two persons stopped the tonga on the road and said, 'We are also going to the court. There is no transport available. If you don't mind giving us a lift . . .'

'Not at all. Come and sit.'

The tonga driver took the tonga to a lonely spot. The two fellows got off the tonga and beat Azim Bhai to a pulp. He was skinny and fell to the ground at the first stroke. They beat him some more and left with the driver.

When Azim Bhai came to his senses, he got up with difficulty, took a tonga and returned home. 'The tonga tumbled over,' he told everyone. But Ishaq Bhai, who was a police sub-inspector, was not fooled by this story. He pointed out that his wounds were different from those that could be inflicted from falling off a tonga.

'How many fellows were there?' he asked him quietly.

'Two, and the tonga driver.' Azim Bhai admitted the truth.

The next day the newspapers said that British laws might be ineffective in Jodhpur but Islam was a living religion there, and that Muslim youths had not yet worn bangles on their arms.

On the following day Ishaq Bhai, Bade Mamu and Chhote Mamu met a gathering of Muslims in Jodhpur and negotiated the truce— Azim Beg Chughtai would go to the mosque to prove that he was a Muslim and burn the book, and the community would forgive him.

Azim Bhai's fever had gone down but he could not walk without support. He had his bath, dressed up and went to the mosque in Bade Mamu's car. He said the prayer, did tauba and asked for forgiveness. A fire was lit under the staircase of the mosque and copies of the banned book were thrown into it. The Muslims showed utmost generosity in forgiving him and choked him with hugs. Azim Bhai's comment was that a couple of lashes would have been better than those hugs.

When the details of this incident were published in the newspaper Azim Bhai received hundreds of letters, some commending him and others protesting against the incident. One of these letters was from Asghari Begum. Her letter was one of those that Azim Bhai responded to, and they continued to exchange letters for some time after that. With one letter she attached the manuscript of her autobiography that was not likely to be published by any publisher, as it could have incited people once more. Azim Bhai would share interesting mails with me. Asghari Begum's life story had a deep impact on me. I recorded the details of the autobiography in my diary. This diary continued to inspire me, allowing my pen to spew both poison and nectar.

Asghari Begum was an extremely intelligent and beautiful woman. She faced life with great courage. She brought out a journal, *Tanveer*, from Bombay. She was adept at both poetry and prose. Her struggles impressed me. I told Syeed Sahib about her and read out some parts of her diary.

He was stunned and said rather irritably, 'Look, I do not poke my nose into affairs that might cause trouble. I would also advise you that it is stupid to hurt people's sentiments for the sake of titillation. You can't bring people round to your way of thinking by making fun of them. Do you believe in individual freedom?'

'Absolutely.'

'Then you should leave people alone. Let people think and do as they like. What right do you have to object to their ways?'

'And what about people who hurl abuses at educated girls? Don't the abuses stick? I do have the right to respond! The restrictions that stifle me . . . the people who have spoiled so many lives. My blood boils . . .'

'And then you begin to let off steam.'

'Shall I pour embers over them?'

'Bade Bhai Sahib, this humble brother of yours begs your pardon. The mood is totally spoiled after bandying words with you so bitterly. Let's have a round of guava chutney. After that you could pop some neem pills into your mouth . . .'

But we continued subconsciously to allude to Asghari Begum.

I had not only the guava chutney, I also had my lunch there. Apa had come over with the children. Chhoti Bi doted on them . . .

Asghari Begum wrote a letter to Azim Bhai. It was a letter in name only; actually it was a novelette. He gave it to me to read. I was terribly impressed by her.

When a woman falls on bad times, she usually tries to get out of the hell with the help of some man. This has been true for hundreds of years and for all the countries of the world. Even today, not only in India but in Europe and the USA too, girls run away from home only to fall into the hands of depraved characters who lead them astray. It is one of the most important issues in the US today. The police are helpless. Young girls run away from home, not because of poverty, but because they get fed up with the excessive doting of their parents and feel irresistibly drawn towards the glitter detailed in obscene literature and films. They reach big, bad cities where powerful mafias hold them in their grip and they are trapped. They are promised the romantic, glamorous life of models and film heroines. Then they are turned towards drugs. As they become dependent on it, they are made to sell drugs, undertake prostitution and commit many other crimes.

In this trade criminals get the better of the police, because lower-level officials are hand in glove with them. These officials are, in fact, at the beck and call of big criminals, who have access to senior officers and even magistrates. People holding key positions consider it good and profitable to carry out the order of the cartel. Honest officers find it difficult to survive. Thinking of their livelihood and their children, they often have to compromise. If they don't, they lose their lives. However honest the police intend to be, they are helpless.

For centuries in India, young girls have been lured and led astray. No scheme for social reform seems to have been successful. These young girls fulfil the needs of the red light areas, while the kidnapped youths fulfil the need to establish oppressive regimes of plunder. This illegal regime [the underworld] is thriving in small towns in small ways, and quite brazenly in big cities. Not just weapons and machines, but ideas and policies of commerce are imported from the West. In big cities, the hand of the West is seen in the use of these young girls for purposes of commerce.

Today, when I revisit the streets and lanes of my past, the present is also before me. I have studied the condition of these young girls in Bombay, Delhi, Lucknow and Calcutta. It has been three years since I made a round of the villages too. I also met parents whose children were lost in cities. I gathered information about the red light districts in the big cities. I met pimps and gained their confidence after much effort. They accepted me as a friend, showed me great regard and gave me information that I had not expected. Many boys and girls come to meet me. I introduce them as needy artists looking for jobs. I do not think poorly of them, but curse the system that exploits them in various ways.

Amidst a thousand stories of the fall of women there were some stories of a different kind which indicate to me the nobility of human beings. Ala Bi, the founder of Aligarh Girls' College, told me about many incidents that she experienced simply because she and her husband brought the college into being. These incidents have not been recorded in detail by Papa Mian, aka Shaikh Abdullah, either in his own biographical accounts or in those of Ala Bi. However, during conversations Ala Bi would talk about girls who had taken refuge with her, got an education and became successful. Among them there was this girl—I won't name her—whose husband and mother-in-law were trying to force her into prostitution. She had run away from some village in Punjab. She was pregnant. It was her good luck that in the train she ran into a lady who was taking her daughter to the Aligarh school for admission. She took pity on the unfortunate girl, took her under her wing and, on reaching Aligarh, handed her over to Ala Bi.

Ala Bi was alarmed. She could not let her stay in the boarding. She could not admit her to school as she did not know even the alphabet. She told everyone that the girl was her distant niece and entrusted to her the responsibility of running the house. Even Ala Bi's sons came to know the truth when they grew up. She had given out that the girl was a widow. The girl gave birth to a son and everyone doted on him. Like other children of the family, the boy carried the tag 'Abdullah' with his name. That boy turned around his life and now lives in comfort in Pakistan.

Ala Bi narrated another incident. One day three girls landed at the Aligarh station and then reached her house. The eldest of them was eighteen or nineteen years old, the second one was fourteen or fifteen and the youngest one was only four years old. Ala Bi was alarmed. Several girls lived in the boarding without paying any fee. It was run with great difficulty, through donations, borrowing and cutting corners. After all, it was a boarding, not an orphanage. Anxiety about the girls robbed Ala Bi of her night's sleep.

'If you do not give us refuge, the three of us will set fire to our dresses and burn ourselves to ashes before your eyes, or jump into a well and drown,' the eldest of them had threatened.

Ala Bi was really frightened. A girl could get lost in the boarding and no one would know where she was. The parents of the three girls were alive. The eldest had been married to an aged contractor who already had two wives and had fathered about a dozen children. The unfortunate girl worked like a maidservant. On top it, the brother of one of her co-wives tried to lure her. When she resisted they branded her as a woman of loose morals and beat her within an inch of her life. She could read the Quran and knew Urdu. She had read about Aligarh Girls' School in some journal and came here, looking for refuge.

The second sister was married to another aged and pig-headed baker who treated her abominably. And all this happened even though all the sisters were beautiful and had fine features.

Someday I will recount the chronicle of how these sisters came out of darkness to light, changed their lives completely and led successful lives.

Asghari Begum's life story reminded me of these three sisters.

I could never forget her.

HELL

The aristocrats and government officers of Bahraich reached the station to greet Baaji's wedding party. No one had seen the groom. The nikah happened at night while the children were sleeping. Only Nanhe Bhai knew what the groom looked like but he was trailing behind the party. First, a handsome, tall man about thirty-five years old got off the train. He was wearing a sherwani of green brocade, tight pyjamas and a green Rampuri topi at a rakish angle. Everything around him looked faded and withered.

People took him for the bridegroom and promptly garlanded him.

The man let out a thundering guffaw, and said, 'Gentlemen, I am Sohrab Khan, uncle of the groom. Safdar Mian is over there.'

Seeing Safdar Mian, Abba broke into a sweat. He looked like a tuberculosis patient, lanky like a bamboo pole, with stubble on his chin. His forehead was crisscrossed with wrinkles and his eyes looked tired.

I remember this much: A bevy of fair women, with anklets tinkling, disembarked at the entrance and were skimmed with sticks. I picked up a neem stick and lashed at the ankles of the samdhans as the ghouls had come to take away my Baaji. Someone dragged me away and I sat beside Baaji, clinging to her. Baaji coughed so loudly people could hear her from afar.

Long after this, one day Chhoti Apa told me that there had been an earlier proposal for Baaji. The son of a zamindar, the would-be groom was a dissolute whoremonger. He was some Khan. He had committed a murder or two. His family had a small estate. He was not educated, but was boastful of his family jewellery and gold anklets. When Khan's mother came with some other female relatives and an elaborate retinue

239

of maids and slaves, they brought silver trays and boxes stuffed with paan. She spoke more about gold and pearls than her son.

'May God not let me tell lies. Here I hold my ears with my hand and tell you, an offering of five sers [of gold] and fifty thousand in mehr will be given. The small haveli has already been made over in the prince's name. May Allah protect him, he is the only son of the family.'

When she left, Baaji muttered, 'I'm not going to marry that dog.' She could be brutally blunt.

'Hai, hai, shut up, you perverse girl! Think before opening your trap before me. I'll burn your face.'

'Just try! I'll tell Abba.'

'Fear God's wrath, Munni . . . if people get to hear what you are saying . . .'

'What if they do? I don't give two hoots for anybody.'

And then one day, when Amma had gone to Hakimonwali Gali, Doctors' Street, to Safi Nana's house, Khan's mother chose to land at our house.

'Ai bhai, where's our samdhan? Ai samdhan, Bi samdhan!' she hollered.

'What is it?' Baaji came out to see who was calling.

'Hey girl, where's your mother? Don't you have any regards for your mother-in-law? You're strutting and swaggering!'

'Are you Khan's mother?'

'Oui, just see her cheek!' She plopped down on the settee.

'I am not going to marry your depraved son, for sure.'

The woman was stunned. She could not have imagined such a turn of events in her wildest dreams.

'Have you lost your wits, girl?'

'You've lost your wits, old woman!'

'Ask for God's forgiveness, girl.'

'Your son is a worthless debauchee.'

'That's enough! May God forgive us! Come, you bastard,' she called to the maid. Slinking away, she muttered to herself, 'God's curse! Is she a girl or a red-hot chilli pepper! My darling son! Many will offer their daughters on a platter for him. I spit on her, what a girl Nachchu Bi has begotten!'

When Amma came home and heard what had ensued she was flustered.

Baaji laughed heartily. 'If she dares come again, I'll bash her up,' she said, striding up the stairs to the attic and losing herself in the manoeuvres of kites. Baaji flew kites secretly and the threads would snap. That is why Amma was in a hurry to marry her off. Girls are usually considered a burden for parents. And a brazen girl like Baaji, may God not give such girls even to one's enemies!

Abba also got a whiff of what had transpired but kept quiet. What could he have said, after all? He had no love lost for Khan. Abba was friendly with some zamindars with whom he had business transactions as well. If a baby was born to their families, guests would arrive from distant places to celebrate the occasion. Courtesans would be brought and music and dance soirées would be held for two or three days. Abba loved both dance and music and the soirées were truly glorious!

However, he hated the practice of visiting prostitutes. He also opposed the custom of having more than one wife. Quite a while ago, when only seven of my siblings had been born—Shamim, Chunnu and I had not been born yet—Abba had taken leave from his job to build our house in Agra. One part of the house, where he lived, was ready. Amma and my siblings had not yet moved in. No one knew why Amma arrived there one day with Chhote Mamu and Munne Bhai. Munne Bhai's cough was really bad; it had been going on for the past couple of months. The change of climate and Safi Nana's potions had brought some relief. Amma would spend most of her time in Hakimonwali Gali; occasionally she would come to Panje Shahi. The people of the mohalla would invite us frequently, and almost every day we would visit some family or the other.

This happened in the house of Badi Amma, who owned a buffalo: One day Amma was lounging on a cot under the chameli vines. The women were chatting about the usual topics of love and the infidelity of husbands.

'My husband is like a piece of gum, stuck to me. He doesn't even look at other women! Well, we have had so many children that he does not have any time for other women!'

'Hear, hear! God forbid!'

'To tell you the truth, I often ask him to take in another one.'

'Nachchu Bi, sometimes words that come out of your mouth become real.'

'I don't believe that.'

'Banno, do you have any idea which way the wind is blowing? I was thinking how to break this to you. I was dumbfounded when I heard this!'

'What are you talking about?' Amma was slightly flustered.

'It's all the doing of Badshahi Khanum, your darling nanad.'

'I have no idea what story you are cooking up, Badi Amma.'

Then Badi Amma explained to Amma that constructing the house was a mere pretext. Only the debris had to be removed, but Mirza Qasim Beg did not want to budge from Agra.

'Did you ever think why?' Badi Amma asked.

'What is there to think of?'

Badi Amma broke the entire story. Rahat Aunty was the younger sister of the wife of Bade Abba, Ibrahim Beg Chughtai. She had become a widow at a young age. Her husband had left her considerable property. She was fairly well-versed in Farsi and Urdu and had some interest in poetry. She must have been older to Amma by two or three years. Amma could have been twenty-three or twenty-four at the time. She was an attractive woman with plump features, a golden complexion, curly hair and liquid eyes. Rahat Aunty was tall and slim and had long, silky hair. She was an image of melancholy and sadness. When she recited Urdu poetry in her rhythmic, lilting voice, listeners would nod their heads in appreciation. Sometimes poetry evenings would be held in the kothi. Abba Mian too could occasionally scribble lines in Farsi and Urdu. But he would never read them to anyone. His urge for poetry had probably been stirred up in the company of Rahat Aunty. It was so contrary to his usual life with the noise of children, the responsibility of his position, poultry, chicken, horses, buffaloes, goats. In contrast to these, he now had the pleasant evenings of Agra, the beauty of rose bushes in full bloom, the newly built, peaceful house, romantic silence and elegant poetry. Abba Mian was a complete man—he rode horses at top speed, played tennis, tended gardens, entertained friends and let out hearty guffaws. And the melancholic beauty of Rahat and her lonely life . . . She had no greed for wealth, she was thirsty for sweet words, charming couplets, Omar Khayyam's quatrains, and the verses of Anwari, Fani, Hafiz Shirani, Mir, Ghalib, Zauq, Ashufta . . .

Amma lay still. It was as though she had stopped breathing, as though she was afraid of moving from her position lest she break to pieces which would be difficult to put together again.

When she returned home, food was laid on the table. Abba Mian was reading the newspaper.

'Where on earth had you gone? I am starving.'

Amma made a violent gesture with her hand and the plates came tumbling down from the table.

'You will have to eat my brain!'

'Begum!' Abba Mian had never seen this spitfire image of Amma. He had a guilty conscience, and felt scared.

I cannot keep my pen steady as I write these words today. The person who we considered to be second only to God and His prophet, one who we always regarded as sacrosanct and steadfast! Can my pen today show the audacity to point a finger at the solitary error, weakness and deviation from principle by Mirza Qasim Beg Chughtai, one who had lived an unblemished life so far? I do not remember any other error, injustice or false step by him. From every angle I found him to be a complete human being.

Rahat Aunty's name was usually invoked in jest. The poor woman left this world, lonely and abandoned, probably before I was born.

This story came to light one day when Shamim snatched away some money kept by Amma on the paan tray. This was when my BA results had come out. Abba, who had had a paralytic stroke and recovered from it, was sitting on the reclining chair.

'Hoon, so you have passed,' he said.

'Yes.'

'I see. Begum, shall we arrange for a dinner to celebrate?'

'Forget about a dinner in this season of scarcity. Hey, give my money.' But Shamim had already put the money in his pocket and was walking away.

'Look, put the hundred rupees back. Otherwise, I won't give you any food.'

'Kofta has been cooked, and kheer of sweet potato.' I supplied the information.

'And rice and fish curry have come from Bade Mamu's place.' This was Bhabi who was clearing away watermelon seeds.

'What a stingy mother you are! Look, Abba Mian, you snapped your ties with Rahat Aunty for no reason. Our mother is such a tyrant that for any little thing she threatens to stop food and water. Did Hazrat Uthman have ties with any tyrant?' The family tree from our mother's side began with Hazrat Uthman, the third caliph.

'Hey, don't talk rubbish. Shameless fellow, God's curse on you! Your younger sister has passed BA and you are still rotting in the tenth class!'

'Just see! She has only curses and harsh words for me. If it were Rahat Aunty . . .'

'What if? Get a brand new mother for yourself now!'

'I see. Do you really mean it?' Shamim posted himself behind a column and said, 'I will get a co-wife installed in this house, or my name is not Shamim Beg Chughtai.'

Shamim would often indulge in such vulgar jokes, but he did it with such flair that no one could help chuckling. He had pronounced the threat with such a serious face that neither Abba nor Ammi could stop laughing.

Shamim siddled up to me and whispered, 'Just see how the old fellow is beaming. The thought of becoming a groom is making his heart bloom.'

'Run, you naughty boy!'

'Why, am I saying something funny? Just a dash of dye in his hair and he would look young. There's no wrinkle on his face, nor are his hands chapped.' Then he said loudly, 'The shariah allows four. Really, if a new mother came she would look after us better.'

At that moment Mamu arrived and food was laid on the table.

After the meal I asked Amma, 'Bi, what is this story about Rahat Aunty?'

She then told me the entire story, from beginning to end.

After turning over the food on the table, Amma had begun to cry while Abba sat quietly with his head bowed. Then he had said, 'Begum, I plead guilty for my mistake. I have married her.'

'I know.'

'I will accept whatever punishment you give me.'

'Call all my children here. I will stay in Agra.'

'What are you saying, Begum? How can I live without you and our children?'

'Your darling . . .'

'You are my darling, my life, my past and future.'

'You did not remember all this while marrying her . . .' Amma's voice choked. 'A father of seven children . . .'

'I had no idea where I was. When I came to my senses and saw my signature on the marriage document I lost my wits. I left the spot at that very moment.'

'The nikah took place at Phupi Badshahi's?'

'Yes.'

'So her desire was fulfilled, after all. She has been able to take my husband away from me.'

'I am still alive, Begum. I wish I were dead. No, I do not have the right to die either. I want to live.'

'I know. Badshahi Khanum must have fed you something.'

'No, Badshahi has not fed me anything.'

'Then? You are not a baby!'

Amma did not know how often human beings turned into babies. They are reduced to ciphers. But Abba was not telling a lie. Human beings build walls in their mind for their defence. They do not want to think about the consequences that might flow from their actions and take recourse to self-deception. For a principled man to break his principles is a challenge, like sleepwalking while awake. Like silkworms, they make shells for themselves.

'I hope you won't divorce me?' Amma asked in a choked voice.

'Divorce, Begum!'

'My children will be branded a divorcee's children. No one will accept my daughters. People will say, "Like mother like daughters. There must be something wrong with her that Qasim Beg Chughtai had to divorce her." Place your hand over my head and swear that you won't divorce me.' She picked Abba Mian's hand and placed it on her head.

'I have not touched her, and I swear that if I ever touch her then I am not from the lineage of Mirza Karim Beg Chughtai.'

'Oh no! Oh no! . . . this will be a sin.'

'If my conscience does not approve of something then it is a sin for me.'

'For God's sake, do not act like an apostate. God's wrath . . .'

'I will bear with it.'

'This is kufr. The sin will be visited on the children.'

'There is nothing like that in the divine scheme of things. Every individual is accountable for his own actions.'

'Sarkar!' Amma said after a pause.

'Yes, Begum.'

'You can marry a thousand times now, I do not care.'

'Why are you saying this? Don't you love me any more?'

'It is not like that. Good wives do not love their husbands, they worship their spiritual god.'

'Begum, people worship stones. I am a human being, your very own.'

'Then let's leave this place right today. To hell with the kothi—it will be built any which way.'

The same day Amma had left for Kanpur along with Abba.

The communal tension in Kanpur was increasing. Abba Mian had a strange policy. He had cordial relations with the aristocrats and officers. He also visited with his sons various mosques of the area for the Friday prayer, and engaged the mullahs in debates about Islam, fiqh and hadith. He was not a practising Muslim but he had an interest in different religions and read about them. His detractors would spread word that he was an atheist and try to take advantage of it, but were discomfited by his strategy.

Hindus would befriend him readily as they considered him an atheist. The roots of Abba Mian's friendship were always strong and lay quite deep. The friendships would extend to families and the wives, sons and daughters would join in. When Amma invited her Hindu friends, she would employ a Hindu cook and send for fresh utensils. Even children would not be allowed to peer into the kitchen. The wives would themselves make the puris and lay out the plates made from leaves after washing them. Usually, the veranda would be washed to serve food. We were not particularly bothered by this awareness of pollution by touch, and thought it was fun. The elderly people were self-conscious and would stay somewhat aloof. It was as though if we so much as touched them they would be reduced to ashes.

'These are all kafirs,' Jugnu would declare ponderously. 'If I recite ayaat-ul-kursi,* they will burn to ashes.'

'No, Jugnu. Please don't. Sheela is my friend; if she is burnt to ashes I will die. In the last puja, she hid a tiny piece of sandalwood from watchful eyes, and gave it to me. It stayed in my fist all day, emitting a sweet scent. The scent lingered even the following morning.'

Jugnu was a pukka Muslim. He had read the Quran before any of us. I did not even know how to say namaz; I only observed fast, that too for only part of the day.

The notion of untouchability had seemed somewhat romantic and mysterious to us. The poor fellows were scared lest we touch them and some calamity befell them. We did not realize it was because they thought us dirty. When I grew up and learnt this I felt terribly angry.

---

* Verses from the Quran that are believed to be specially efficacious to ward off evil.

When Abba Mian got to know that during Muharram both the parties were making preparations for a skirmish, he approached the Collector for pre-emptive steps, but the Collector dismissed it altogether. He exhorted Abba, 'You're simply imagining things. Don't spread such ideas. It is precisely this attitude that leads to skirmishes.'

The Collector withdrew all pre-emptive measures. But as Abba was in touch with both the groups he felt alarmed. The plan was to build the tazia so high that it would not pass from under the peepul tree by the road; its branches would block the way.

'Sarkar, this is a secret; but you are one of our own.' The chap who had made dovecots for pigeons and cages for chicken would also make the structure for the tazia during Muharram. Thinking that Abbu was of his party he let out the secret to him. 'The tazia will be one and a half feet higher this year.'

'Can it pass under the tree if it is one and a half feet higher?'

'The height of the tree has been measured with great care, Sarkar. Along with the branch even the stem has to be chopped off.'

Abba Mian went out on the road on horseback. The tree was really old. It looked majestic with its dense foliage. A square platform had been made near its base. The bark of the tree was tinted yellow and a stone which was decorated with coloured powder and colourful pennants was placed at the bottom. It looked like the Shivling. People would occasionally make offerings of sweets. Often a diya would be lit too. Passers-by would rest under its shade and bow to it in reverence. Leave alone others, our own Pathani Bua had the firm conviction that if a pregnant woman made an offering here on Thursdays, she was sure to give birth to a son. For sometime people had started taking unusual interest in the tree. They had begun making offerings of sweets which the beggar on the street would grab immediately. If anyone else wanted to claim a share there would be a scuffle and the sweets would go to the dogs. That year there was great enthusiasm at the time of Muharram. Wayward youths from Lucknow were travelling without tickets. Drummers, jugglers and flame bearers were brought from Kakori and Malihabad. In sum, there was great excitement everywhere. Abba Mian had sleepless nights. He consulted his friends from both the communities, cultured and well-respected members of society. They held the view that the government was trying to ignore the importance of this discord. Abba was known to be a loyal servant of the government. People respected him for it, while those opposed to the British government hated him. Abba was a true Indian, even though his job was dear to him. He was afraid that the discord might lead to bloodshed.

After much thought it was decided that large numbers of people from both sides should participate. Crowds would gather on the road on which the tazia procession would move. If anyone could not make it, he should at least send some hefty youth and his servant.

Abba had talked with some zamindars, who sent some of their lathi-wielding strongmen; they came in groups of twos and threes before the actual day of the procession. Amma had no clue. Nanhe Bhai, Ishaq Bhai and two of his elder brothers Shafqat and Maqbool, Chhote Bhai, sons of Abba's friends, Adham Usman and Adham Suleiman, whom he had brought up from an early age, were there. In addition, there were cooks, watermen and Muslim watchmen, who were instructed to join the tazia procession when it passed through the neighbourhood and to stay close and to offer to carry the tazia, should the opportunity arise.

The washermen, sweepers, grass cutters, milkmen and their assistants and the odd-job boys took their position near the tree, along with other Hindus, and stayed there.

'Will there be gun fights, Sahib?' they asked.

'No, guns won't be used. But there will be soldiers, the police inspector and the police superintendent. We will stay close to the procession. Most of the soldiers are Muslims but we have not been able to talk to them. We haven't spoken with any government officials. Our main objective is to stop any skirmish that might break out.'

'But, Sarkar, they have brought strongmen from faraway places.'

'They may have brought ten or twelve troublemakers. Well, that's enough to kick up trouble. We have got to know their exact number, more or less. Once trouble starts, these troublemakers will slink away and stupid, impetuous young men will jump into the fray.'

Nanhe Bhai was young but quite sturdy. The other boys were also quite young but they were in that phase of life when the smell of a fight excited them. Some made the suggestion that the youths should carry knives with them but Abba refused categorically.

'Not even a cane?'

'Not even a splinter. Or else, don't go. If you are so afraid for your dear life, stay at home.'

Amma would observe Muharram with great fanfare. She would take off her bangles and would drape a white dupatta over herself till the tenth of Muharram, the ashura. On the first, fifth, seventh, ninth and tenth, she would give away sherbet, leavened sweet bread, kebab and halwa to all and sundry.

On the night of the ninth of Muharram, Abba told Amma that he had been entrusted with the duty of preventing riots. Amma started mourning the moment she heard this and clung to Abba.

'Now it is evening. I cannot even resign from service. It was a mistake to tell you.'

'If something happens . . .'

'Nothing will happen, I'm telling you. Have I ever told you a lie?'

Amma seemed convinced. But in the morning when he was going, the consecrated goat was tied to the neem tree. Amma visited the bathroom repeatedly. All the girls, the maids and the women of the mohalla had gathered and, after reading the Quran, blew in the direction of the road, miles away and on which the tazia procession would pass and over which the angels of death hovered.

As Abba was stepping out of the house, Amma ran towards him, caught him before he crossed the threshold and brought him back. She made him salute his mother, and then made Abba's aunt and Amma's grandma bless him. After that she made him sit with his face towards the qa'ba* and asked him to read ayat-al kursi.

_____

* Mecca.

'Look, I don't remember it. It's getting late. Why don't you read it, Begum?'

Amma hardly remembered anything. However, she seemed to mutter a lot of prayers and blew on Abba. She then made all the children sit and recite the Quran.

Dozens of drums were making a deafening noise and the anklets of drummers were pounding the eardrums. Policemen with bells tied around their waists were running with the spears held up in the air. And hordes of children always seemed to come out of nowhere on such occasions.

The superintendent of police was an Englishman; his face was red as beetroot. The soldiers were walking in two rows. To control such a huge procession, there were just a dozen lathi-wielding soldiers. The inspector of police was a Hindu and the sub-inspector was a Muslim. In the entire police there were only three or four Hindus, the rest were either Muslim or English. The event took place as the plan was hatched. The tazia had advanced only a couple of inches and those carrying it were walking gingerly and respectfully. They were hefty fellows; even then there was the question of six to seven inches. There was no way besides chopping the branch. Two or three overzealous youths climbed the tree. A scuffle ensued.

Abba Mian thundered, 'Stop there!' It was as though an elephant was roaring.

He stood below the branch and looked up.

'If we do not chop the branch the tazia cannot pass.'

'If . . .'

'The tazia cannot be lowered. It will be an insult.'

'No, the tazia won't be lowered, but it can pass.'

'How?'

Two or three fellows emerged from the crowd with spades in their hands.

'We will dig the road.'

'The road . . .? It's newly laid.'

'It can be laid again.' Abba began to dig with the spade. The cook promptly snatched the spade from him and began to dig. Abba saw that around him there were many of his dear friends who were ready to help.

'What is this nonsense? Why are you spoiling the new road?' This was the police superintendent who was terribly angry.

In an instant a veritable grave, one and a half yards long and a foot deep, was dug and the sectarian strife was buried in it. Abba leapt to lend his shoulder to the tazia. He was short and the other end was supported by the water carrier. Several others also leapt in to give a hand. To keep the balance of the tazia the others had to bend their knees slightly. There were neither gunshots nor bloodshed.

The English officer kept fuming for a while. But he gradually calmed down and then planned a hunting trip with Abba the following Sunday. Abba Mian had the knack of making long-lasting friendship in seconds.

Abba Mian's strategy had the town talking for days. Those who fomented trouble were always few in number; most people wanted to live peacefully.

People thought that Abba Mian would be rewarded with a promotion for his innovative handling of the situation. He would be made a Collector; the title of 'Khan Bahadur' had already been conferred on him in 1911. People were stunned when, on the contrary, he was suspended and an inquiry was slapped on him.

'Did you know that there would be trouble?'

'Yes,' Abba Mian replied.

'Were you involved in it?'

'No.'

'Then how did you come by such authentic information?'

'I have access to it. I maintain cordial relationship with both the communities in the town. I keep my mind alert and ears open.'

The committee members were all British except for one Hindu and one Muslim who sat quietly and nodded their agreement to everything.

'The strife was stopped because of the steps I took and the troubles that were supposed to break out in other towns as a result of this also lost steam. Either they did not break out at all, or if they did they soon fizzled out.'

'That's all right. But you did not take permission to dig up the road. Whatever plan you had you did not put it up before us and take our approval. This indicates a rebellious disposition which could be a great threat to the administration.'

Abba Mian's lawyer said, 'As a citizen whatever steps my client undertook proved to be right. Only in the matter of digging the road the committee can question him and slap a fine.'

'For government officers, the rights of citizenship should come later. The first question is about duty and protocol. Everything should be done according to rules. Breaking rules points to a rebellious bent of mind.'

At that moment Abba remembered the lines of the English poem 'Charge of the Light Brigade':

Theirs not to reason why
Theirs but to do and die

When the lawyer, who was an orthodox Hindu, repeated the lines in a muffled tone the committee members were very annoyed, but Abba Mian looked content. He was not promoted. The order for his dismissal was revoked and he was transferred, as Mishraji had threatened that he would go as far as London to plead the case. The matter was sorted out and Abba left his friends at Kanpur for Lucknow where he had done a stint earlier. In fact, Chhoti Apa was born there.

My memory takes me back to Bahraich. Our first house was an ordinary one. There were some houses in the neighbourhood which made Ammi happy, but not Abba. I remember the tamarind tree which was there behind the wall, in Sughra and Batul's house, and half of it bent over our courtyard. There was no harvest field or forest close by. There was the road outside the gate, so the guard did not allow children to go out. There were only two horses left. Two buffaloes too. Chickens had also come in cages in the railway train.

The courtyard was not too big, but if anyone jumped over the wall there was a desolate mansion right there.

Guru had told us that the place was infested with ghosts. People from my mother's side were all great talkers. Jugnu also liked spinning yarns. He frightened us by telling us about the ghosts, spirits and ghouls of Jaigarh. He characterized monkeys as the relatives of Hanumanji and made us salute them. We were greatly impressed by Hanumanji. We would implore Jhangri Ram, the coachman, to tell us stories from the Ramayana.

Hanumanji burnt the entire island of Lanka with the flame in his tail. Since my childhood whenever I listened to a story the entire drama would be staged in my imagination. Now I have seen it in movies, but even in my childhood by listening to the kochwan I could see Hanumanji burning the Lanka in my imagination. Monkeys indulge in stupid antics but to me they look very clever. I felt as if they would start speaking any moment. Then there was this miracle of holding an entire mountain on the fingertips. When Lakshmanji got wounded in the war, Hanumanji scoured the entire mountain for the life-giving herb, sanjeevani booti. When he could not find it he brought over the entire mountain. I thought this was incredibly smart. Whenever anyone asked me to fetch a thread or a needle I brought the entire box to avoid fetching the stuff again and again. Instead of appreciating this clever step people would reprimand me and call me lazybones. I would take the box back to its place and keep thinking about whether Hanumanji had to return the mountain to its original position. I always forgot to ask the coachman.

The coachman's body would sway a lot as he recited a story from the Ramayana. He would close it with the invocation, 'Bolo Shri Ram Chandra ki jai,' and all of us would repeat it. For us the best part of the story was this invocation which we blurted out at the highest pitch. The coachman would tell us if one took Ram's name even once we would be blessed.

But Jugnu would tell us if I said the invocation my tongue would burn in dozakh, the Muslim hell. I was frightened of this hell and would be shell-shocked. Jugnu portrayed a terrifying picture of hell and I would see in my imagination people being fed blood and pus, burnt in coals, split with a saw, swallowed by snakes. I would scream in my sleep. I was not ready to go to hell under any circumstances. The coachman, on the contrary, told me that if I did not invoke Ramji then I would go to narak, the Hindu hell, which was also a pretty frightening place. There were snakes, scorpions, burning embers and the equipment to slash the human body there. Just imagining them would petrify me.

I was in real trouble. Indira told me that if I did not kneel before the statue of Jesus Christ and make a confession of my sins I would go to hell. I was not ready to go to any of these three terrifying places. But Jugnu said that I would be beaten and taken there by force.

'I will run away.'

'How can you escape from angels? They are everywhere.'

As long as Baaji was there, if anyone threatened me I would run to her lap for shelter. But where was Baaji now? She had left for her in-laws' house with her bamboo pole of a husband. I cursed all the in-laws of the world. This would be the fourth place of torture, akin to dozakh, narak and hell. At the Bhabo's there would be a well-attended majlis every year, and Sughra and Batul performed maatam, i.e. the fervent mourning. I, along with other children, would go to the majlis for the lure of the tabarruk, the consecrated sweets, though I would be bored to death listening to the recitations of marsiyas.

When I grew up a little I tried to follow it closely but could not make much sense of it. But one day I was moved by the description of Ali Asghar's martyrdom. An innocent baby of six months, his body was pierced by an arrow and he was bathed in blood.

All the women were weeping loudly. I also joined them. The women were crying in a subdued, rhythmic way while I was just screaming wildly. My voice was always a pitch higher than the mass mourners. Along with screaming, I also began to roll on the floor. This way of protest never failed to make its impact.

But on this occasion it was different. I was brutally dragged out of the majlis. Other children who were with me were also dealt in the same way. When I reached home my brothers reported me to my mother.

'The ghoul began to writhe on the floor there. They turned us all out, without giving us any sweets.'

'Why were you writhing there?'

'Why did they kill him?'

'Who? You luckless vixen.'

'A six-month-old baby, the poor child!'

'Hey, whose baby died?' Khala Amma stopped snoring and blurted out.

'She's just being crazy, the ill-fated brat!'

'Why kill the baby?' I insisted.

'Hai, no one can make out what she's blabbering. Get lost.'

I left, weeping, for the room where the quilts were stored. There I rested my head against the dirty bolster and cried my heart out. At night I was afraid to sleep alone.

'Shekhani Bua, can I sleep beside you?'

'Come over.' She moved to one side to make room for me. After Baaji, it was Shekhani Bua who would pick out lice from my head whenever she had time. She would also tell me the story of the princess and the five flowers.

'. . . one day six flowers were placed but the balance did not tilt.'

'Why? Did she grow fat? Did the princess eat too much?' I too ate a lot.

'Oh no! She'd seen the prince in her dream.'

'Did the prince make her heavy?'

'No, baby. The fact is, she fell in love with the prince.'

'What is love, Bua?'

'Hey baby, you keep picking my brain. Get lost, I will not tell the story.'

Uff! This 'what' of mine has been a great spoiler. I asked Shekhani Bua why they killed Ali Asghar.

'Can't say.'

'Who killed him?'

'Yezid.'

'Why?'

'Oh baby, how do I know? He was a bad man and he killed the baby. Now go to sleep.' I went to sleep but at night I was startled a couple of times and let out several screams.

It is only a couple of years ago when I heard the account of the martyrdom of Imam Asghar that I realized it was Hazrat Anis's great elegiac poetry that had overwhelmed me . . .

Shamim complained to Abba about me.

'Abba Mian, this pig performs maatam!' Shamim was naughty, always reporting against others to Abba.

'Do you do maatam?' he called me to his side and asked. I nodded yes.

'Show me how you do it.'

I made a demonstration.

'This is not the way.' Abba Mian caught both my hands and slapped them with force against my chest. 'The more forcefully you do it, the more merit you earn.'

'Oye, why are you indulging this evil brat? As it is, she is crazy enough. To do maatam is strictly prohibited, it is sinful,' Amma said.

'Do you remember how deeply you mourned when the cat ate your myna?'

'Well, I did not beat my chest.'

'But you beat your head, didn't you?'

'Come on, I was so young at the time.'

'Well, this poor girl has not become an old woman yet. Begum, is it sinful for young children if they are frightened by accounts of terrible oppression? Of course, you earn a lot of merit through your offerings which will be enough for all of us. I got to know that at the time of my kidney operation you had promised a chaddar in Ajmer. Not content with that, you had arranged for the Satyanarayan Katha, and given Panditji a dhoti and a doshala as gifts. I did not ask you why you did this. I did not ask you whether what you did for me was sinful or meritorious, whether it was permissible or impermissible in religion.'

I was in a fix. The coachman was reluctant to tell me a story.

'Shabari fed half-eaten berries to Ram Chandra . . . Tell me that story,' I implored him.

'Will you say, "Sia Ram Chandra ki jai?"'

I acceded to the condition.

'Shabari fed the berries to Ram Chandra, but she had split them in halves . . .'

'Why?'

'She wanted to check whether there were any worms inside. She gave Ramchandra only the good ones and threw away those that were eaten by worms. Now say, "Sia Ram Chandra ki jai."'

I looked right and left and intoned the words. Otherwise, he would not tell me the story of the slashing of Surpanakha's nose. I looked around before saying it because, according to Jugnu, saying 'jai' was a great sin, and angels would pierce my tongue with thorns and burn it in a raging fire.

I was afraid of the nights. Nightmares tormented me. I saw in the dreams that my tongue was fluttering like frogs over live coals. I screamed and then someone punched me and I woke up. After that I was scared to close my eyes. Jugnu felt that I should roll quinine on my tongue. But as Amma kept quinine locked up in the drawer I purified my tongue by rubbing salt in it. I was petrified of dozakh, the coachman's narak and Sheila Thomas's hell; all these three were terrifying. I decided that I would go only to heaven.

'Just see, the angels will just throw you into dozakh,' Jugnu terrorized me.

'I will run so fast that . . .'

'Where will you run to, baby?'

'I will hide in the quilt room,' but I did not say this to Jugnu. He pronounced everything so confidently it seemed as though he wielded great power. He had finished reading the Quran, after all. I was still stuck in the first chapter.

Really, the whole question of my salvation was a difficult one.

LIGHT

I first went to Aligarh on my way to Lucknow. I had no clear idea how to get to Lucknow. So, on my way from Jodhpur I first stopped at Aligarh. There were some people in Aligarh who would encourage me in the step I was taking. Before undertaking this new enterprise I wanted to talk it over with Papa Mian and Ala Bi. Instead of staying with my aunt, I took Khatoon Apa's permission to stay at the boarding house. Naseer had left for Kinnaird College, Lahore, a year earlier. Hamida Islamuddin was in the first year; I had stayed with her earlier. I realized that no girl from Aligarh was going to Lucknow, so I headed for that city alone.

The station platform itself looked more impressive than the one in Aligarh. At that time Aligarh had only pebble roads and all of them were uneven. In Lucknow I saw cemented roads for the first time. Jodhpur was still a backward city. Lucknow looked like Paris in comparison with these cities.

When the tonga stopped in front of the portico of the college I stood still for a couple of minutes, staring at the high columns of the portico. It was the first time I had seen such a splendid structure. IT College was the most magnificent among all the women's colleges in Asia, and it may still be so. I had not seen another women's college so grand and imposing. Years later I saw a more magnificent university in Moscow that impressed me much.

When I presented myself before the principal, Miss Shannon,* she got up to shake hands with me and welcomed me as though I were an honourable guest. An impressive six-footer with an innocent face, a

---

* Mary E. Shannon, Principal, Isabella Thoburn College, Lucknow, 1925–39.

rosy complexion, deep-blue eyes and a crown of silvery hair on her head, she had a well-endowed physique. She shook my hands with such force that my fingers crackled.

I chose a double room lest I felt lonely in the college, which was desolate. I had no idea what kind of roommate I was going to have. I was among the few students who had newly arrived. The boarding house was still vacant. The matron gave me permission to choose my own room. There were two bedsteads there. I dumped my bedding on one and draped the bed with a bed sheet that was embroidered in bright colours in Marwari style. Then I arranged my clothes in the cupboard.

I did not know what to do. I just wandered around with a serious face as though I was on some important assignment and would stop only when I had reached my destination. A couple of girls who were talking and laughing among themselves passed me by. It was as though they had not seen me at all. I felt terribly lonely.

I had no lunch at noon, as I didn't know where the dining room was. I felt like crying. When the bell rang for the afternoon tea I got up and tried to follow the direction of the sound and indeed reached the dining room. There were only a few girls sitting, scattered in groups of two or three and talking informally among themselves.

I was starving, otherwise I would have skipped the meal. Loneliness was eating into me.

'Are you a Punjabi?' a plumpish, short girl asked, as she sat facing me.

'No.'

'I am Punjabi—Elma Mohan Lal.'

I blurted out my name with great difficulty.

'Well, you look like a Punjabi and I, a Hindustani.' As a rule, Punjabis characterized other Indians as Hindustanis.

'What subjects have you opted for? I have chosen politics and economics.'

'Those are my subjects too!' Elma said excitedly. 'Which hostel are you in?'

'I am in "Nishat" and I have opted for a double room.'

'Oh boy, I'm in the dormitory.'

'Why don't you come to my room?'

'Oh no, it's expensive. Why don't you come to the dorm? It's only one rupee per person. We are six and there are two more beds. Come along, we will have great fun. We could study together.'

There were three hostels in all, Nishat, Naubahar and Maitri Bhavan. Nishat was the newest and the most expensive, then Naubahar. Maitri Bhavan, which housed dormitories, was the oldest. I went along with Elma to her dormitory. The five other girls were already there. One of them, Zohra Abul Hasan, had come from Aligarh after completing her matriculation there. She was Naiyer's class fellow and a day scholar at Aligarh. I had a passing acquaintance with her but I was truly delighted to find a girl from Aligarh there. I brought her to my room. She was from a rich family and was pampered by her parents. But she was pitch dark, lanky and had very poor looks. Seeing her shabby appearance Miss Shannon had sent her to Maitri Bhavan.

The boarding house of IT College was divided according to class. Rich or European girls stayed in Nishat, those from middle-class families stayed in Naubahar and Maitri Bhavan had a majority of girls who were Christian or from poor families. Being a missionary college, the Christian girls enjoyed many privileges here. Many were exempted from paying tuition fees, and for some meals were subsidized. Almost all the Christian girls received scholarships. Hindu cooks refused to cook beef, so the entire kitchen staff consisted of Christians and Muslims. There were about half a dozen sweepers, gardeners and watchmen who were harijans and had converted to Christianity. The Muslims among them were quite supercilious. They would sometimes show displeasure towards the Muslim girls while at other times they would try and be partial to them, for instance, giving them toast dripping with butter.

The European teachers showed contempt towards the Indian Christians because of the class from which they came. They could not enter the dining room. There was a separate table for the British and American girls. They were served English food. There were some Anglo-Indians in the group too, such as Indira Dayal, the perfect, fair-complexioned daughter of Dr Girija Dayal and his white wife who was a doctor. She had lived in Europe for sometime and wore skirts and frocks. Her mother had delivered most of my siblings. She was a close friend. Whenever Abba was transferred to a new place he would manage to get Dr Girija Dayal also transferred to the same place. We had known them from our days in Bahraich; their eldest son Bhao would tease me no end. He'd leave me alone only when I howled and screamed.

When Indira reminded me of all this the first thing I asked her was the whereabouts of her brother, who was extremely lanky and fair. Then I brought her to my hostel. On the third day Sultana and Amina also came over. I saw them while they were still in the tonga, took them under my wings and got them allotted a double room which was on the front side of my room. We would go to one another's room through the one in between. This annoyed the senior girl staying in that room and she shifted to Maitri Bhavan, where the girls were all studious. She was in her BA final year. After she left, Sultana and Amina shifted to her room, adjacent to mine. Zohra, Sultana and Amina were in the first year of FA, but we all hung out together because of our Aligarh connection.

The things that had the greatest impact on me were the library and the reading room. Never before had I seen such a beautiful and massive library. In Aligarh, we had four almirahs in a room where English and Urdu books and a sprinkling of dictionaries and encyclopedias were kept. There were several thousand books in the IT College library. I spent the first few days looking through the shelves. There were still a couple of days for classes to begin. The girls took about a week to collect. They were playing whatever games they wanted. Those who wanted to participate in other games were writing their names on the notice board. The four of us signed up for all the games on offer. We had played basketball, volleyball and badminton at Aligarh. Football, hockey and tennis were new for us.

There was only Dr Tucker in our hostel. She was eighty and responsible for teaching us English. She was short, ordinary-looking and very fair. I saw for the first time in my life that a fair complexion could look ugly. She had short, boy-cut hair and wore very simple dresses.

Dr Tucker had earlier taught at the University of Cambridge, Harvard University and in California. She had been leading a retired life when she came to Isabella Thoburn College for a residency. After spending her entire life teaching students, she could not stay away from it for long and began to teach again. Her students had included senators and ministers, generals and commanders-in-chief. Her knowledge of her subject was really very deep. Shakespeare was her forte. Once she started her class, she did not need to open her book to look at the text. The same with Bernard Shaw and the poetry of the English poets. The girls would open the book while she would pace on the dais and teach them. Her style of teaching had the girls spellbound.

In Aligarh, Khatoon Apa was regarded as the best English teacher. What she taught had a deep impact on one's mind. But when we met her teacher, Dr Tucker, we felt as if she were a river overflowing with knowledge. I will always remember the day when she taught us Wordsworth's 'Little Match Girl'* and 'We Are Seven'. First, there was absolute silence in the class, then there was muffled sobbing and then girls began to cry loudly. Dr Tucker was glowing like a red-hot ember and her tamarind-seed eyes had brimmed over with tears. She would get so wrapped up in the feelings evoked by poems that her own hands and feet would begin to shake all over.

When the girls from other classes stood outside the door we would realize that the period was over. In all the classes taught by Tucker, the girls would remain glued to their seat, oblivious of time. Girls from other classes resented this.

Girls would surround Dr Tucker if she happened to pace up and

---

* This poem is actually by William McGonagall.

down on the lawn. She could speak on any issue under the sun and little windows opened in one's mind when one listened to her. She had a cheerful temperament. If she was in the mood she would play some comic character with such perfection that we'd split our sides laughing. If sometimes she played Falstaff, at other times she played Mr Barkis of *David Copperfield*. She played Shylock, Portia, Cleopatra and Bernard Shaw's Candida. She also knew the Bible fairly well. She had not yet decided which plays of Shakespeare and Bernard Shaw she would teach in the final year. She had to select one each out of the three listed in the syllabus. Similarly, in the poetry paper she had not yet decided which poems by Milton, Wordsworth, Shelley, Byron, Keats and Matthew Arnold she was going to teach. 'Read up all the plays of Shakespeare. The complete works of the poets are available for two rupees each in the cheap edition in Hazratganj. Buy them up and read all of them fast,' she told us.

My English was weak even by Aligarh standards. This was because I had started learning English quite late and had rushed through the process. I had mugged up one or two poems of the English poets which were listed in the course. As far as the meanings went, I tried to come to grips with them, partly through classroom lectures and partly through 'keys'. But even though I knew the facts, I couldn't write well. My language was not felicitous enough to convey adequately what I meant to say. My spoken English was also weak which meant that I could not narrate fluently. I would translate each word while speaking in English. If your mind is full of ideas and you have no proper outlet for them, you feel suffocated. In college, though, the 'keys' were a blessing that helped tackle the difficulties, as there was no lack of enthusiasm on my part. The dictionaries too were of much help.

Whenever I entered the library I would feel intoxicated. The aroma of the old and the new books assailed me from all sides. For hours together I would turn the pages of books and inhale their odour. I don't know why even now when I open a book or a journal I smell it first. Chinese and Russian books used a kind of glue that smelt like stale meat, which was nauseating. When I sprinkled eau de cologne over them they smelt more horrific. Only I know how I read those books by stuffing my nostrils. I love books. I feel uneasy if I don't have books and journals scattered on my bed. There are books in every nook and cranny of my house. Even the bathrooms are stuffed with comics and magazines of all kinds. The same is true of my daughters. My grandson too is crazy about books. He falls asleep with books lying on his chest or by his side. Shahid also loved books. He would hold a cigarette in one hand and a book in the other. He used to buy books like crazy. There was hardly a month when he did not buy books worth two or three hundred rupees. He bought rare books from old bookshops. He had put together an excellent collection of books. Reading them changed my life completely. He did not find much time to read.

I did not buy any books during his lifetime. There was no need. It was not easy to go through so many books. May God look after the book thieves who lifted many of them. To save the books from thieves I stored the important books in iron shelves and put a lock on the shelves. No one except me knew where the keys were.

I read Shakespeare, Bernard Shaw and the complete works of all the poets. After finishing some of them I didn't need the 'keys' any more. As for fiction, I began with the Brontë sisters and then read many Russian writers, such as Chekhov, Tolstoy, Gorky, Dostoevsky. Then I read Charles Dickens, Émile Zola, Balzac, Maugham and Hemingway.

I often looked wistfully at the shelves packed with books and thought that one needed several lives to read all of them. Then I had my regular study for the college. The light had to be turned off at the appointed time. Sometimes it got difficult to tear myself away from the book I was reading when the bell went out for putting out the light. Then the matron would appear and would not budge as long I had not turned off the light. This would annoy me no end! Often I would have to pay fines. Then I would take refuge in the room of a senior girl from BA final or MA or BEd. If I heard the approaching footsteps of the matron there too, I would take refuge in the bathroom. Uff! I was so stubborn.

Dr Tucker added to my troubles. She stayed in a room not far from mine. In old age one can hardly sleep. When she returned to her room after dinner I'd lay in wait for her. I'd wish her and we would get talking. Then she would call me over to her room. The bell for going to sleep would ring out, but we would keep talking. Time would tick away—five minutes, ten minutes, fifteen minutes, but I would still thirst for more of her conversation. The following day I would look for the characters in books that she alluded to in her conversation. Besides, she had introduced a feature of after-dinner conversations. Those who wished could come to her room and participate in a question and answer session. The girls would crash into her room. Her small room would be overcrowded. We would sit on the floor. Sitting on the armchair she would read out a poem or an extract from a play, or talk about Virgil and Homer; sometimes the discussion would centre on the Bible's commentary. Some girls spread the canard that the old woman was trying to convert us to Christianity. Whatever the truth, she was certainly adding to our knowledge. One day she talked to us about English music. In every hostel there was a drawing room with a piano. Girls practised on it; sometimes the professors would also entertain themselves by playing on the piano. Our ears were not attuned to Western music. We had sung 'God Save the King' when we were at Aligarh; we really just yelled out the words without any consideration for rhythm. Abba Mian loved music but no one in our family knew even Indian music, let alone Western music.

When Dr Tucker sang for us in the session on music appreciation we could not suppress our mirth. The Western tunes sounded strange to us and we stuffed our mouth with dupattas to stop our laughter. Dr Tucker's face turned red. She told us that the song was sung by a black singer named Paul Robeson and it was considered a masterpiece. She played the record again and again and exhorted us to listen to it carefully. 'You can hear the tumult of the Volga river in his voice. Close your eyes and imagine that you are in the boat and trying to cross the Volga river. A violent storm is coming—the tumult of giant waves, the clapping of thunder, and the boatman alone and helpless. The helpless, luckless black boatman, whose life is also caught in the maelstrom.'

Embarrassed, we went on listening. The third time, when she turned off the light and played the record, we felt our hair standing on end.

Then she asked us to read about the black Americans, the wars in the north and the south, and the plight of the blacks caught in those wars. Then I read *Uncle Tom's Cabin* and grasped the strength of Paul Robeson's voice.

My second subject, politics, gripped me from the very first lesson. Miss Chacko, who taught politics, was a south Indian. With her smooth, velvety complexion and curly hair, she looked like a Negro. Her hair parting was broad and straight, and her big, bright eyes sparkled. She had drawn eyebrows, thick, cloud-coloured and slightly dilated lips and sparkling white teeth. She had a shapely physique with a long swan-like neck. Most of the white professors were old, ungainly and short-statured. Miss Chacko moved with the dignity of a black swan and in their midst seemed like the princess of some country.

Many girls of the college were crazy about her. We all doted on her as her lectures made a deep impression on all of us. She wore Madrasi sarees in bright colours, like purple and blue, which made her look both sober and mysterious. She laughed but rarely. Usually she would break into laughter when a student committed some error or lapse.

Along with politics it was necessary to study history.

And, from a worm to a frog, from a monkey to human being; in other words, the theory of evolution and its different stages.

'Kun fayakun,' God Almighty said, 'Let there be,' and the world came into existence. Then Hazrat Adam was created and angels were asked to prostrate before him. The chief of the angels, Iblis, was bent upon rebellion. He refused to prostrate before an ordinary lump of clay. But he was given permission to lead human beings astray as long as the world lasted.

When Adam got bored in paradise, Eve was created for his entertainment. The Woman as the plaything of Man.

Iblis knew that Adam was not going to listen to him, so he incited Eve and, willy-nilly, Adam too ate the fruit of the forbidden tree. Induced by Iblis, Eve led Adam astray. Woman is the handmaiden to Satan! As a result both were flung away to earth.

Adam and Eve gave birth to a son and a daughter every day. These children became adults in a day but were not permitted to marry each other. They could marry those who were born on the following or the previous day. However, the wicked Qabil lusted after the wife of the godly Habil.* Satan taught him how to kill. Thus Qabil became the first murderer on earth, for a woman. A brother shed the blood of a brother.

Woman is at the root of discord!

While studying politics as a subject, it was necessary to study history as well. Miss Chacko, who was a nun, taught us the theory of evolution very competently; from a worm to a frog, then from monkey to human being. The previous week, during vespers, that is the evening prayer, she had related to us the anecdote related to 'Let there be and it was'. My mind raced fast and I expressed my thoughts.

Miss Chacko's derisive smile could devastate anyone. Her big, heavy-lidded eyes would start spewing venom. For a few moments there was total silence in the class.

'Don't mix belief with history.' She craned her neck to look at my notebook and was upset by what she saw there.

'What is this you're writing?'

'Notes,' I replied in a feeble tone.

'But . . . this!' She picked up the notebook and showed it to the class.

'This is Urdu,' said Kishwar.

---

* Qabil and Habil are Cane and Abel, two sons of Adam and Eve in the Bible.

'I would expect some seriousness in my class.' Miss Chacko slapped down the notebook.

'The script is Urdu but the words are those of English.' I read out the notes I had taken of the lecture.

'But . . .'

'Miss Chacko, you speak quite fast. I cannot keep pace. I take notes in Urdu which I render later into English easily. Urdu can be written fast, it's a kind of shorthand.'

Miss Chacko was pacified after hearing the notes. The other girls would fill in the gaps in their notes with the help of my notes. This allowed them to concentrate on the lectures. This strategy had stood me in good stead. The Hindi alphabet too is not as short as the Urdu one, so the girls studying Hindi also would seek help from my notes.

For several days we discussed the first chapter of the Bible. The woman has to carry the burden of all transgressions, which is her secondary existence. We felt it was a personal attack on us. We felt both sad and angry.

If this were so, then why did the books listed in the syllabus undercut religious beliefs? Why were students taught two contradictory things and asked to believe in both? The theory of evolution says something different from the Bible. If the examiners were to judge a question on faith how were they to tackle it?

The Stone Age, then the discovery of iron. For thousands of years man lived on trees and in caves like monkeys. Then the concept of home developed and human beings began to live together in tribes. They learnt cultivation and animal husbandry. They invented weapons for hunting that were also used in inter-tribal skirmishes.

In the beginning, men and women had a more or less equal status. In terms of physical strength too there was not much difference. Division of labour was implemented in the conduct of daily life among the tribes. Women produced children who strengthened the tribe, so they had a position of prominence. Before the institution of marriage came into vogue, children were identified by their mothers. Women had multiple husbands and there was no way children could be identified except by the mother. They got their names from the mother. Women used to be the chief of tribes. Slowly, the quest for comfort made them physically weak. Just as the rulers wallowing in luxury lose their kingdoms and become kings in name only, women lost their importance and were turned into machines for producing children. They were gradually relegated to working at home.

As the tribes were engaged in constant warfare—after all, what else did they have to do except kill their rivals and grab their possessions— women who filled in the losses suffered, in terms of lives lost, were themselves turned into booty. Along with livestock, they also became objects of plunder. The person with the most women in his control had the largest family and would become the chief of the tribe for his strength in terms of numbers.

Women were also collected as booty along with other objects. For an equitable distribution of the booty after any occupation, the people of the tribe would count the number of women, along with goats and rams. When a new woman was brought, it was notified to the tribe that this property belonged to a specific person. Later, this arrangement assumed the form of marriage. To avoid future complications and to make known who the property belonged to, people beat drums or made rounds of the village. Later, the same custom was transformed into marriage rituals.

Members of a tribe not only fought against other tribes, they fought amongst themselves too. The stronger of the father and the son killed the other when he got the opportunity. That is why the value of kinship relationship was stressed. The father would bring up the son with care and affection; in return the son was expected to be grateful to the father, and respect and obey him.

After the death of the father the son would inherit the property of the father. Along with it, he also acquired rights over his father's wives. There would be squabbles and bloodshed. Usually, the eldest son of the oldest wife was stronger than the rest. He was closest in age to his father and was able to make others recognize his importance. That is why the eldest son was accepted as the heir apparent. It also made his mother win respect and attain the status of queen mother. The first wife of the tribal chief, the First Lady.

Such a mundane interpretation of marriage threw cold water on our notions of love and longing. It was as though a wet blanket was thrown on our colourful dreams. Women were looked after like harvest and cattle. Separate values developed for the possessor and the possession to live by. Man became the provider and woman's spiritual god. It became a woman's duty to serve the man. She did not have to face the challenges of life. As long as she kept her man pleased and produced more and more soldiers, she led a secure and peaceful life. After that she met the same fate as that of old, worthless cattle. That is why women are scared of old age and conceal their age; so far she has been dependent on the kindness of her husband and sons.

Old age, when you cannot look after yourself, invites people's contempt. Man-eaters first devour the weak and the aged. Some clever old women were spared to train young girls in manners and etiquette. They would teach them how to win the hearts of men. And, they would teach them lessons of love so that when their children grew up they would not move away from them. 'Paradise is under the feet of the mother'— this was sought to be imprinted on children's mind.

The older generation had the view—and it still holds the view— that girls should not be educated much. This brings ruin to them; they lose the capacity to be good wives and mothers. One does not know why this rule is not applied to men. If education is dangerous, it must be so for every living being. It can never be that while women die of snakebites, men will survive the same. What is poison to one cannot be elixir to the other. What a stupid axiom people have developed!

Apart from two Indian teachers who had families, all our professors were unmarried. Dr Tucker, Miss Shannon, Miss Pearson, Miss Johnson were all unmarried.

One day we asked Dr Tucker, 'Why didn't you marry?'

'No one fell for me,' she said.

'Why not? You must have been a stunner in your youth. Were there fewer young men around?'

'Oh yes. There were fewer youth. In every country more women are born than men. In my own country, England, the youth were engaged in consolidating British power in far-off colonies. Only the aged and the worthless were left behind. The wives of those who had been out of the country for years led more wretched lives than unmarried girls. If they accompanied their husbands, they could not cope with the difficulties. Besides, British men had begun to take an interest in native women even if they avoided marrying them. Women kicked up a row over this. As a result, the government placed restrictions on the whites establishing liaison with native women. Women themselves visited the colonies in search of husbands and faced great difficulties. Men are required to fight and kill and women had to retire to the home country. Women could not get married which led to the spread of women's education. Our family was well-off. Education was not so expensive. Two of my brothers died in Africa. Plans had been afoot for their marriage when the call of death came. My younger sister became a widow. The situation was such that besides education there was no option. But you must marry.'

'Why?'

'So that you can give birth to intelligent children. In my family, only a sister married and she had three children.'

'Was she educated?'

'Yes. At the age of thirty-eight she managed to find a bridegroom with one leg for herself. Ellis was a schoolteacher. Her children received a good education. Her grandchildren are spread over every corner of the world. For a country to develop, educated mothers are needed. Can you give me one example where the mother is a graduate and the sons and daughters are illiterate? A family that has educated women cannot but have educated men.'

Today, when I remember Dr Tucker's words and look about myself, I find that none of the children of those she taught is uneducated. 'The milk of brainy mothers is conducive to the growth of intelligence in children,' Dr Tucker had said.

Then one day preparations began to welcome the freshers. Now we were fully acquainted with the values and traditions of IT College.

Terminal exams were about to begin. Before they started we were made 'residents' of IT College.

It was announced that all the girls would sport dresses of the IT colour, a mix of white and gold. Most of the girls had bought white cotton sarees with a yellow lining. As Saturdays and the Sundays were off, the staff and the students gathered on the portico on Friday afternoon—the new girls stood outside the portico and beneath the staircase, the staff and senior students on the portico. Large crepe paper bands of white and gold were tied to the columns to block passage. At some distance the memorial piano was emitting a tune. Miss Shannon took the oath in a solemn tone. We repeated her words.

'We shall abide by the rules of the college.'

'We shall make no distinction on the basis of caste, creed and colour and treat everyone with love and friendship.'

'We shall regard the property of the college as our own and use it carefully.'

'We will regard the library as a house of worship.'

'We shall regard the professors as our senior friends and seek their advice unhesitatingly in times of difficulties.'

'We shall do nothing that would impair the reputation of the college.'

'We shall be punctual.'

Our hearts were beating fast and our hands were getting cold.

After this, Miss Shannon untied the golden ribbon, and said, 'Today you are going to enter the college in the real sense of the word and become members of the family. We promise to pass on the knowledge bestowed on us by our own teachers to you, so that you may pass it on to others, and thus this transaction of knowledge goes on. We welcome you.'

As we climbed up the stairs there was a big lump in our throat. It was as though we were entering a house of worship. We were welcomed with thunderous claps.

Then there was the dinner and the college song was sung. After that we shared some jokes and laughed to our hearts' content. The year that had passed proved to have been a good one. One thing was, we had had the opportunity to see Mahatma Gandhi. IT College was an American institution. We could protest freely against the policies of Great Britain. We could talk openly about the revolution of 1857 and the British raj. We talked about how America, which was a British colony, put an end to British rule. We were not only allowed but exhorted to listen to the speeches of the Indian leaders. America had not yet become an imperial power, and was sympathetic to people under British colonial rule. The American people were open-minded, outspoken and sincere. There was no trade of weapons as yet, and trade with other nations had not become so widespread. The production was enough to meet the needs and it had no evil designs on the raw materials of any country. American products needed new markets.

And the funny thing is that America's current rival Russia had its full sympathy at that time.

We had collected clothes and money to help out the Russians, as Miss Shannon had told us that the winter was very severe in Russia and people were facing great difficulties. During those days a film *Rasputin* was doing the rounds. Before it was shown to us, a lecture on the Tsar and the Tsarina was organized. It showed how the Tsarina was crazy about Rasputin and thought him to be a prophet. Girls from aristocratic families also expressed their love for him. He also doled out his favours to some. Similarly, before the screening of *Catherine the Great* teachers helped us gather material on her and there were fierce debates in the class.

If a celebrated personality was invited to speak at the university, we were permitted to go there. After meeting Khalida Edib Khanum at the university, we invited her to the college. We read up the available literature on her. When she actually arrived, we asked her many questions. We talked to her regarding the revolution in Turkey. If a professor of economics or politics came on a tour, we regularly attended the lectures and then debated the issues in class.

When we went to the university for the first time Miss Shannon told us in the assembly hall that as we were going to sit with boys for the first time we had to be careful. Some ill-mannered boys might crack vulgar jokes, and we should not behave in a way that would give people cause for complaint. People were not yet ready for co-education.

Usually, I was not the one to listen to sagacious advice. But the professors of IT talked to us in such a friendly, personable way that I would listen to them attentively without showing my rebellious streak. Their manner of speaking did not smack of authority or coercion.

I took interest in everything. I was thoroughly absorbed in imbibing the spirit of freedom and enlightenment that the environment offered us. New doors and windows were being opened in my mind. If one could assimilate even a tiny bit of the education and wisdom that was available here, one's future would be illuminated. I had clashed with stone walls, but there was no scratch on my head. I could see my consciousness developing into something new and the whole world looked precious to me.

The problem is that there is the body to think of along with the mind. Sometimes a clash ensues between the body and the mind, and this clash might lead one astray. One cannot keep balance. The death of one spells doom for both.

In Lucknow I got the opportunity for the first time to move around freely in the bazaars. I also met boys. In Aligarh, the college boys were a distant, faded dream. The fear of the other sex that is planted in a girl's mind in her childhood has very deep and complex ramifications. As I was brought up among a host of brothers and cousins, and my father was close to me, boys did not seem to me a threatening presence. And if a girl from a good family had no fear for boys, she was not considered to be good. Sultana and Amina too were neither scared of nor impressed by men. In every family there were some men who were worthless. Compared with them, all the received wisdom on women's supposed inferiority falls flat. It is not against the natural law for women to take precedence over men, and the accepted truth that women are inferior to men appears to be a stupid precept.

Nevertheless, it is a given in human nature that the battle of the sexes rages everywhere. This awareness made us girls stick together while going to the university, because a group has greater strength for its defence. In the university lecture hall, if the lecture was interesting we would get so absorbed in it that we'd forget about the other sex. However, if the lecture was boring, our eyes would begin to wander and common human failings would surface. But that would happen but rarely, because even if the speaker did not have a grip on his subject he would not brook such behaviour. Usually, we went to the university only when some reputed intellectual came for a lecture and we'd get so wrapped up in it that our attention would not waver. The boys and girls would prove themselves mature students.

But as we'd come out of the hall, the magic of the lecture would melt into the air and the smell of gunpowder would fill the atmosphere. The girls would walk separately in a group, followed by the boys who appeared like a pack of wolves. There was one boy, in particular, Hiri, who was every girl's heart-throb. The girls referred to him as 'haay' and called him Medusa. Medusa was a mythical creature and anyone who cast his eyes on it turned into stone at the first sight. Hiri was more than six feet tall, with heavy-lidded eyes and a honey-coloured complexion, from his European mother and Bengali father. His teeth were like a set of pearls dazzling through his ashy lips.

The fear of Hiri was strong in the minds of the girls. He had preyed on several women already. When he was at school he had violated the chastity of a nun. For some time now he had been following the IT crowd up to the gates of the college. It was also said that he was partial to the group from Nishat Mahal. In our group there was Sultana and several other head-turners. Sultana was very naughty but her younger sister, Amina, was a simpleton and delicate as a rose. She was very studious and oblivious of the existence of the other sex. She was the youngest, but the most sober and serious. She would give advice like an elderly person to others about adhering to principles, the importance of education, etc.

One day we were sitting on the stairs and guffawing when Amina came out of her room with a grimace on her face and reprimanded us. 'You don't study yourselves and don't allow others to study either,' she said.

'OK, grandma, we'll seal our lips now,' I retorted.

Amina broke into tears and ran into her room. In the morning she refused to talk to me.

Two or three days passed. We were always together, eating or chatting, but she kept mum whenever I asked her something. I wondered what happened.

'She says that you have called her names.'

'Called her names?'

'Yes, you called her grandma.'

'Oho, my grandfather's wife! But he died a long time ago!' I don't know why, but I had a fit of laughter. This flower-like girl and my grandpa, who was lying buried under tons of earth in Agra and I was looking for a mate for him! I explained to her with much difficulty that it was an idiom I was using, that when small children talk like elderly people they are derisively called 'Grandma'. It took a lot of work to coax a smile out of her.

Whenever we went out, Amina would be placed in the middle so that no boy could jostle her. One day a boy bumped into me and I leapt to give him a mighty whack on his back. It was so sudden that my own action left me stunned. The boys broke into a guffaw and the culprit ran away. Elma was with me and gave me a piece of her mind.

When Shamim beat me, my hands would automatically rise against him. Anyway, when people made a big issue of it, my own action seemed improper to me. Word went about and reached the teachers, but none of them raked it up nor reprimanded me. In class, teachers sometimes looked at me in such a way that I felt like burrowing into a rat hole. I had hurt female dignity. But someone in some corner of my mind told me I had done nothing wrong.

I do not remember if anyone ever teased me. When I walk on the street I talk to my companions so animatedly that I cannot hear anything except the sound of my words. Or I get lost in contemplating the distant horizons, and I can neither see nor hear anything. Often I've narrowly escaped being run over. In my mental state, I never hear the hooting of cars. I often lose my way and end up somewhere I hadn't intended. When I wake up from my trance, I take a U-turn and hasten towards my destination. I look around myself to see if anyone has caught me out in my stupid act. Well, who would know that I have wandered away from my path?

I've solved complicated problems during these long walks, edited stories, warded off difficulties. Even now, when I am stuck on something I go for a walk along the sea on Chowpatty Beach or Marine Drive. If I run into someone I know I present my situation to him as the plot of a story or someone else's problem and we discuss the pros and cons of the situation in an impersonal way. The tense threads begin to ease.

At the end of the year when, true to the tradition of IT College, the senior girls of BA were given a farewell dinner, there was again a festive atmosphere. The rituals were gone through in a fashion wrought with emotion. All the furniture of the hall was tucked away near the walls. The outgoing girls stood in a group in the centre, and the final-year girls stood behind them. The girls standing in the front were holding multicoloured candles in earthenware bowls. The candles were burning. After the college anthem was sung, at the end of the rituals, the senior girls passed on the candles to the junior girls.

'These candles of knowledge that our senior sisters passed on to us, we pass on to you.'

'Let these lamps not die out.'

The girls burst into tears. The eyes of the professors also became moist.

The light of these candles is still stored in my mind.

Family Tree

Ismat Chughtai's father, Khan Bahadur Mirza Qaseem Beg Chughtai (born circa 1861), was a deputy collector, and later a magistrate in the employment of the Maharaja of Jodhpur. He died in Jodhpur in December 1936. Ismat's mother was Nusrat Khanam/Rukhsana Khanam who was nicknamed Nachcho. She was born circa 1878 and died in Aligarh in April 1967. They had six sons and four daughters:

1. Rifat Khanam (Bari Apa)
2. Nazeem Beg (Nanhe Bhai)
3. Azim Beg (Munne Bhai)
4. Farhat Khanam (Baaji)
5. Azmat Khanam (Chhoti Apa)
6. Waseem Beg (M Bhai)
7. Jaseem Beg (Jassu)
8. Shamim Beg (Shanna)
9. Ismat Chughtai (Chunni)
10. Aseem Beg (Chunnu)

Ismat's father had two brothers and one sister. The sister, Badshahi Khanam, immortalized by Ismat in her story 'Bachchu Phupi' was married to Masood Ali, and gave birth to two daughters, Musarrat Khanam and Hashmat Khanam. Musarrat Khanam was married to Shaikh Zafar Husain Usmani who was Ismat's maternal uncle. They had three children—Mazhar Husain Usmani (Ismat calls him Mazhar Bhai), Azhar Husain Usmani (Jugnu) and Shaukat. Shaukat was married to Naseem Beg (Nanhe Bhai).

Source: Sukrita Paul Kumar and Sadique, *Ismat: Her Life, Her Times* (New Delhi: Katha, 2000).

GLOSSARY

alif, bey	initial letters of Arabic/Urdu alphabet
Asavari	a raga
ayats/ayat-al Kursi	Quranic verses
baraat	wedding party
baree	gifts, mainly of dry fruits, taken to the bride's house
behn	sister
bhaath	ceremony during a wedding when brothers give gifts of dress, jewellery, etc., to sisters.
bhutni	female spirit
chakki	grindstone
chaprassi	attendant
dada	grandpa
dalia ki phatki	a device that involves attaching a hanging basket with a rope in such a way that when the birds come to nibble at the grains placed before the basket, one tug of the rope traps the birds inside the basket.
dastarkhwan	cloth on which food is spread
devar	husband's younger brother
dulhan	daughter-in-law; bride
gharara	baggy skirt
ghilman	heavenly creature
halal	permissible in Islam
haram	forbidden in Islam
kalmohi	black-faced one
kochwan	coachman

kufr	apostasy
lota	tumbler
majlis	a gathering of people, for a specific purpose; it could be social, administrative or religious. In its usage here it indicates a gathering of Shia Muslims for the remembrance of Imam Husain ibn Ali, the Prophet's grandson.
maatam	the act of self-flagellation during Muharram
moonhbola/ moonhboli	adopted
Mullaniji	lady teacher
nana	mother's father or uncle
nand/nanad	husband's younger sister
nauha	a sub-genre of Marsiya depicting the sorrow felt by Shia Muslims at the martyrdom of holy imams
nikah	A Muslim marriage
panda	Hindu pundit/ priest
phupi	father's sister
suhaag	the blessed state of wifehood
taya	father's brother
tauba	repentance
thaan	length of cloth
udankhatola	literally, flying saucer
walima	the dinner/reception at the groom's house following the wedding
wazifa	a special kind of prayer
wazu	ablutions

Acknowledgements

Githa Hariharan, for suggesting the title and looking through the manuscript. UGC Special Assistance Programme, department of English, Jamia Millia Islamia, for infrastructural help.